HOPPING

Also by Melanie McGrath

Motel Nirvana:
Dreaming of the New Age in the American Desert

Hard, Soft and Wet

Silvertown: An East End Family Memoir

The Long Exile:
A True Story of Deception and Survival
amongst the Inuit of the Canadian Arctic

HOPPING

*The Hidden Lives of an East End
Hop Picking Family*

Melanie McGrath

FOURTH ESTATE • *London*

First published in Great Britain in 2009 by
Fourth Estate
A division of HarperCollins*Publishers*
77–85 Fulham Palace Road
London W6 8JB
www.4thestate.co.uk

love this book? www.bookarmy.com

A catalogue record for this book
is available from the British Library

ISBN 978-0-00-722366-4

Typeset in Perpetua by Palimpsest Book Production Limited,
Grangemouth, Stirlingshire

Printed in Great Britain by Clays Ltd, St Ives plc

Mixed Sources
Product group from well-managed
forests and other controlled sources
www.fsc.org Cert no. SW-COC-1806
© 1996 Forest Stewardship Council

FSC is a non-profit international organization established to promote
the responsible management of the world's forests. Products carrying
the FSC label are independently certified to assure consumers that they
come from forests that are managed to meet the social, economic
and ecological needs of present and future generations.

Find out more about HarperCollins and the environment at
www.harpercollins.co.uk/green

For Tai,
who looked forward to this book.

'Kent, sir – everybody knows Kent – apples, cherries, hops, and women.'

CHARLES DICKENS, *The Pickwick Papers*

PREFACE

A few years ago I wrote a memoir of the lives of my grand-parents, Jenny Fulcher and Leonard Page. In the telling of my grandparents' story I wanted to capture the essence of two ordin-ary lives and to tell the story of the East End of London during an extraordinary period which saw it transform from what Jack London called the 'abyss' – a hive of poverty and deprivation whose dimmed population toiled in sweatshops, factories and in the docks – to the less impoverished but more socially fragmented place it is today; a place associated not so much with economic depriv-ation (though there is still far too much of that) as with a hip art scene, vibrant Banglatown, Canary Wharf city slickers and, most recently, with the massive regeneration programme in disguise that is the 2012 Olympics.

Having told that story in *Silvertown*, the most obvious next step would have been to have continued my family story into the present day. To have done that, though, would have been to ignore completely one of the greatest of the East End's many great traditions: hopping. Every summer throughout the eight-eenth, nineteenth and much of the twentieth centuries, hundreds of thousands of East Enders made the trip to the hop gardens of Kent to pick hops. My own family were among the minority who didn't regularly go on these trips. My grandmother, Jenny Fulcher, regarded hopping as common and, as concerned as she was with respectability, avoided it. My mother went once or twice, but the hop never became part of her life.

But it *was* at the centre of the lives of many, if not most, East Enders; so much so, in fact, that the annual hop was referred to, not without irony, as 'The Londoners' holiday'. It would hardly count as one today – the hoppers, mostly women and children, worked long hours in sometimes difficult conditions – but the annual hop constituted a break from the smoke and grime of the East End and as such it became the nearest thing to a holiday that most would ever see. Mothers, in particular, looked forward to bringing their children down to the countryside for their health, and for many East End children the annual hop was their only opportunity to run about unhampered by roads and vehicles and noise, to breathe air uncontaminated by factory waste and smoke, to watch the sun go down and look out across wide open spaces to the horizon beyond. The money East End women earned by picking hops was usually the only part of the family income over which they had control, and it was often used to buy children the boots and coats they would need for the coming winter.

The tradition of employing Londoners to pick hops in Kent began in the mid-fifteenth century when Flemish weavers first began cultivating the bines in the Kentish weald, though it's possible that cultivation itself began long before, since we know that the Romans, who marched into Britain through Kent along what is now the A2 Dover-to-Canterbury road, brought hops with them. The first *recorded* hop garden in Britain was thriving at Westbere near Canterbury in 1520, and hops were still growing on the same site more than 450 years later.

The hop plant, *Humulus lupulus*, a relative of cannabis, is a fast-growing herbaceous perennial which dies back to its rhizome in the winter. Although vine-like, it is strictly speaking a bine, the stout stems being covered with little hairs to assist in its clockwise clambering habit. Though hardy, it requires deep, well-draining loamy soil and shelter from the wind, and in the soft undulations of the Kentish downland, Flemish weavers found the perfect growing conditions. At that time, hopped beer was virtually unknown in Britain, but it had long been popular in central and northern continental Europe. All over medieval Europe, beer was a relatively safe substitute for water, which was often contaminated. In Britain, people tended to drink ale, a much heavier, sweeter drink, brewed without hops. Adding hops to beer not only imparts a grassy, bitter flavour and a spicy aroma, but the acids in the hop resin have a mild antibiotic effect which assists the work of the yeast and, along with the alcohol itself, helps preserve the beer for longer. Hopped beer can thus be brewed with a lower alcohol content than ale, which makes it a more practical substitute for water.

There were numerous early attempts to restrict hop production in Britain – Henry VIII forbade his own brewer to use such foreign fripperies and his Catholic daughter, Mary Tudor, condemned the hopping of beer as a nasty Protestant habit. All the same, the popularity of hops grew with the practically minded British, and many growers also became brewers, planting hop gardens for use in their own breweries and building drying oasts, the word taken from Flemish. During the sixteenth and seventeenth centuries, gardens were planted all over southern and central England, but the hops continued to flourish best in Kent, where there was a ready supply of sweet chestnuts with which to make poles to support the bines, the enclosed fields provided shelter, and the hops did not have far to travel to the vast breweries of London. So important did Kent become in hop production that in 1681 the London hop market moved from Little Eastcheap to Borough to be nearer to the main thoroughfare to Kent.

During the fifteenth and sixteenth centuries, troops of indigents, Gypsies and Irish and a few Londoners poured into Kent to pick the hop crop, staying on to pick the apples, pears and plums that also flourished in the 'garden of England', but the real inflow of Londoners began after the mid-seventeenth century, when Londoners took to drinking beer rather than the gin they had previously favoured, and Kentish farmers began to plant more hops to meet the demand. At first, only the poorest and the most desperate for work came, either walking the fifty or so miles from the East End of London to the Weald or, for the few who could afford the passage, travelling by boat as far as Gravesend and on foot from there to the gardens in north and east Kent. On the way, these new migrants slept in cart and cow sheds and in pigsties on mattresses of old hopbines, or, if there were none around, under hedges.

By the end of the seventeenth century Britons were consuming 300,000 hundredweight of hops every year, more than half of which were grown in Kent. A hundred and fifty years later 40,000 acres of Kentish loam were being put down to hop gardens, each acre requiring 200 pickers, numbers that could be met only by bringing Londoners down in their thousands.

As luck would have it, the hop boom coincided with the development of the railways. By the 1850s the Southeastern Railways company and the East Kent Company were putting on special hoppers' trains in the season, using cattle trucks as carriages, and the Joint Transport Committee of Railways and Farmers began printing postcards that farmers could send to London hoppers, allocating them a picking spot and a place on one of the 'hoppers' specials'. By 1867, demand was so great that Kentish farmers started using hiring agents actively to recruit hoppers from the poorest districts in London: Poplar, Whitechapel, Limehouse, Bow, Stepney and parts of Hackney to the north of the river and Bermondsey and Southwark in the south.

Families began returning to the same farms every year, often giving up their jobs and homes in order to do so. Whole neighbourhoods came en bloc, and set up their London streets in the rows of hop huts. By 1878, 72,000 acres of Kent were laid to hops and 250,000 mostly women and children were making the three- or four-week trip into Kent every year to pick them. Of these, nearly half were Londoners. And so a social and cultural event unique to Britain was born.

As I was researching the 'Londoner's Holiday' and thinking I would like to write about it, a letter arrived from a man who had read *Silvertown* and knew of my grandparents. For the purposes of this story, I am calling this man Richie Baker. A relative of Richie's had worked in my grandparents' greasy spoon for a while, and his aunt, who I'm calling Daisy Crommelin, counted my grandmother, Jenny Fulcher, among her friends. At some point in the 1970s, Daisy and my grandmother stopped seeing one another. Whether they disagreed over something or the friendship simply ran its course, I don't know. Jenny Fulcher outlived Daisy Crommelin but I'm pretty sure Jenny did not go to Daisy's funeral; the friendship clearly died some considerable time before Daisy herself.

From such seemingly tenuous connections, Richie and I established a regular correspondence, during which Richie began to reveal, bit by bit, his family story.

Daisy and her husband Harold Baker, Richie's uncle, led ordinary lives in extraordinary times. Using Richie's letters and doing some research of my own, I began to piece together the story of their relationship. For Daisy, the annual hop was a kind of Oz, the place where life meted out most of its magic. It is no exaggeration to say that, along with her family, hop picking was one of the central pillars of Daisy's life. Harold had other pleasures, as we shall see, but he was no less of a family man. On the surface, the marriage between Daisy and Harold could be seen as a pact between two people driven together by common wounds and a shared sense of fragility, the feeling that they were never more than a beat away from disaster. The contrast between the delicacy of their position and the harshness of the conditions in which they lived was one of the habitual ironies of survival in the East End in the first part of the twentieth century. As I dug around further and came to understand them more deeply, though, I realised that pain and practicality alone could not explain the bond these two people shared.

Theirs was, I believe, a great love affair, not in the Hollywood style, an explosive melange of sentimentality and sex, but in a much more profound and, perhaps, old-fashioned way. Harold and Daisy lived by the same principles. To survive and flourish in a place and at a time that offered little other than fellow travellers and almost nothing by way of second chances, they understood that happiness in life was to be found by making the most of whatever small, bright joys might flit by. For Harold and Daisy, as for many couples, the joys were not always to be had from the same things, but they tolerated each other's small claims on happiness and thereby created much for themselves. Theirs was a marriage of affectionate solidarity. Like all couples, they made compromises, but unlike many, they kept each other's confidences. They proved their love through unshakeable loyalty.

The story here belongs first and foremost to Daisy and Harold. They are not here to give their consent to my telling their story but, knowing their lives are worth the telling, I have taken the liberty of doing so. To protect their posthumous privacy I have changed their names and many others of people in this story. Like many people living in straitened circumstances in the East End of the twentieth century, Harold and Daisy did not leave a written record of their lives. There are no diaries or extensive correspondence, few official letters or documents. Richie knew them, of course, and there were others who remembered them and the events of their lives, but no two people's recollection of any event is ever identical. My correspondence with Richie and subsequent investigations are the canvas on to which I have embroidered. Some of the facts have slipped through the holes – we no longer know them nor have any means of verifying them – and in these cases I have reimagined scenes or reconstructed events in a way I believe reflects the essence of the scene or the event in the minds and hearts of the people who lived through it. Had I stuck strictly to the knowable and verifiable facts, the lives of Daisy and Harold, and many of the other people in this story, would not have been recorded on paper. To my mind this literary tinkering does not alter the more profound truth of the story. The lives Daisy and Harold led were in some ways emblematic; they were lives that, in their broad sweep, could have been lived by any number of hundreds of thousands of East Enders born in the first quarter of the twentieth century. Their struggles and triumphs were, if not the same, then similar enough to countless others to allow Daisy and Harold in some way to stand in for those who left no records and who may already have been forgotten.

Harold Baker and Daisy Crommelin were good, ordinary people. They were not celebrities or champions of anything, they achieved nothing of public note and left little behind when they died. Their lives were the most ordinary, least likely kind of lives to be put down on paper. That is why I have chosen to record them.

CHAPTER I

It was on a Monday in the early winter of 1913 that ten-year-old Daisy Crommelin's childhood came to an end. The day began ordinarily enough. At six or thereabouts, Daisy and her younger sister, Franny, were woken by their mother Elsie, and creeping from their bed so as not to disturb the lodger, Mrs Anderson, and her daughter, Maisie, who were sleeping beside them, the two girls threw on their overcoats and made their way down the rickety stairs to the scullery below. The room was dank and smelled of stewed trotters from the night before. Elsie had made their usual breakfast of mashed bread in milk and was now applying Union Jack corn paste to her feet and tutting over her chilblains. The girls' father, Joe, Freeman of the River, was rinsing off his cut-throat razor in an enamel bowl beside the sink, singing to himself and trying to ignore his wife. Seeing Franny, of whom he was particularly fond, he said:

How's me little princess?

Today, as always, Daisy tried not to mind her father's favouritism. She told herself that you couldn't expect to be loved as much when you weren't the pretty one. In any case, her father might love Franny more, but she, Daisy, had loved him longer. She brought over the two bowls her mother had prepared and sat them on the table. Joe Crommelin finished up his task and sat himself down before the plate of fried bread and faggots Elsie had made for him. Franny clambered on to his lap and all three tucked into their food in contented silence. At a quarter to seven

1

Joe Crommelin rose from the table, threw on his blue serge lighterman's garb and kissed his daughters goodbye. As he reached the door, Franny called out:

Kiss me again, Dad, and Joe, delighted by the pretty little creature he had helped bring into the world, turned and said:

Dad's gonna bring you something nice home.

Then he waved, went out of the front door and joined the general flow of men and women making their way towards the river.

Daisy watched her father go with the usual tug of pride. Just before she was born, so her mother said, a group of dockers had set on Joe on account of the free water clause which made it legal for ships to bypass the docks and unload directly into lighters. The dockers supposed that lightermen like Joe were taking their jobs. Joe had suffered horrible injuries, and the shock of it, so Elsie said, not only brought on Daisy's birth too early but was in some indefinable way responsible for her oafish ears, her spindly neck and fuzzy brown hair.

With Joe gone, Elsie put the washing copper on to boil with a handful of carboxyl then fetched herself some Beecham's Powders on account of it being a Monday and her nerves playing up. On Mondays, Elsie did the family laundry and took in neighbours' washing and was usually rather grumpy, and the children knew better than to risk vexing her further. Daisy plaited her sister's velvety hair and turned her attentions to the washing up. Just before eight, she laced her boots, which were too tight, rolled up the sleeves of her winter coat so she could see her hands, said goodbye to her mother and sister and went out into the rusty air of Bloomsbury Street.

At this moment in her life, Daisy Crommelin's world – which she took to be all the world there was – comprised a huddle of streets, riverside factories, railway yards and docks about two miles long and a mile deep, flanked on the western side by the district of Limehouse and to the east by the River Lea. This was the parish of Poplar, five miles to the east of Tower Bridge, in London's East End.

A few hundred years earlier Poplar had been a sybaritic little fishing settlement on the banks of the Thames. The river currents carved a natural deep basin on the eastern, seaward, side of Poplar at what is now Blackwall, and by the fifteenth century it had become an anchorage for the trading ships discharging their cargoes on to barges. Soon enough, a pier was built and named Brunswick after its chief financier, and in 1606 it was from this pier that the Virginia Settlers set sail to found the first permanent colony in North America. A company of shipbuilders set up shop nearby and continued to build ships at Blackwall for three centuries until the last remnant of the old business closed in 1980.

The settlement came to be called Poplar after a single tree which lay on the road leading east out of London towards the sea, and by the late eighteenth century it had a permanent population of 4,500 and was temporary home to thousands of sailors working on the tea clippers moored up on Brunswick Pier and Blackwall Wharf. To the west of the anchorage, a number of smart terraces went up, and at a polite distance from these the East India Company built almshouses for the seafaring poor. By then Poplar was a bustling, prosperous little place, growing plump on the proceeds of marine trades, its tarry turnings connected by a web of rope-walks. In 1802, anxious to protect its cargo from pilfering, the West India Company opened its first large inland dock in Poplar and added a new waterway, the City Canal, dug from marsh on the Isle of Dogs on Poplar's southern side. The new West India Dock was a wonder of modern engineering, with space for 600 clippers, each up to 1,000 tonnes in size, and nine five-storey warehouses, protected by 20-foot-high walls and looming gates. Four years later, the East India Company followed suit, opening its own dock just a few miles east at Blackwall and building two new roads, the East India

Dock Road and the Commercial Road, to connect the docks to the city.

Thousands of impoverished rush cutters and weavers from the dwindling Essex rush beds, eel fishermen and agricultural labourers flooded into the area to take up navvying jobs in the construction of the docks. Among these were Daisy's ancestors on her mother's side. Gradually, the shipowners and merchants of old Poplar slipped away to quieter, greener districts and their once grand houses were soon split into multi-occupancy lodgings. Speculators threw up tenements and turnings and dingy rents on the marshy ground and the place began, bit by bit, to accumulate the flotsam and jetsam of human desperation. Drinking and gambling dens appeared, brothels looked out on to open sewers, and poorhouses, missions, soup kitchens and charitable lodgings soon went up to serve the most basic needs of the fallen and destitute. The river became a dumping ground for sewage, industrial waste and the leavings of slaughterhouses.

In the middle of the nineteenth century, the area changed again, when the North London and the Great Eastern railways arrived, chopped the little place in two and blanketed it in coal dust, smuts and grease. A giant gas works went up in the east, beside the River Lea, followed by sawmills, a jam factory, chemical works, a corn mill, a metallic cask works, breweries, a paint works and a factory making incandescent mantles. People joked that in a prevailing westerly wind, you could smell Poplar all the way to France.

Exiles from remote wars and famines and distant pogroms began pouring into Poplar, and by the time Daisy Crommelin was born, in 1903, the district was the poorest in London; 40 per cent of Poplar's inhabitants lived with their families in a single room.

The Crommelins had escaped the worst of the poverty. Joe's trade, piloting lighters across the Thames from ship to jetty, was protected by a guild and, though his wages were modest, they were regular. Elsie had been in domestic service until Joe had rescued her with his offer of marriage, and she now supplemented the family income by taking in laundry and assembling silk flowers. They occupied the scullery and the downstairs front room of number 7 Bloomsbury Street; the girls shared their bedroom with Mrs Anderson and Maisie and the second bedroom was rented to a distant cousin. There was a yard with a yard dog and a privy shared with next door. Modest thought it was, the Crommelins were proud of their home, knowing it to be several steps up from some of the rat-, child- and scandal-infested sinks in the street. Only two doors down lived Helen Reid. No one had ever seen a Mr Reid and one of 'Mrs' Reid's four children was a half-breed. The Reids shared their house with old Flossie Lumin, who could regularly be seen out at night picking drunken fights with anyone who came by. Then there were the Greenbergs on the corner, not only Jewish, but anarchists too! Elsie had it that Bloomsbury Street got more common the farther down it you went. According to Elsie, the most distant end, which she called The Deep, was a hotbed of ruffians, criminals and loose women, and she forbade her two girls from going there or speaking to anyone who had. To distinguish her family from the residents of The Deep, Elsie spent much of her time scrubbing, whitening, blackening, polishing, mending, ironing, sweeping, dusting and bleaching. The Deep and the dirt were close bedfellows, she said. Respectable folk kept them both at bay.

In Elsie's opinion, the only close neighbours who passed muster, despite being Irish, were the Shaunessys next door at number 5. Marie Shaunessy was a sweet-hearted, only mildly bossy woman who had married a hard-working French polisher called Patrick, and they had a son, Billy, who, unbeknown to Elsie, was a crybaby and a pincher. Billy Shaunessy would often wait for Daisy in a little alleyway a few blocks farther down the street then fire pieces of coal at her with his catapult, but when

Daisy had once tried to wrest the catapult from him, he had pinched her then burst into tears in such an alarming manner that Daisy thought it better, on balance, to put up with the barrage of fired coals than risk Mrs Shaunessy finding out what a hopeless booby she had for a son, for Daisy loved Mrs Shaunessy. She and Franny would often go round to the Shaunessys' while their mother recovered from one or other of her digestive and nervous complaints, and the two Crommelin girls viewed Mrs Shaunessy as a sort of maternal stand-in. Many were the nights that Daisy would lie in bed wishing that she and Franny could be Mrs Shaunessy's daughters. Maybe their mother could have Billy in return. A year or two before Daisy was born, Elsie had birthed twin boys, but they had both died very shortly afterwards and, in accordance with East End custom, Elsie hadn't attended the funeral.

If I'd only seen me twinnies laid in their boxes, she would say, *I wouldn't suffer these bonce aches, and this gnawing in me bones.*

The arrival of Daisy, on 17 March 1903, *as blue as a monkey's arse*, as Elsie put it, only seemed to remind Elsie of the loss she'd suffered.

The gel's got her father's elephant ears and doggy chops, Elsie would announce, cheerfully, to Mrs Shaunessy. *Ain't no one gonna mistake her for no Mona Lisa.*

Oh, I don't know about that, Mrs C, Mrs Shaunessy would reply. *That gel of yours is a regular sweetheart. Good as gold, not a mean or nasty hair on her head.*

Later, Elsie would complain to Joe about their neighbour.

I ain't saying she ain't good to us, Elsie would say, mustering her righteous indignation. *But she should mind her p's and q's. I ask you, what kind of woman thinks she has the right to tell a mother about her own daughter?*

Now, Else, Joe would say, hanging up his jacket and cap and sitting down for his tea, *calm down, old gel, there's plenty worse at sea.*

Elsie would slap down her husband's tea of brawn and boiled greens.

Like you'd know, Joe Crommelin, she'd say. *What's never bleedin' been at sea but spouts so much sailor talk you'd think he was Sir Walter Bleedin' Rally.* Then she'd turn back to her daughter.

Eat your tea or the Sandeman'll eat it for you.

The Sandeman lived in The Deep and sometimes spirited naughty children away. Whenever Daisy vexed her mother, Elsie would hold her head in her hands and swear that if Daisy didn't start being good in short order, the Sandeman would appear and snatch her up and there wouldn't be a thing Elsie or anyone else would be able to do about it.

When Franny came along, Elsie's sourness softened, at least for a while. Daisy's younger sister was a peach, with a head of light brown curls and dimpled little hands. When Elsie took Franny out in her pram, people would stop and coo and say what a darling baby she was and Elsie, endeavouring to look modest, would explain that she'd lost her twinnies and given birth to a plain girl, but Franny was proof that bad luck only ever ran in threes and her arrival had made up, at least in part, for Elsie's earlier disappointments.

Sensing from early on the power her physical attributes gave her, Franny quickly developed an alarming determination to use them to her advantage. Though neither of her parents seemed to notice, Daisy realised early on that her sister was turning into a canny little manipulator, but in the light she brought with her Daisy could see Franny faintly illuminated a fragile path to Elsie's heart, and she could not find it in herself to resent her sister. She was everyone's darling.

Now Daisy walked along Bloomsbury Street in thin rain and stopped at the corner to wait for her best friend, Lilly Seldon. Elsie didn't approve of the liaison, insisting that Lilly was as rough as pumice, but Elsie was like that about almost everyone Daisy showed an interest in.

Common is as common does, she'd say, but she did not prevent her daughter from seeing her friend. Lilly and Daisy had been friends since their third week at Culloden Street School, when Lilly had backed Daisy into a corner and asked her why her ears stuck out. Later, Lilly said she was sorry about the ears and that she herself had a big nose, and even though she wasn't a Jew, she had often wondered where that had come from too.

'Ere, Lilly said, *a penny says you can't guess old Peasewell's nick-name.* Miss Peasewell was the teacher who daily struggled to inculcate into her pupils a sense of respect for their betters, who numbered almost everyone.

I don't know: Pease Puddin'? Daisy ventured, conscious that her future in some way depended on the answer.

Pease Puddin'? Lilly snorted. *Pease Puddin'? What a doze you are. Pease Puddin' ain't a name.*

Daisy shrugged and said she couldn't think of any other name.

Pigswill, silly, said Lilly, landing a friendly punch on Daisy's arm. *Old Piggy Pigswill, ha ha ha.* Then she looked up at Daisy and saw those ears and relented. *I suppose Pease Puddin' ain't so bad, though*, she said.

And after that, the two girls became the best of friends.

Four years of education had not served Daisy well and she often relied on Lilly to dig her out of the holes in her learning. She could read and write well enough to check a pawn ticket, though, or decipher the numbers on the tallyman's chit, and she knew just by looking at the coins in her hand whether or not a trader had short-changed her; already she sensed that these skills were likely to be most of what she needed to reach the low horizons mapped out for girls like her. She would stay on at school until she reached twelve and join the half-and-half system, spending half her time at school and the other half working in a factory. A year or two later, if she was diligent and lucky, the factory might take her on full-time, or she might find work sewing collars and cuffs or wrapping bars of soap. If not,

8

she would become one of the 30 per cent of working women who were forced to leave their homes and families and find work as domestic servants. She'd heard enough about life as a domestic from her mother to find the prospect terrifying: the slavish hours, the removal from family and friends and the complete dependence on the whims of strangers. She knew she wasn't sharp like Lilly, but what she lacked in brains she determined to make up for in diligence. One day, she hoped Keiler's or Peek Freans or some other factory would see how hard she applied herself and want to take her on.

At midday, she packed her slate and headed back home for her lunch. A warm, fatty smell greeted her at the door of number 7. Elsie was in the scullery shuffling the piles of drying laundry she had been washing all morning. It was no longer raining and Franny was shut outside in the yard with the dog. Elsie opened the door and called her in, then, making a space at the table, she slopped down two bowls of bacon barley soup and, announcing she had a bonce ache so bad it felt like a horse had kicked her in the head, went to lie down for a while.

Whenever the family needed a bit more money than usual, Elsie would keep Daisy back from school in the afternoons to help her with her flower-making. From one o'clock to six o'clock they would sit on the floor in the scullery, twisting and wiring and stringing, starching and curling, delicately painting spots and shadings on scraps of silk until what had been nothing more than a pile of brightly coloured fragments had been transformed into the silk irises, forget-me-nots, violets and roses that would adorn the hats of women and girls more fortunate than themselves. While they worked, Franny would be dispatched to Mrs Shaunessy, or sent to play in the yard, or, if the weather was bad and Mrs Shaunessy wasn't in, locked in her room to prevent her from messing up the scraps of silk and delicate fixings.

It was piecework and poorly paid; on cold and damp days Elsie would complain that her finger joints knitted together and on warmer days the silk dust scratched at both their lungs and brought on bronchitis. By the end of the afternoon, their eyes were often so irritated by glue and fibres that they swelled and oozed with yellowish fluid. But there were worse jobs for the homeworker, like making matchboxes or stitching newly tanned leather for shoe soles, and, as Elsie liked to remind Daisy, there were plenty of women and children down in The Deep who were at that very moment busy doing them.

On weekday evenings, after work or school, Elsie expected Daisy to play outdoors, and she and Lilly would pass the time spinning tops, or playing pat-a-cake or skipping games, or they would simply walk about the streets of Poplar, hanging off the street lamps and gazing in the windows of the shops. In winter, Mrs Shaunessy would sometimes take pity on them and let them warm themselves at her fire and give them a slice of parkin or a rock bun.

The one exception to this was Friday afternoon, when Daisy was expected carefully to wrap the week's flowers in tissues, arrange them in a series of old cigar boxes and place them inside a tea chest on to which Joe had grafted some old pram wheels, then help her mother push the chest three miles west along the Commercial Road to Leitkov's millinery in Aldgate, where they would collect their payment for the week's work and pick up a new allocation of silk scraps, ribbons, wire, beads and paints. These Elsie stored in a large keel-shaped basket woven from Kentish willow which she kept beside the fireplace to keep the silk from getting damp.

You ever touch this basket without my say-so, Elsie would warn her daughters, *and the Sandeman will carry you off to the orphanage so fast you won't know what's hit you.*

So they never did.

Daisy always looked forward to Friday evenings, when Joe

would often bring them some treat he'd lifted from his lighter cargo – a few locust beans or carob pods, some liquorice twigs, a handful of monkey nuts or even a crab or two. While he ate his tea, he would regale his daughters with all that had happened to him that week on the river. Sometimes the tar boats caught fire and the whole of the river would become a wall of blue and orange flame or the water would freeze into a slush littered with icy diamonds. Other times, great fish would rise from the water and tell stories about all the drowned sailors who lived in huge cities at the bottom of the sea, or Joe would uncover a smugglers' den or spot a mermaid stranded by the tide.

Saturday mornings were taken up with chores, but on Saturday afternoons Joe would take his girls to the Sally Army concerts in Tunnel Park and afterwards treat them to a piece of cold fried fish or a little waxed cone full of whelks and a jam jar of lemonade. On Sundays Elsie would boil up a sheep or pig head. On special occasions she would take a piece of gammon ham or a pork leg to the bakers to roast and follow it with a steamed syrup pudding or a spotted dick. Sunday nights were lived in dread of Elsie's Monday feints and tantrums.

Today was no exception. If anything, Elsie had been even more grumpy than was usual on a Monday. The Friday before, Leitkov had given Elsie and Daisy twice the usual amount of silk and ribbon and finishings so they might complete enough flowers for the Christmas rush, and Daisy and her mother had worked late on Friday night, then again on Saturday and Sunday, but by Monday morning they had made barely a dent in the piles of scraps and pieces of ribbon in the willow basket, and Elsie decided to keep her eldest back from school in the afternoons so they could get the job done. Now she was ill with one of her innumerable, vague complaints, and Daisy was left trying to get through the task alone.

At five, Elsie rose from her bed in a fluster, glanced at the mantelpiece clock, started muttering to herself about the time and getting Joe's tea, then, throwing on her coat, announced she was going to fetch a piece of pork belly or maybe a spot of jellied trotter, leaving Daisy with instructions to begin boxing up the flowers and to make sure Franny remained in her room until they were all safely packed away. In recognition of her daughter's efforts she put a halfpenny in Daisy's hand, telling her to spend it on muffins or a toffee apple from one of the vendors who paraded their wares around the streets on open trays, accumulating smuts and factory fumes.

Now you be careful while I'm gone. The Sandeman's watching and don't you forget it.

Daisy began gathering up the flowers and scraps of unused silk, but within minutes of her mother's departure, she heard Franny crying and begging to be released from her room. For a while Daisy ignored her, but, eventually, her heart pricked, she climbed the flimsy staircase and opened the bedroom door, thinking she would set her little sister in the yard to play with the dog. When they reached the back door they saw that a greenish fog had come down and Franny shook her curls and screwed her delicate little face into a fist, and Daisy, who could never bring herself to do anything that made her sister unhappy, sat her at the table and told her to sit as still as the clock on the mantelshelf and touch nothing.

No harm might have come of this minor infraction of the rules had the toffee apple man not turned into Bloomsbury Street at precisely that moment, crying:

Apples and flats, apples and flats!

Flats, the discs of toffee that pooled from the toffee apples when they were left to set, were the two girls' favourite treat, and it was so rare for them to have any money with which to buy anything, that Daisy could not resist the impulse to go out into the street and get some.

Don't touch nothing. I'll only be a minute.

Despite the weather, a line of wide-eyed children had already formed around the toffee apple man's tray and it took Daisy a while to push through the crowd, claim her prize and hurry back to the house. When she did, she realised immediately the mistake she had made in leaving her little sister alone. The scullery looked as though a high wind had passed through it. Silk scraps lay scattered across the lino flooring and between the scraps broken flowers lay, their petals wrenched out or torn or bent at strange angles. There was ribbon strewn across the table, torn and knotted in places. The air was dense with fibres and silk dust and the sheets and pillowcases that had been hanging on string lines beside the fire were spotted all over with little pieces of silk, whose bright colours were already creeping their way across the whiteness of the cotton. And there was Franny sitting in the midst of it with her hands in the basket.

Oh, my knees and knuckles, Daisy said, *Franny Crommelin, what have you done?*

You said sit still as the clock, Franny cried in a voice ripe with indignation, *but the clock moved!* Daisy glanced towards the mantel-piece, where the clock was still in the place it had always been, its spot marked out on the mantel in dust and smuts from the fire. But ten minutes had passed and the hands of the clock had indeed moved.

I want the flowers! Franny screamed. *You always have the flowers.*

Suddenly, Daisy understood why her sister had done what she had. Franny had torn up the silk because she didn't want Daisy to have anything she didn't have, and because she knew she could. Already so sure of her power over the family, Franny knew that, whatever she did, her older sister would somehow always shoulder the blame. The thought of it was unbearable to Daisy, yet at the same time she knew it was true.

This time she had gone too far. Half lifting, half dragging, Daisy forced her sister through the scullery, and pushing her out into the yard. As she stumbled on to the flags, Franny uttered a low growl, the sound, Daisy remembered later, of a cornered cat, full of defiance and contempt. She shut the back door behind her, turned the key in the lock and leaned on it, trying to catch her breath. After all she'd been to her little sister, it hadn't been enough. Franny resented her, hated her even, and wanted her to fail. She began scurrying about, picking up silk scraps, pressing them back into shape with her hands, scooping up the pieces of feather and red and green ribbon, trying to salvage what she could from the mess, but pretty soon Franny began a piteous wailing in the yard, and all the love and protectiveness Daisy felt for her little sister flooded back and she felt disabled and ashamed. Opening the door, she said:

All right, all right, there, there.

You said to stay still as the clock, Franny said sulkily. *You said it, but the clock moved.*

Daisy nodded. Franny was right. What had happened was her fault. It was all her fault. She returned to the clearing up. It very soon became clear that most of the flowers, the silk scraps and ribbon were ruined and the laundry was dotted about with blooms of transferred dye. Daisy dreaded her mother's return.

When Elsie saw the mess she screamed so loudly that Mrs Shaunessy came rushing round, thinking she was being attacked, and after she left, Elsie pounded and thumped Daisy so hard that her breath came in rasps as if from an old kettle.

I wish the Sandeman would come and take yer. I wish he would, Elsie raged. *'Cause you ain't no good to me, yer blue-arsed little weakling with yer elephant ears. I wish you'd never been born. I wish the Sandeman would take yer right now so that I wouldn't ever have to trouble me eyes with you again.*

As she swore and rampaged about, Franny sat at the table, perfectly still, with a little smile playing on her face.

What Daisy did not know and could not know then was how far and with what shocking speed this event would tumble into another, and another and another, until only the thinnest barrier, as fragile as eggshell, separated the Crommelin household from catastrophe. She did not know this because she did not consider her family to be poor – hadn't Elsie always said they were respectable? – and because she had no notion yet of how vulnerable they were, and because she had not been alive long enough to understand the relentless cruelty of the East End tides, which daily washed in the hopeful and the desperate and daily dashed their hopes. She did not know, yet, what Joe Crommelin knew and had not thought to tell her, because she was not a boy, that to survive you had to steer your course mid-stream, where the water was deepest and ran fastest, that you had to paddle fast, as fast as you could, to stay there, to stay still in the rushing current, because the price of failure was to be washed up on the beach or be dashed to pieces on the wharves.

On Friday, Daisy walked alone to Leitkov's, but instead of the usual boxes of jaunty irises and delicate roses, she carried the Kentish willow basket with what remained of the scraps. Listening to her story, the milliner sat impassively for a while, then reached for his account book and started totting up figures in his head. Eventually he said:

Tell your mother she owes me eight shillings and sixpence and there'll be no more work till she's paid it. I'll be sending my man around every Friday to collect two and six. Tell her that.

Daisy returned home with the news. She sensed that, from now on, Friday evenings would never be the same.

For a while, Elsie struggled to pay back the money she owed Leitkov. She took in more laundry and kept Daisy back from school to help her with it and for days together the scullery reeked of carbolic and borax and Mrs Anderson complained that the plashing sound of the dolly peg and the rhythmic scraping of the washboard disturbed her sleep, but they never seemed to be able to make enough to pay off the collector when he came on a Friday. The experience seemed at once both to harden Daisy's mother and render her more fragile, as though she'd been fired in a kiln at the wrong temperature. Elsie began to look around for things to hock. The first thing to go was the mantelpiece clock, then after that the china Elsie had been given as a wedding present by the woman in whose house she had worked as a maid. Next was Elsie's overcoat, then Daisy's, followed by some bed blankets. On Monday mornings it was now Daisy's job to fill the cart that had once contained silk flowers with blankets and coats and set off for the pawnbroker, and as she walked by Helen Reid with her half-caste son, past the Greenbergs, it seemed that all that lay between them and The Deep were a few front doors.

Not long into the New Year, Elsie stopped eating, and at the same time she took up cleaning and polishing and scrubbing and bleaching and sweeping with more vigour than ever, and often at the oddest times. It was nothing to find her whitening the step at six in the morning, or hunched over her scrubbing brush in the middle of the night. When he got home from work in the evenings, Joe tried to comfort her, but she beat him off with her fists, and told him he could *bugger off and take his bloody children with him*. He began to spend more and more time in the pub after that.

The spring of 1914 arrived and patriotic flags began to appear in the shops. In May 1914 Joe came home with the news that the dockers had refused to handle German cargo and Mrs Shaunessy reported that Burrelli's paint factory, where Mr Shaunessy worked, had dismissed all its German workers. By early summer, the more usual advertisements for flu powders and meat tea pasted on to Poplar's billboards began to be replaced by recruitment posters and men in uniform were seen outside the East End's pubs and cafés. Billy Shaunessy started catapulting boys and girls in the street and shouting:

Halt, friend or foe?

By late summer, columns of men had begun marching up and down the East India Dock Road most days, and queues of men gathered at the recruiting station in Poplar High Street, waiting to volunteer for the standard six-month tour of duty which was how long everyone was saying it would take to defeat the Hun. It was said that one fifth of those signing up were of German descent, keen to prove their patriotism or maybe to save their skins, for German butchers were having their windows smashed and anyone with a German name was in danger not just of losing his job but of being set upon in the street. At Culloden Street School Old Pigswill introduced an air-raid drill and taught potted histories of the calumnies of the Boche. In early September a sign went up at the general store around the corner offering *credit for volunteer families only*. The following day a great oval-shaped cloud floated across Poplar and in class Old Pigswill explained that airships would help defeat the enemy. Later that week a policeman rode by on a bicycle shouting *Take cover!* and sirens sounded and Daisy returned home at lunchtime to find her mother locked in the understairs cupboard shouting *Give me back my twinnies!* with Mrs Anderson rapping on the cupboard door and threatening to fetch Joe and the police and the doctor all at once. That night Daisy heard Joe and Mrs Shaunessy talking about her mother in hushed tones, Mrs Shaunessy every now and then clicking her tongue against her teeth, as though she were measuring the march of the Sandeman, advancing toward them.

Later that week Daisy returned home from school to find Mrs Anderson cooking faggots in the scullery.

Your mother's gone for a little rest, poor duck, said Mrs Anderson. *But never you worry, Mrs Shaunessy's going to be taking you and yer sister on a nice long trip to the countryside.*

CHAPTER 2

Mrs Shaunessy trudged forward in the gloom before dawn, trundling her hop box on a borrowed barrow. For the past three months she'd been stashing away the odd jar of Bovril, a sugar cube or two and a few packets of flour in the box that Paddy Shaunessy had fashioned from an old tea chest, and the night before she'd filled it with a bucket, a tea towel, a scrubbing brush and other domestic paraphernalia. Behind her Daisy pushed a pram containing Franny, who, at four, was far too big for the lacy bonnet Mrs Shaunessy had insisted that she wear as a kind of disguise (for what purpose she would discover later), and a half-dozen tins of corned beef. Billy Shaunessy trailed behind with a Union Jack sticking out of his pocket. Ever since Mr Shaunessy had signed up, Mrs Shaunessy considered it a matter of filial duty that Billy demonstrate the family's patriotism at every opportunity, and the flag was intended for this purpose. Whenever men in uniform passed, heading towards the docks, Mrs Shaunessy would turn her head and say:

Wave that flag, Billy! And give our men a cheer!

And, scowling, Billy would jab the flag in the air and issue a half-hearted hoorah. As they neared London Bridge the number of soldiers increased, and by the time they reached the bridge itself poor Billy was jabbing and cheering like a mad thing. Mrs Shaunessy strode on ahead across the bridge, singing 'Onward, Christian Soldiers!'

The tide was up and the wide black water tumbled beneath

them, but they did not stop to admire the dark cords of lighters bobbing around on the tarry surface, nor the belching little tugs slicing through the currents, nor even the elegant tea clippers that sat outside the London Dock in the Lower Pool, their slender masts lit by the light of paraffin lamps on passing tugs. In all her eleven years, Daisy had never been so far from home. She tried to remind herself that Poplar was just there, just a mile or two downriver, and in a few hours' time her father would be somewhere on this water, sculling between ship and shore, but she felt frightened and a little homesick and she missed her mother and could not help but feel that she was in some way responsible for everything that had happened.

They reached the end of the bridge and Mrs Shaunessy led the little party along Tooley Street, through a set of immense yellow columns and into London Bridge Station. Inside, they were greeted by a great hoot of noise, a bluster of men and women and a whorl of pearly smoke. Everywhere there were women and children dragging carts and boxes or standing beside towers of cheap cardboard suitcases, some singing, others shouting instructions to the porters, but everyone seemed good-spirited and happy and for now, at least, Daisy was reassured.

Mrs Shaunessy collected her charges together beside a large crudely painted sign, reading *Hoppers' Specials!*, and with three fingers pointing to, respectively, the High, Central and Low Levels.

Now, she said, *me and Billy is going to run along and get the tickets so you stay there. Don't you move none and don't speak to no strangers.*

Daisy felt a sly, hard pinch on her arm. She moved over very slightly and stamped on Billy's foot. The boy shot her an evil look and bit his lip, but said nothing and moved off with his mother, limping slightly.

Ever since she'd known them, which was all her life, Mrs Shaunessy's family had gone hop picking in the late summer.

Mrs Shaunessy said the fresh air and exercise were good for children, and the space and time apart were good for husbands and wives. There was nothing like the freedom that you felt on a long evening with the fires burning and someone striking up a song, she said, knowing that the next day there would be no step to whiten, no coal to heave, no blacking of the range, no boiling laundry or wiping smuts from windows that would be smutty again twenty minutes later.

Most of the Crommelins' neighbours went to the hop. In fact, almost everyone Daisy knew, including Lilly, had at least one hopper in the family. Daisy didn't know why the Crommelins had never been. Her mother had once said she thought it was common, so perhaps that was it. Perhaps it had something to do with her mother's poor health.

The Shaunessys returned in a flash, Mrs Shaunessy carrying two slips of paper, and they soon found themselves on a long platform beside which stood an immense, sooty train. Daisy and Franny heard them coughing along the railway tracks at Poplar, but they had never seen one so close and looking so huge. Mrs Shaunessy parked her hop cart and began looking up and down the platform, then she turned to Daisy and said:

When I say to get on the train you do it and sharpish. Not a second early, not a second late. Billy here will help me with the pram.

She leaned down into the pram again and, pretending to fluster with the baby blanket, whispered:

And not one tiny word from you, miss, not a bleep or a toot. Babies go free and for now you're one of them, or your father will be paying the price of your ticket.

Soon a whistle blew and Mrs Shaunessy lunged forward. Elbowing several women out of the way, she swung open the door of the carriage and hissed, *Now!* Billy, for whom this was an annual routine, leapt to the top of the steps, and helped his mother yank and heave the hop box on to the train, then did the same again for the pram.

They took up a bench in the middle of one of the emptier carriages. Mrs Shaunessy parked the pram beside her so that the hood was facing outwards into the corridor and Franny's face was obscured. Not long afterwards the train hooted and began to lurch from the station.

Now Daisy, ducky, Mrs Shaunessy said, laying her overcoat and a blanket on the bench and spreading her skirts across it, *you just creep under here and don't make no noise.* She lifted the coverings. *And don't you come out a second before I tell you to, or you'll be bringing a whole heartful of trouble down on me. No noise, mind, quiet as mice.*

Under Mrs Shaunessy's overcoat and skirts it was dark and foisty and the prevailing smell of damp and mothballs was so penetrating that for a while Daisy felt as though she might be sick. The train gathered speed, some minutes passed, then she became conscious of a man's voice asking for tickets, after which there was some hasty movement of Mrs Shaunessy's skirts and she heard Mrs Shaunessy saying:

Only me and the boy, mister, plus the babe there, but she goes free, now, don't she?

Eventually, she became accustomed to the cloying whiff and the warmth and the gentle tick-tocking of the train did their work and she remembered nothing more of the journey until she was pinched awake by Billy Shaunessy and, surfacing, saw to her astonishment that they had left the world she knew and had entered a new and strange one. The sun was rising but instead of the dun glimmer that signalled the start of the day in Poplar, everything was bathed in the colours of silk freesias. All along the carriage women and children were gazing from the windows and a hushed silence had fallen of the sort Daisy usually associated with the moment her mother put hot food on the table. She clambered to the window and took her place at it.

At first she saw only a blur of unfamiliar shapes within which she could discern no building, no factory, no street or row of shops, no market or press of people. When she tried to focus on a single object outside the train it raced away from her. Gradually she began to pick out gentle slopes, wooded knolls and copses, and stands of trees. Between the trees, she could see now, the great green swell was divided here and there by little green walls enclosing streets of gnarly trees or bushes, and dotted inside these walls were cows like the ones she'd once seen at Limehouse dairy. A few lonely-looking buildings, which Daisy took to be factories or poorhouses, were dotted about. Some of these were circular and topped with cones on which sat white dunce's caps. She remembered with a jolt what Billy had once said about her mother: *Me mum says your mum's jigged in the bonce and got put in a fool hasylum.* She wondered whether these, too, were hasylums. The distance to the horizon took her breath away. She hadn't imagined the world could be so big. Where the sky met the land there was a ribbon of such vivid blue that it reminded Daisy of the turbans of certain Lascar sailors.

Soon, they were passing streets of red-brick houses and the train began to slow and, for an instant, until she saw the sign on the platform, which read *Faversham*, Daisy thought they were back in London. A great many women and children stepped off the train and there was a short commotion of baggage and shouted instructions before the carriage doors slammed and the engine began to heave itself from the station once more. They hadn't been going long before there was a loud whoosh of air and they were crossing a bridge with a high embankment painted with pink and yellow flowers, then descending towards a tiny cluster of houses separated by meandering paths banked with hedges. It all looked so empty and old and crooked, Daisy thought, like the pictures on biscuit tins, only without the courting couples.

Soon Daisy felt the engine begin to slow again and she noticed Mrs Shaunessy fussing with her things. They helped Franny out of the pram and the train came to a halt beside a neat brick and clapboard building decorated with fancy cut-out work. From this hung a sign reading *Selling*. Billy Shaunessy opened the door, leapt on to the platform and reached back in to receive the hop box and the pram. Once everything was unloaded, Mrs Shaunessy signalled for the children to follow her down the platform. A party swung by laughing wildly and chanting:

> *Oh, they say hopping's lousy*
> *I don't believe it's true.*
> *We only go down hoppin'*
> *To earn a bob or two,*
> *Oooohhhh, with an ee-aye-o, ee-aye-o, ee-aye-ee-aye-o*

Among them, Daisy recognised familiar faces. She was struck by how much smaller everyone looked out here, in this new world. It was as though the countryside had reduced them all to dolls.

Despite all the jollity, or perhaps because of it, Franny was unimpressed with their new surroundings.

I want me dad, she wailed, shuffling in close to her sister. *I wanna go ho-ome*.

But Daisy knew there was no hope of going home soon. London was an almost infinite distance away, behind endless hills and trees. The air felt thin and cutting, its smell something between river mud and the salted cabbages Jews sold out of barrels. She took in a deep breath, picked up her bag, grabbed her sister's hand and began to shuffle down the platform towards the station building.

We're here now, Franny, she said. *Let's make the best of it, eh?*

She spotted Mrs Shaunessy up ahead, waving, and they stepped through the station building on to the soft ooze of a cinder path, its give under the feet strangely unsettling, like the grass in Tunnel Park after the river had flooded.

Opposite the station stood a handful of red-brick cottages spread out along a flinty road coloured rosehip pink in the early sun. Up ahead, Mrs Shaunessy was making her way towards a rustic wagon watched over by a solid-looking carter, who wore the kind of thick, crescent-shaped beard Daisy had only seen before on the very old men who lined up outside the Sally Army soup kitchen waiting for food. The carter was directing two nut-brown assistants in billowing shirts as they hoisted hop boxes and suitcases into the wagon, and when that was done, he shouted, *Hoi, hoi* to his horse and the wagon began to trundle along the flinty road and away.

Mrs Shaunessy took hold of the pram and began striding off after it, and they made their way through the village, which seemed to consist of a single row of modest houses whose red bricks had grown speckled from the salted wind swooping in from marshes a few miles to the north. The houses did not give directly out on to the street as they did in Poplar, but were fronted by neat little plots planted with vegetables and fruit bushes. Everywhere there were trees, leaves clattering alarmingly in the breeze like panicked hoofs on distant cobbles.

Ah, save us, said Mrs Shaunessy, breathing in deep. The cabbagey, empty smell had been replaced now by a thick and tarry aroma. *If it ain't the hops.*

Just then the wind blew up again, scattering pieces of straw across the road.

It stinks, shrieked Franny, burying her face in her sister's coat. *I want to go home.*

Billy Shaunessy raised his eyes to heaven and kicked a stone.

Listen to Little Miss Muck, Mrs Shaunessy said, not unkindly. *Before the week's out she won't want to be nowhere else. Ain't that right, Billy boy?*

Billy grunted and kicked another stone.

They passed a road sign reading *Neames Forstal* and Mrs Shaunessy explained that Selling station wasn't actually in Selling, but not to worry because everything would become clear.

Pretty soon they had left Neames Forstal behind entirely and were progressing along a deeply rutted road that slid between hedges embroidered with the lace umbrellas of hogweed and pink bladder campions. Others joined them, greeted each other and exchanged gossip. Every so often, when someone she recognised overtook them, Mrs Shaunessy would shout out:

Flossie Felcher, well I never! or *Janey Simpson, now don't you look a picture. You ain't never had another little 'un!* and the two women would look one another up and down, shake their heads over the general state of things and vow to have a good catch-up later on.

After a while, they crossed a footpath that dipped down into a little valley filled with apple orchards, and these in turn gave way to a wood. They could still see the wagon up ahead, the carter slapping his horse from time to time with the reins. The hedgerow here was lined with wildflowers between which danced pretty little blue and brown butterflies.

Look, Franny said, momentarily forgetting her misery to toddle along the bank scooping at the creatures with her hands. *Baby birds!*

They walked on, past a huge grey house and a cluster of smaller cottages, the most distant of which gave on to fields sprinkled with the cone-hatted houses. Far to the north was the glittering strip of blue Daisy had seen from the train.

They stopped finally, beside a mossy oak gate guarding the entrance to a large grassy field. The carter and his assistants were already unloading the bags and boxes and piling them up on the verge and there were women and children reloading their belongings into wooden wheelbarrows. Beyond the gate, the field rose before them. At its farthest fringe sat a row of white-washed huts, and outside the huts there were women moving to and fro and children playing. Fires had been lit and some of the women were stirring pots hanging over the flames. Mrs

Shaunessy located her hop cart in the melee and was busy pulling it towards the pram, guarded by Billy.

Well, don't just stand there like a pair of pickles. Get pushing! she said.

They were part-way up the slope when a girl came running down to meet them.

What you doing here, Doze? It was Lilly Seldon. So relieved was Daisy to see her friend that for a moment she thought she might burst into tears.

Lilly took the pram handle and began helping to push.

Daisy said that for some reason to do with the war and her mother, they had come with Mrs Shaunessy. When she'd asked for an explanation, Mrs Shaunessy had placed her finger on the bridge of her nose and shaken her head, saying, *Now, now, nosy parker. Curiosity killed the cat.*

I suppose your mum'll fetch you when she gets back, Lilly said.

Daisy looked up, past the huts through the thicket of trees to the cloudless sky above.

I suppose, she said. She looked down at her feet. Talk of her mother sent a pulse of shame through her, then another of guilt for the shame. She knew it was something more than rest her mother needed. Perhaps Billy Shaunessy was right and Elsie was in a dunce hasylum. A leafy stalk had attached itself to her boot and when she bent down to pluck it off, the stem stuck to her fingers. She pushed it away only to have it attach itself to her leg.

Goosegrass, you doze, Lilly said, laughing. She plucked it off between two fingers and flung it into the hedgerow. *I'm glad you've come.*

Like all the other huts, hop hut number 21, about halfway along the field, was put together from rough planks set on to a strip of concrete and roofed in tarpaper. It had a window roughly glazed and a stable door made from whitewashed planks fixed with padlocks, which Mrs Shaunessy was busy unlocking. She passed Daisy a bucket and told Lilly to show her where to fetch water. A queue of children stood noisily beside the single tap serving the huts. As Lilly and Daisy waited their turn, Lilly pointed out the cookhouse, the path leading to the hop gardens and, at some distance away, a shed that served as the privy. When they returned with the water, Mrs Shaunessy handed them each a rag and told them to begin wiping the walls. Inside, it was dark, the air was oddly still and there was a familiar smell of dampness overlying another, earthy aroma. Cobwebs lay across every surface and, as they scrubbed, huge spiders, evicted from their homes, scuttled away into the darker corners. While they worked, Mrs Shaunessy laid a piece of lino on the mud floor. That done, she began hanging pots and cups on hooks and stringing a makeshift curtain at the window, instructing Daisy and Lilly to busy themselves stuffing a palliasse with straw from a bale left outside the hut. Pretty soon, a man with a lazy eye and a squint and a plump, homely-looking woman arrived. It seemed that the man was Mrs Shaunessy's brother, Alfie, and the woman, Joan, was his wife. Later, an old woman with metal hair rollers and a witchy-looking goitre fetched up and sat herself down on a sawn-up log outside the hop hut next door. This was Nell, with whom Daisy, Franny and the Shaunessys would be lodging.

By five their chores were done and they sat on the grass outside, which was long, unlike park grass, and ate jam sandwiches and drank hot tea. Franny asked whether they were having a picnic and Daisy said they were but then Franny said her sandwich tasted of grass and began to cry.

Tired, overexcited, said Mrs Shaunessy, carrying Franny into the hut and shooing the older children off to play.

Lilly took Daisy along a pathway that ran into the wood beside the huts. There were fairies there, she said – she knew because she'd seen them. Light fell through the leaves and lit the path with little sparkles. The stillness and quiet inside the woods were so peculiar and so daunting, Daisy had to keep blinking to make sure she wasn't caught in some odd dream. A thousand ideas flipped through her mind. They walked in silence for a while, reaching the edge of the wood and skirting a field. How many trees were there? Daisy wanted to know. Had Lilly ever counted them? Did the fields go on for ever or was it possible to reach their end? Why did the wind blow so fiercely and everything move? What was the point of houses that stood on their own? But Lilly only answered her with a shrug.

That's just the way the country is, innit?

They emerged from the wood into an area of rolling fields, their brows studded with copses and with orchards and hop gardens nestled in the more sheltered places. Here and there they could see the bright painted cowls of oasts.

Daisy cast her eyes around the scene. The wind had died down now and nothing moved. She thought of the men in uniform heading for the docks, of Old Pigswill and the policeman shouting into his megaphone and her mother, in an asylum somewhere, at war with herself.

It's all right here, ain't it? Lilly said.

Daisy didn't answer because she didn't know.

By the time they returned to the huts, the air had begun to darken. The hoppers were already lighting smoky paraffin lamps and the sound of singing rose up in the sharp, leafy air and tangled in the trees. The two girls separated, each returning to her party. Nell was still sitting on her log and someone had studded the fire with roasting potatoes. They drank a cup of cocoa and sat round the embers listening to the adults gossiping. By the time Mrs Shaunessy packed them off to bed there were stars in the sky and in the branches of the trees bats were stirring, waiting to begin their night-time journeys.

From inside the hut, they could still hear the noise of laughter and singing. Franny fell asleep almost immediately but Daisy lay awake for a while, her sister's breath warming her neck. She felt strange, expanded somehow, and wondered whether this was what happened in the country – there was so much space that you had to grow to fit it. Gradually, though, the extraordinary events of the day began to drift off and she felt her breathing deepen. It was still dark when she was woken by Franny's little hands prising open her eyes. From outside came a faint panting sound and a tap-tapping. Sufficient moonlight filtered through the gaps in the boards to give Daisy a dusty impression of the interior of the hut. Old Nell was lying next to them, now, asleep, and on the palliasse beside lay Mrs and Billy Shaunessy.

I don't like it here, Franny whispered.

Daisy held her younger sister and stroked her head.

Ssh. Tomorrow I'll take you to where the fairies live.

I don't want to see the fairies, Franny said, *I want to see the toffee apple man.*

When they next woke it was only half dark in the hut. Daisy thought she heard a man shouting, then his voice became fainter. Nell was no longer lying beside them and the smell of wood burning drifted in from outside. Daisy pulled on her clothes and boots and went out. It was only half light but already Alfie had a fire going and Mrs Shaunessy was busying over it with a tea kettle. The grass was hung with white cobwebs. Down by the long drops rabbits scudded along the fringes of the woods, their bobtails bloody with the sunrise. Daisy returned to the hut, woke her sister and helped her to dress, and Mrs Shaunessy set down a breakfast of bread and marge and warm milk, but Franny pushed hers away, saying she couldn't eat with the trees watching.

After breakfast the girls followed old Nell, Alfie and Joan, and Billy and Mrs Shaunessy out of Pheasant Field, and along a small flinty lane and past another row of huts that Mrs Shaunessy referred to as the Dovers, because the pickers from Dover were staying there, to the dip that marked the boundary between Big Kit and Old Ground. Here, there was a fence of wide stakes which acted as a windbreak – Mrs Shaunessy called it a

Poll Loo – and beyond the Poll Loo Daisy became aware of a great swell of talk and song and they found themselves at the entrance to a sort of country factory whose walls were made of leaves. Here dozens, maybe hundreds, of families milled about, laughing and chattering, and there was a slightly nervy, competitive air, which reminded Daisy of Chrisp Street market at half past seven in the evening, just before the costermongers began reducing their prices. Many of the families carried paraffin stoves, baskets of food and jars of tea, and most seemed to have covered themselves with sacks or heavy aprons. Among the throng, Daisy recognised Lilly, who waved and gesticulated. Then Mrs Shaunessy drew some sacks from her bag and, ignoring Franny's protests, she began tying them round the girls with lengths of string, before covering herself. Not long afterwards, a man arrived on a chestnut horse and opened the gate and the women and children surged forward, elbowing and pushing anyone who got in their way.

Hold hands and don't lose me, shouted Mrs Shaunessy, but this was easier said than done in the general scrum, and even though Daisy and Franny were used to crowds, even though they wandered daily through the most overcrowded alleys and rookeries in a fiercely overcrowded city, it was as much as they could do to keep themselves from being heaved upwards by the crowd and flung down and trampled.

The leaf factory was divided into long alleys marked by a kind of high fencing of poles and wire, along which the hop bines curled upwards to a height of 20 feet. Men were moving about directing families down the passageways, at the ends of which sat huge baskets. Up ahead they saw Alfie waving and shouting.

This is our drift.

Mrs Shaunessy turned to the two girls and through the din signalled them to wait and not do anything until Billy showed them how to pick. Not long afterwards, the man on the chestnut horse drew a large handbell from his saddle pouch. At the sound of the bell, a roar rose up from the crowd of the sort that Daisy had only ever heard before outside the football grounds, as hundreds of women and children dived as fast as they could into one or other of the green alleys, shouting and jostling. Alarmed, Daisy followed Billy, dragging Franny behind her as Billy elbowed his way inside the alley. The air suddenly felt dense and musty. Sprinkles of sunshine fell from the roof but otherwise the only light came from the now distant ends, and when her eyes had adjusted, Daisy saw Billy standing beside them with a thin twine in his hands, from which soft leaves flapped, like pieces of brushed cotton. Between the leaves hung bunches of papery grey-green buds. Billy dropped on to a piece of sacking. With his left hand he held fast on to one end of the twine, then quickly he ran his right hand along the bine, applying force whenever he reached a bunch of cones.

Strip and pinch, strip and pinch. See? There ain't nothing more to it than that.

When the bine was stripped and the cones had accumulated in a dip in the sacking, he gathered them up and threw them into an upturned umbrella that sat between himself and the spot where his mother stood, pulling down the cut ends of bines from the high wire around which they were entwined, then he grabbed another bine and began to repeat the procedure.

Daisy picked up a bine of her own. The soft stem, still coiled clockwise, felt downy and wet. She moved her hand along it, reached a short stem from which a few cones hung, and pinched. The cones did not give way immediately and she was surprised at how hard she had to squeeze her fingers to maintain a purchase on the short stem. So this was where Billy had perfected his pinching technique. No wonder he was such a master at it. She carried on down the bine, stripping and pinching, until she reached the end, then, copying Billy, she lay the naked bine neatly down in the alley and reached for another. Franny sat beside her, playing at picking, but for every cone she removed from its stem, she picked a half-dozen leaves. The work wasn't arduous exactly, but neither was it as simple as it had at first seemed. From time to time Billy took up the umbrella and emptied it into the basket at the top of the alley. Every so often a pole puller came round with a wooden pole on to which was bound a curved knife. With this hop dog, he sliced at the bines caught in the roof of the factory, and having cut them, he yanked each in turn until they tumbled to the ground. Over in one corner of the garden, a family had begun singing.

> They are lovely hops
> When the measurer comes round
> Pick 'em up, pick 'em up off the ground
> When he starts to measure, he don't know when to stop
> But we don't care, we'll pick some more
> Cause they are lovely hops
> Oh! Lovely hops they are
> They are lovely hops.

Soon they were joined by others, until the song spread right out across the garden.

After an hour or so there was a great cry of *Tally!* from the top of the drift and Alfie shouted *Hover up!*, at which Billy Shaunessy dropped what he was doing and raced to the basket. By the time Daisy reached it, he was already elbow deep in the hop basket, pulling up twigs and leaves and turning over the hop cones so they sat lightly on one another and filled more of the basket.

Two men appeared at the top of the Shaunessys' drift. One of them scooped out the cones into a smaller basket, then tipped them into a long, cylindrical sack, while the other handed Alfie a wooden tag and made notes in a book. A family followed behind, collecting up the cylindrical sacks, sealing them and heaving them up on to the same wagon that had brought their bags from the station.

Over the course of the next few hours, Daisy began to refine her technique, speeding up the pinching action until she was picking almost as fast as Billy. Before long, she realised that the bines were coated with tiny claws pointed in a downward direction. If you pushed your hands upwards, the claws pricked and the skin soon became very irritated and sore, but so long as you kept your hands moving towards where the root of the plant would have been, the claws didn't bother you. Once she realised this, she noticed that Billy Shaunessy was meticulous about avoiding being pricked but had not bothered to warn her. Well, never mind. After a day or two's practice, she would have perfected the art of pinching. Then he'd better watch. There was not much between hopping, she thought, and assembling flowers. Though the flowers were fiddlier, both required the same complex hand movements but demanded no particular mental effort, and pretty soon she found she was free to allow her mind to wander. She thought about her mother then, and how much she was already missing her father. At midday another bell rang and everyone immediately stopped picking and set about preparing lunch. While Mrs Shaunessy handed round slices of Dutch cheese and raw onions, wrapped in sacking to protect the food from the bitter tar now covering everyone's hands, Joan put a kettle on the paraffin stove and made everyone a cup of tea sweetened with condensed milk. Heated discussions broke out about the heaviness or lightness or houseyness of the cones, whether they were larger or smaller than usual, and whether they were softer or crisper, ripe or unripe. Half an hour later the bell rang to signal the end of lunch, and bit by bit the women and children vanished back down the green factory walls.

By mid-afternoon, the sun was beating down hard through the canopy of leaves and the gardens were sultry and filled with dappled light. A nearby family began a rendition of 'Only a Bird in a Gilded Cage' and others joined in, some in rueful tones, but everyone seemed in good humour. At five o'clock, when Daisy's arms and shoulders were aching and her hands were dark as fury and the fingers needly and stinging, the man on the chestnut horse rode by and called out *No more bines* and, a few moments later, Daisy found herself in the flow of women and children heading out of the green factory and back along the flinty lane towards Pheasant Field.

Lilly was waiting for her outside hop hut number 21.

So?

Daisy looked at her blackened hands.

Oh, that ain't nothing to fuss over, Lilly said. *Here, you wanna come blackberrying?* Daisy glanced over at Franny but she seemed to be busy with some game, so she left her there.

The two girls started down Pheasant Field hand in tarry hand, washing themselves in the trough just beside the gate, then they continued on until they reached Featherbed Lane. Turning north, they marched along the flints, grabbing at delicate umbrels of cow parsley and scatters of pink bladder campion as they went, as far as Danecourt Bridge where the railway line formed steep shoulders lined with hazel and elderflower and brambles, stopping every so often to plant blackberries in their mouths, and by the time they returned to the huts, Pheasant Field was already bathed in twilight shadow. There were fires lit and some families had made torches from bulrushes, which gave off a magical, orange light. Someone was playing a piano accordion, and outside number 21 Alfie was cursing the wall-eye that left him unfit for duty and Mrs Shaunessy was talking about the letters she'd already had from Patrick. It wasn't all rosy. Some of the letters the sweethearts sent to the soldiers made them laugh. In one, Patrick had said, a young wife had asked her husband how many times the soldiers had managed to get out to the pictures. Patrick Shaunessy was trying not to be too downhearted, though, because the war would be over soon. He was sorry not to be able to visit the hop that year, and he missed it, since to him the hop was the merry in England and the great in Britain all combined. Still, he said, Marie was to keep his place for him, because as sure as eggs is eggs, he'd be there next year.

Alfie said he'd drink to that and the adults all raised their mugs of tea and Mrs Shaunessy started up 'It's a Long Way to Tipperary'.

The following morning Daisy woke to a dewy dawn full of cobwebs and pink-tailed rabbits. At seven thirty she and Franny set off once more with the others through the oak gate towards the great green factory. Daisy picked quickly from the start now, methodically stripping and pinching until she had a rhythm going. After a lunch of bread and cold sausages, Mrs Shaunessy told Franny to go and play, and without the distraction of her sister, Daisy found she could work faster still, her fingers and hands knitting the delicate movements together with such proficiency that by the time the man on the chestnut horse had called *No more bines*, she was confident she had perfected her technique, and she sensed from the care Billy Shaunessy was taking with her that he knew it too. If nothing else, hopping had given her a pinch to be reckoned with.

That evening, Mrs Shaunessy told them to go off and play, so Lilly took Daisy to the old gravel pit where a colony of feral cats was chasing butterflies, and they gave each cat a name – Big Marmalade, Smuts and Ship's Cat. Daisy noticed not only how many butterflies lived in the country, but also how many birds there were, so many that even if you rolled your index finger and thumb into a tiny circle and looked through the hole, there would always be birds trapped inside your fingers. They were returning back across the fields when they saw Billy coming towards them with a smirk on his face, saying Mrs Shaunessy wanted Daisy to return immediately to Pheasant Field.

There they found a great hullabaloo of women, with Franny, red faced and weepy, at its centre.

What were you thinking? said Mrs Shaunessy, grabbing Daisy by the shoulders and giving her a good shake. *Leaving your sister like that?*

The little girl had been picked up by the carter, who had seen her dangling her legs over the platform at Selling station. When questioned, Franny had said she was waiting for the train to Poplar, but the carter, surmising from her accent that the little girl was an East End picker, had brought her back to Gushmere Farm.

She could have been killed, and then what'd I say to your poor ma what's already lost her twinnies and ain't all there in the head? Lord save me, Daisy Crommelin, if you shouldn't be bleedin' well shamed of yourself!

Daisy had never heard Mrs Shaunessy swear before. It was rather alarming. She felt rage and shame in equal measure. The injustice of it, when it was Mrs Shaunessy who'd told them to go and play! But she knew such thoughts were dangerous. It had been thoughts like these – like thinking she deserved a toffee apple flat and had a right to one – which had set off the train of events leading to Elsie's absence and their current exile. Whatever happened, Franny was special, and it was Daisy's responsibility to look after her, particularly now, when they were away from their mother and father.

Mrs Shaunessy never heard the full story behind Franny's flight but Lilly heard it later from another girl and passed it on to Daisy. Billy Shaunessy had taken Franny to one side and told her that a giant lived at the top of the beanstalks in the hop garden waiting for little girls to eat. So terrified had she been by this news that she had run directly to the train station to wait for the next train home. It was only fortunate that no train had come, or Franny Crommelin might have found herself alone at London Bridge.

From then on, Daisy did her best to keep her sister in her sight. During the day, while she picked hops in the Shaunessy family drift, she had Franny stay beside her and play with some dolls Daisy had made for her from twigs and pieces of rag. At five every day all picking would cease. This was the time Daisy loved best, when the evening stretched out before her, plump with possibility. She would take Franny and with Lilly they would go blackberrying or swimming in the dank little pool the locals called Ghost Hole Pond, or they would sit at the rim of the chalk pit watching the antics of Big Marmalade and Ship's Cat or the swallows diving for insects and dandelion clocks rising up on the summer thermals. At other times they would clamber across the downed oaks in Winterbourne Wood and climb to the top of Iron Hill and watch horses and carts and the occasional steam tractor or thresher lumbering along the Roman Road, and Franny would say *Is that the tram?* and Daisy would laugh and reply:

There ain't no tram in the country, silly, and gazing out across the beamy hills and wooded nooks of the Kentish Downs, Daisy would comfort herself with the thought that here, where the horizon stretched out as far as the eye could see, the tumult of war and even her mother's illness seemed so fantastically remote it was hard, sometimes, to remember them. She began to miss her old life less and less; Elsie, flower-making, Old Pigswill and sickly-coloured fogs. All she longed for was Joe, and his stories.

And so the weeks passed until, one day in September, it started raining. It rained so hard that the bines dripped with drowned insects and the hop cones softened and clung to their stalks; it rained on the huts until tiny ropes of water snaked along the walls and on to the palliasses and the cinder paths until they ran in muddy streams; it rained on the evening fires and on the washing put out to dry. And it rained the next day and the day that followed that. By the end of the third morning, Franny was coughing green phlegm and by the afternoon a fever had set in. The next day the hop doctor called, announcing himself, as he always did, with a cheery *Bring out your dead!*, but he had nothing to offer except to tell Mrs Shaunessy to keep the girl warm and dry, two things which, given the weather, had become impossible. Old Nell suggested taking the invalid to the vardoes for a Gypsy cure, and having no better idea herself except to pray, Mrs Shaunessy bundled the little girl into her hop cart and, with Daisy and Old Nell helping to push, trundled along Vicarage Lane towards Poppington Bungalow, where, scattered among the trees, were a dozen or more gaily painted caravans.

Franny was too ill to protest about the intrusions of the Gypsy women as they ruffled through her hair, pulled up her eyelids to inspect the eyes and prodded the tiny ribcage, and too ill to notice the taint of their herbs in the spoonfuls of treacle Mrs Shaunessy doled out to her. But whatever the Gypsies gave Franny it worked. By the following morning her fever had gone and she was no longer coughing up phlegm. By the end of the week she had never looked so healthy, and though she continued to complain about almost everything, she never again repeated her flight to Selling station, nor spoke much of going home.

As September drew to a close, the annual hop wound down. There was a party with jugs of beer and three whole roasted pigs. Bit by bit, women and children drifted back to the city, but the Shaunessy party stayed on to pick plums, apples and pears. The leaves began to turn, and each morning in the hop huts seemed a little colder than the last. In the first week of October Lilly left, and not long after that, a telegram arrived for Mrs Shaunessy. They were at the hop huts preparing breakfast when the man on the chestnut horse rode up. On hearing there was a telegram for Mrs Shaunessy, Old Nell and Joan came bustling over, with grave looks on their faces. Mrs Shaunessy took the telegram, read it and fell over. After Joan had picked her up, the man took Mrs Shaunessy back to the farmhouse on his horse. Nell looked after the two Crommelin girls and Billy

Shaunessy for the remainder of the day, and burned the onion pud. The next day they heard that Patrick Shaunessy had lost both his legs and was being discharged, as a consequence of which Mrs Shaunessy would be returning to Poplar the following afternoon, taking her son and the Crommelin girls with her.

Though Daisy longed to see her father, she didn't want to leave. She spent her last evening saying goodbye to Big Marmalade and Smuts and Ship's Cat, to the hop gardens and to Ghost Hole Pond. At the pond she noticed something red lying in the water and, poking at it with a stick, saw that it was a Union Jack flag on a stick. She thought she could guess whose it was. That night, her last in hop hut number 21, she lay awake listening to the screech owls and the barks of the foxes, wondering how she could ever have found them strange or frightening. The next morning she woke early with a feeling of dread. The rabbits were out, and old Nell was fixing breakfast. In the six weeks she had been away, she realised that she hadn't once thought about the Sandeman in The Deep, but now that she remembered them, she had no doubt that they were both still there, and that she was about to go back to them.

CHAPTER 3

Henry Baker began his working life in the West India Docks the year after the Great Dock Strike in 1890, at the age of twelve. He started by fetching and carrying ropes, winches, dockers' hooks and whatever else the breaking gang he worked for needed shifting. Once the gang had broken up and cleared the cargo, young Henry would be lowered into the ship's hold to sweep and clean, an experience that left him with an abiding horror of dark, enclosed spaces. At the age of fourteen he graduated to breaking, becoming one of a small team within the gang responsible for dividing the cargo, attaching rope strops to it and seeing it out of the hold. It was dangerous work. Cargo routinely loosened and shifted at sea, and even the most experienced breaker couldn't tell exactly what he was dealing with until he was standing beside it in the hold, as a result of which barely a month went by without someone being crushed by a bale of rubber or a cord of timber. In common with most of the gangs working around the docks, Henry's gang had set up a funeral savings club to which everyone contributed tuppence a week. Nothing shamed a docker more than the thought of a cheap funeral.

At the age of twenty-one Henry married May and took her out of domestic service. In short order they had a son, Jack, then, three years later, another, Harold. Jack was handsome and reckless and got himself into trouble from an early age for petty theft and dipping. Harold was his opposite, born small with an odd, enlarged head which stayed that way as he grew. Poverty added rickets, the disease of dark, sunless places which Jack had somehow been spared. The disease gave Harold bowed legs, knocked his knees and made half his teeth fall out. Yet despite these afflictions, young Harold was a remarkably upbeat, optimistic and stoical boy, with no trace of self-pity, so unlike the noisy, blustering, self-centred Jack that it was almost as though they had come from two different broods.

Growing up, the two boys saw very little of their father. Henry left the Baker family house in Gaselee Street at six thirty every morning in order to be at the docks in time for the seven o'clock bomp-on, when he would learn whether there was work for him that day. The Great Dock Strike had been in part a response to the casual cruelty of the bomp-on system, where men would have to compete – and sometimes even physically fight – one another for an hour or two's work. Since dock work was both unpredictable and highly seasonal, some dockers would find themselves unemployed for months with no means of keeping their families from starvation. Henry's father had been among these, and this had made Henry a staunch union man. After the strike, the bomp-on had been modified. Dockers were now required to register, it was no longer possible for shipowners to hire a man for less than four hours, and those dockers who were attached to gangs, like Henry, had at least some protection from the ravages of a casualised labour market.

When there was no work at the docks, Henry would offer his labour on the cheap to the nearby goods station, hydraulic works, timber store or knacker's yard. If that failed, he'd spend the day in one of the dockers' clubs. One way or another, he was rarely back until seven in the evening, when he'd bolt down the tea May Baker had prepared for him before going out to the pub or to the bare-knuckle fights at Wonderland in Whitechapel that were his weakness.

Despite the fact that he rarely saw them, or perhaps because

of it, Henry remained the most powerful presence in his sons'
lives; more powerful certainly than May, who was a bitter, silent
woman; more powerful too than the railway, which thumped
and ticked all night beside the house in Gaselee Street where
the Baker family lived; and more powerful even than the docks
themselves, which stretched out broad and filthy not a minute's
walk away, their cranes so close that Harold would lie in the
bed he shared with Jack and imagine them reaching through the
window and plucking him up.

From the moment they were born, it was assumed that
Henry's sons would follow him to the docks. It was a matter of
familial pride that they did so. In the East End, as elsewhere,
docking ran in families. It wasn't something you did, it was
something you were. In 1914, at the age of fourteen, Jack
followed convention and went into the West India with his father,
but by then it was already clear that Harold would never join
them. Four years before, in 1910, when he was seven, Harold
had suffered an accident, and ever after he walked with a
pronounced swagger brought on by one leg being much longer
than the other and the shorter one being calipered.

While Harold and Jack were still at school together in
Union Street, Jack protected his younger brother from the
worst of the teasing from his schoolmates. Jack grew up tall
and well built and with a reputation for toughness and reck-
lessness. No one wanted to mess with him. Once Jack left for
the docks, at the beginning of the Great War, Harold was
considered fair game. By then, most of his schoolfellows had
grown used to his limp and, knowing him to be a kind and
decent boy, counted themselves as among his friends, but the
arrival of Albie Bluston at the school changed all that. Albie's
father had been killed during the earliest days of the war, and
an elder brother returned home burned the colour of a plum.
Albie had been sent to live with his aunt while his mother
nursed her older son back to some semblance of a life. To

Albie, a boy who had come about his injury without having to fight was nothing short of a coward, and he immediately set on Harold with the specific intention of making his life a misery. All of a sudden, boys Harold had grown up with and considered friends began to trip him up or kick him down for the pleasure of watching him struggle to right himself. When that became a bore, they set wires to trip him up or rolled marbles under his feet, stumbling alongside him in exaggerated imitation of his gait, hurling highfalutin insults, with toffee-nosed expressions on their faces.

I say, look at that blundering blunderbuss.

How outré he is.

Shall we pulverise his bony arse anon?

Still, Harold being Harold, and as generous minded a boy as you are likely to come across, he held no grudges against his former friends, nor even against Albie. He accepted what had happened and, when he thought about the accident, realised he had brought his fate down on himself.

Having no friends to speak of any more, Harold vowed to make the most of the extra time being on his own afforded him. In 1916, Henry was called up, and in his absence, the family had trouble making ends meet. To please his mother and win the favour of his father on his return (for Henry had lost interest in his younger son the moment it became clear that he would never become a docker), Harold took to spending his free time selling second-hand programmes outside the Queen's Theatre in Poplar. Hanging around the Queen's, he soon picked up the words and melodies to most of the popular music hall songs of the time, and he'd sometimes sing one or two favourites to keep the people in the queue entertained and make a little more money. People felt sorry for a boy in a caliper. The song that always got the best response, particularly from the women, though Harold had no idea why, was:

I like pickled onions
I like piccalilli
Pickled cabbage is all right
With a bit of cold meat on Sunday night
I can go tomatoes
But what I do prefer
Is a little bit cu-cum-cu-cum-cu-cum
Little bit of cucumber.

Aside from an occasional attack from a Gotha or a Zeppelin visit and the inconvenience to everyone of air-raid warnings and gas alerts, the East End itself remained relatively unscathed during the Great War, and the event had had none of the terrible consequences for the Bakers that it did for many East End families. As white feathers began to appear in letterboxes, Jack Baker's colour-blindness exempted him from the call-up and Henry was quickly invalided out of service and sent back to the docks. He never spoke about his injury, but it seemed to be of little hindrance to him. In fact, Henry's spell in the army proved positively advantageous. Having served, he was immune from accusations of shirking or cowardice and, having seen what conditions were like and witnessed desperation and guessed at the lonely intimacy of trauma, he knew exactly how to anticipate the returning soldiers' needs and soon saw an opportunity to supply some of them.

While Harold recited his times tables and did his best to fend off Albie Bluston, Jack and Henry Baker were busy establishing a tidy business selling pilfered rum to the East End's growing tribe of war-wounded, gassed and shell-shocked. Not everyone had the ready cash to buy their drink in pubs or the means by which to distil their own poteen, and it was to these men, men at the bottom of the pile, that Henry and Jack extended rum and credit. After all, did they not deserve a drink as much as, or even more than, the next man? Once they'd got drink on tick, the men very often wanted to borrow more money to indulge in cards or women or to gamble on the fights. Neither Jack nor Henry saw themselves as moneylenders or pawnbrokers, but they were happy enough to direct drunk men to a friendly pawnbroker for a portion of the ticket, or to a card sharp for a percentage of the bet, come to that. They usually went to freelance enforcers, though neither Jack nor Henry was above throwing a punch for a deserving cause, and by 1916, their rum and tick business was flourishing.

Harold wasn't particularly keen to join it. He loved his father and his brother very much but he couldn't help thinking there was something a little dishonourable in selling drink to desperate men. On the other hand, it was difficult to see what he would do. At school he had proved himself a diligent student, good at numbers in particular, but who would take on a boy with an affliction such as his when there were crippled war heroes tramping the streets half starved? Nonetheless, as 1916 turned into 1917, and the time neared for him to leave school, he knew that he would have to find something. No one could make a living selling second-hand programmes and singing songs to half-cut women.

A week or two before his fourteenth birthday, when he was expected to leave school, the headmaster, Mr Stuart, took Harold aside for what he called his 'demob'.

You'll not be following your brother Jack into the West India when you leave here, I take it?

No, sir.

You're bright enough, but it won't be easy to place that wooden leg, you see? So what do you propose to do?

It ain't the leg what's wood, sir, Harold said, feeling the need to explain himself, *it's only the caliper.*

Mr Stuart nodded slightly.

Harold expressed his intention to find an apprenticeship until he was old enough to sign up – if the war was still going on.

Mr Stuart tried not to smile.

Well now, listen here, he said. *That's all well and good, but in the meantime, take this.* He scribbled a few words of recommendation on to a piece of paper, named a handful of factories and suggested Harold go to see the foremen there.

So that was exactly what Harold did. At Keiler's jam and pickle works he was asked to sit and wait for a Mr Taylor, who failed to appear. At Venesta's a bulky, flustered man took one look at him and said they wouldn't be taking on any crippled boys. Deciding he might fare better in a shop, Harold presented himself with his letter of recommendation to one establishment after another along the Commercial and East India Dock Roads, then down Poplar High Street, but no one had any positions open for crippled errand boys and he returned home empty-handed. For a while, he rather reluctantly helped out his father and brother, and his mother's cousin gave him work delivering clean laundry, but when someone complained that the corners of their sheets had been dipped in mud on account of Harold's lurching gait, his mother's cousin said she couldn't afford to have him ruin her business and he would have to go on his way. He continued selling programmes, and added to his portfolio by picking up horse manure and selling it to the tenants of the new allotments which had begun being dug all over the East End, and sweeping coal dust to sell to those who could not afford lump coal. In the afternoons, May would send him off to fetch the evening tea. So long as he didn't expect them to employ him, the local shopkeepers were often sympathetic and would slip him an extra rasher or two or a couple of eggs, shaking their heads and saying:

Your poor mother.

It was on one of these expeditions, as he was making his way home with a slice of jelly brawn and some potatoes, that Harold spotted a cardboard sign propped up in the window of Spicer's Grocers and Purveyors of Quality Goods on the Commercial Road. The sign read:

Honest boy req'd.

Tucking the brawn and potatoes down his trousers, which, being Jack's hand-me-downs, were also very big on him, Harold pushed open the shop door and entered. The place was deeper and larger than it had appeared from its frontage. The walls were lined with dark green shelves on which sat tins of treacle, jam in ceramic jars and tea in penny packets. Beneath the counter were four large floor cabinets, two containing bandages, starch, soap, packages of Carter's and Beecham's pills, worm cakes, flypapers, hairnets and all manner of pharmaceuticals and haberdashery. On the counters above the cabinets slabs of butter and cheese were laid out, and behind these were rows of biscuit tins and jars containing honeycomb, toffee and liquorice. Hearing the bell, a plump man with thinning hair, who was arranging piles of kindling, turned to see who had entered and said:

Yes?

Harold felt the man's gaze alight on his caliper.

It's about the position, Harold said, trying to sound bold. The man took a breath and, introducing himself as Mr Spicer, flapped his hand, motioning Harold to approach. Harold did so, aware all the time that Mr Spicer was appraising his leg.

You always been a cripple?

Harold shook his head and gave his usual answer. He'd had an accident, he said. He preferred to remain vague about the details.

Rickets too?

Mr Spicer leaned back slightly and rubbed his chin.

Can you ride a bicycle? I wonder. For deliveries, I mean.

Oh yes, Harold said, though he'd never been on a bicycle and had in fact only ever seen one at close quarters when the air-raid policeman had left his lying in the street while giving chase to a boy who had popped him with his catapult.

Well, said Spicer, sucking his teeth and waving Harold closer, *come round the back and we'll see what your learning's like.*

Harold followed him through a hessian curtain at the back of the shop, then down a damp, dark corridor into a small, draughty room filled with a large oak table at which sat a gaunt woman with a lavender scarf tied around her neck. Beside her, on a stand, a sleek mynah bird swung in a small wire cage. For a moment, everyone looked at one another.

He's come about the position, Mrs Spicer, Mr Spicer said to his wife.

Oh, he has, has he? Mrs Spicer said, though not unkindly.

Give him something to read, Mrs Spicer. Mrs Spicer rummaged for a moment then drew out a single broadsheet. It was an invitation to attend a meeting on votes for women in Limehouse, tea and biscuits served. Harold read without a stumble. As he finished, Mr Spicer coughed and raised his eyes to heaven.

Here, then, Mrs Spicer, he said. *Give this boy one of them accounts books.* Spicer waited until Harold had taken the leather-bound book. *Well, open it then,* said Mr Spicer, *and add up all them numbers in the right-hand column and give me an answer quick!*

Twenty-seven shillings and tenpence ha'penny. Mr Spicer took the book and began to scan the column, mouthing the numbers to himself. After a short while he passed the book to his wife and said:

Here, you check this.

While Mrs Spicer made her way down the column, Harold fixed his gaze on the mynah.

They'll speak, you know, if you train 'em, said Mr Spicer. *Which is just as well since they ain't much to look at.*

Yes, Harold said. He explained that the Baker family had a similar bird and that it, too, wasn't much to look at.

Mrs Spicer confirmed Harold's figure. For a moment Spicer stood fiddling with his moustache, thinking, then he said:

Got family what served, sonny?

Harold explained that his father had been invalided out and that his older brother had worked in the docks for most of the war. Spicer listened with apparent concentration, then tapped the bars of the cage and began to sing 'Laddie Boy':

Goodbye and luck be with you, Laddie Boy, Laddie Boy.

After a little while, the bird began to join in with the chorus and even managed a bit of one of the verses.

Ha ha ha, see? Spicer shook with laughter and wiped his eyes with a mucky sleeve. Mrs Spicer sighed and began very quietly drumming her fingers on the table.

Your father not badly injured, I hope? said Spicer, taking another tack. *Employed?*

Harold replied that his father worked in the docks. He didn't know the nature of the injury because his father didn't talk about it.

What do your bird say, sonny?

Peg leg, *sir*, Harold said.

Spicer pulled himself upright and coughed a little.

Peg leg? Not nothing else?

Spicer gazed at Harold wide-eyed for a moment, then, striding forward, clapped him on the back and said:

Come back tomorrow morning, eight sharp, and, so long as you can ride the bicycle, you can have the job.

When Harold got home and told his mother the news, May said:

So what's the wages? and biffed him round the head when he said he didn't know.

Fishlips! Always ask about the wages.

But when Harold turned up at Spicer's early the following day, Mr Spicer met him at the door and with a grim look on his face said he was very sorry but he'd reconsidered his position and decided that, when there were war heroes without jobs, he couldn't in all honesty offer the post to a boy. Even to a boy like Harold. Especially to a boy like Harold.

And so Harold went home, feeling puzzled about the

world and the dilemmas it offered up. It was true that it didn't seem right to take a job from a war hero, one of those men with a single eye or two missing feet that you saw staggering around the streets looking dazed and ragged. But what was he to do? He had to make his way in the world in some fashion or other. He understood that he was a cripple and with rickets, but did that make him so incapable? Had he not proved himself able to make calculations that even Mr Spicer couldn't manage?

By the time he reached his front door he had decided not to tell his mother about Spicer's rejection. He hated lying to her, but he couldn't bear to tell her the truth. He'd have to tell her that Spicer had asked him to start the following morning and think up some strategy meantime. Never knowing him to have lied, May accepted what her younger son said without a blink, but guilt gnawed away at him so badly that, lying top to toe in the bed he shared with Jack that night, he finally confessed the awful truth to Jack's feet. His older brother sat up and swore a great deal.

War heroes my arse. Ain't our dad a war hero? Don't he deserve his crippled son start bringing in a bit of a wage?

Harold hadn't considered this argument but, considering it now, a flush of pride blossomed on his face.

Don't you worry, Crip, Jack said. Ever since the accident he had called his younger brother Crip, though never in public. *We'll soon sort it out.* Jack turned away and moments later his snores were rattling the mattress.

The following morning, on Jack's instructions, Harold limped to the door of a friend of Jack's, Tommy Bluston, and asked to borrow his bicycle. The wheels wobbled and the bicycle swung wildly about but he managed to remain on the saddle. For an hour or so he practised, pedalling faster and faster up and down the quiet terraces. Pretty soon he had gathered his confidence sufficiently to venture out into traffic and was bowling along the granite sets as though he'd been born to it. It was exhilarating. The rough air of Poplar whipped his face and he had the sensation of being pulled, but the best part of it all was that, on the seat of the bicycle, Harold ceased to be a cripple. On the contrary, he suddenly became someone people admired or even envied. He had only to ring his bell and women would hurry out of the way, dogs would bark, children would point and sometimes even run behind him. So wrapped up was he in his new-found freedom that he lost all awareness of time. Suddenly, becoming conscious of the twelve o'clock chimes, he pedalled as fast as his legs would take him along the East India Dock Road towards the docks. As he pulled up, Jack was standing beside the police sentry box at the entrance to the West India with a cigarette in his mouth.

You're late.

Harold followed his brother, pushing Tommy's bicycle past the workhouse and into an alleyway beside The Resolute pub. Jack tapped on the pub window and nodded to someone inside, then the two brothers went around the back to a latched gate. A dog chained up beside a shed started barking, then, seeing Jack, it quietened down, slapping its tail against the dim concrete of the yard. From the inside pocket of his jacket, Jack produced a key with which he unlocked the padlock to the shed. Immediately inside the door stood a few wooden crates, their outlines dissolving gradually into the gloom.

Now this Spicer cove, Jack said, finally. *He sell black treacle? Coconut mats?*

Harold closed his eyes and tried to reimagine Spicer's shop. It seemed to him that Spicer's sold everything, so much and in so many varieties that he couldn't put names to them all, but he thought he could remember green tins of black treacle sitting beside the sugar loaves wrapped in blue paper.

Good, said Jack, *'cause we got consignments of them both.* He dived into the shed and reappeared with a large basket which he attached to the front of the bicycle with rope. Into the basket they loaded half a dozen tins of treacle and six mats.

You tell that Spicer, this is for free, but he takes you on there'll be more: black treacle, coconut mats, rum, the lot. He'll have to pay, mind, but not half what he'd pay the wholesaler.

Harold stood beside the bicycle, committing this message to memory. Then, for no particular reason, he heard himself say:

Mr Spicer's got a mynah what sings 'Laddie Boy'. He'd heard Jack and Henry singing the song. *He don't know all the words, but he can sing the chorus.*

Jack looked interested. *Oh, our man likes birds, do he? Well, I'll give him birds. Wait here, then, Crip.* He went into the pub by the back door and emerged a few moments later holding a crude wooden birdcage inside which sat a startlingly large white cockatiel with a bristling yellow crest.

Some tyke give me this for a card game. Spotless, this bird. Lovely singer. Tell Spicer if he gives you the job, it's his for six shillings.

Jack tousled his brother's hair.

Listen, Crip. All this cargo what you see here. This is a family matter, all right? Just a little bit of duck and dive. Your dad and me, we like to keep it private, so only tell that Spicer fellow what I said you could.

Harold reassured his brother and went to mount the bicycle. With the mats and the treacle in the basket and a large birdcage hanging from the bars, the bicycle was a good deal trickier to manage than it had been, but Harold set himself to the task and he was soon pedalling north again and hearing his brother calling after him:

And don't forget to tell him your dad's a bleedin' war hero and all.

He made his way back to Spicer's feeling upbeat. His brother's words had settled him. Jack was right. Everyone in the East End made a big play out of being neighbourly, and they were. If you were in some kind of crisis, your neighbours would always do what they could to help you out. That was how the East End was. But no one confused that with family. Family was the core, the essence. Family was what you were, and if that meant doing whatever it took to get a job, knowing there were one-eyed men and limbless veterans who might need the job even more than you did, then that's what you had to do. Ultimately, it was family that counted.

Presented with the treacle, mats and cockatiel, and persuaded that Harold's father was indeed a war hero, Mr Spicer decided he was running a business, not a charity, and hired Harold Baker on the spot for a weekly wage of five shillings and a direct line to his brother's unorthodox grocery wholesalers. Harold's duties included sweeping and dusting, stocktaking, the afternoon deliveries and occasionally helping Mrs Spicer with her books.

The Spicers proved themselves to be kind and reasonable employers and Harold quickly and happily made himself indispensable. In the mornings he mopped and swept the pavement in front of the shop, then dusted the shelves and washed and polished the floor, before feeding and cleaning out the mynah bird. In the afternoon, he hitched up the delivery trailer to Spicer's bicycle and took off along the streets of Poplar, delivering packages here and there. From time to time he would cycle down to the pub beside the West India to pick up consignments of molasses and black treacle, bananas and spiced rum from Jack and Henry's store.

After some months, Spicer sold the bristling cockatiel and bought a breeding pair of Cumberland fancy canaries, and it became Harold's responsibility to put out their white grit and seed every morning and to change their water, wipe their cuttlebone free of droppings, and lay new paper on the cage floor. There was no more talk of war heroes, nor of crippled boys. May never called her younger son *fishlips* again, and even his father seemed to treat him with a new respect. The Spicers, who had no children of their own, developed an affection for their errand boy and were touched by the care he took with everything, and in particular with the birds. Spring came round and Spicer made a breeding box and offered Harold a cut of the sale price of every canary chick he could bring to adulthood. Pretty soon the hen laid eggs, each of which Harold carefully removed with a spoon and replaced with a clay dummy. Once the clutch was complete, he put all the eggs back in the nest together and waited for the hen to settle on them. Of the first brood, he lost three chicks and managed to bring up two, but he was picking up tips at the bird market in Sclater Street now and he knew where he had gone wrong. With the money he made on the two he sold, he bought another breeding pair and successfully raised six chicks. He sold the males, which were the only singers, and kept the females for breeding on.

Summer passed into autumn and on 11 November, the Armistice was signed and, despite the ravages not only of the war, but of the influenza which came in on its coat-tails, the whole of the East End devolved into one giant street party. Young men not yet drafted laughed with relief, children boasted about their fathers, and wartime sweethearts schemed to extricate themselves from their promises.

The curtains opened, the lights came on and everyone remembered their lines. Life was on again.

There followed the briefest of booms as the economy picked itself up from the war and then a deep depression hit.

How's about I pay yer next week, sonny boy? women would say when Harold turned up to deliver their groceries. *Mr Spicer won't mind a bit.* Sunken-eyed mothers would come into the shop with their crying children carrying the most pitiful array of shabby goods – a baby's rattle, a spinning top, a rabbit's foot good-luck charm – to trade for food, and Spicer would have to take them to one side and remind them sternly that it was a business he was running and if they wanted charity they should apply to the Sally Army.

Them politicians have got a lot to answer for, Mrs Spicer said. *Ain't those poor women got enough on their plates? Half of them widows and all.*

But that's just it, Mrs Spicer, Spicer replied, shaking his head at the way of things. *Most of 'em ain't got nothing on their plates at all.*

Things got so bad that on one day in 1921, four members of Poplar council were arrested for diverting the rates into a food voucher scheme designed to protect Poplar's poorest residents from starvation. When news spread of the councillors' arrest, men and women in the docks and factories began putting down their tools and taking to the streets. Spicer watched them moving slowly past the shop windows and tutted with disapproval. Things were bad, he knew, but there was no need to make a public scandal of it. Besides, the demonstrators were putting off his customers.

At lunchtime that day, Mrs Spicer put on her coat and brown cloche hat and announced she was going to the post office. Spicer tried his best to persuade her not to go, but she was insistent. By late afternoon, when the demonstrations and street protests had spread across Poplar and even the rookeries and turnings were jammed with aggrieved men and women, jostling for a view of their leaders, and Mrs Spicer had not returned, Spicer sent Harold out on the bicycle to look for her. For several hours, Harold slowly pedalled through the throng, along the Commercial Road, down the East India Dock Road into Poplar High Street and farther east to Blackwall and the oxbow of land at Bow Creek where the river Gypsies lived, weaving his way through the tides of people, but he saw no sign of Mrs Spicer until, making his way home, he was bicycling down Poplar High Street when he thought he spotted her brown cloche hat among a group outside the town hall. He clambered from his bicycle and, leaving it in the care of a boy in return for a farthing, he made his way through the throng of people until finally there, over on the other side of the street, next to the slipper baths, his suspicions were confirmed. Mrs Spicer was standing with the protesters. She had a banner in her hand and was shouting. He knew then she had never intended to visit the post office but needed an excuse to leave the shop. In her own quiet way Mrs Spicer was a rebel; most likely she'd been a rebel all her life. Harold found the idea exotic. Until that moment he had thought that rebels were all like Jack.

He reported back to Mr Spicer that his wife was nowhere to be seen and that she was probably caught up somewhere in the tide of people, but he saw no need to worry because no one seemed to be much in the mood for violence. It was all right to lie to keep a secret, he thought, to avoid hurting people. Sometimes, it was probably better than telling them.

Later on that week, he lifted his new clutch of young canaries into an old wooden port box, tied it to his bicycle with string, and pedalled along the Commercial Road, past the soup lines at the Sally Army, past thin men standing smoking on the corners, past sallow-skinned women and tearful children to the animal emporium in Sclater Street, where he sold all four, and throughout the whole journey it never once occurred to him that it might be an odd thing, in the midst of such poverty and misery as there was in the East End of the 1920s, that men and women would happily give what little money they had to possess just one of those tiny, yellow gems, whose song recalled sunshine and laughter and better times.

CHAPTER 4

On their return from Kent and all through the war years, Daisy and Franny visited Elsie at her Wanstead Flats asylum once a month with Joe. Sometimes they'd take a rock bun or a piece of Mrs Anderson's tea loaf, but after Mrs Anderson and Maisie left for alternative lodgings nearer to Mrs Anderson's sister, there was rarely anything worth taking. Elsie didn't seem to bother one way or another. Every so often her face would beam with recognition, but most times she seemed confused and mildly irritated, as though their presence interrupted her peace. No one had any real idea what was wrong with her. The diagnoses ranged from nervous exhaustion to hysterical grief and melancholic disorder. She was prescribed complete rest for an indefinite period. Whether she would recover or not was anyone's guess. Still, the asylum was warm, the nurses seemed kind and the food was plentiful, and Daisy often thought her mother was happier in her walled prison, shorn of memories, than she had been on the outside, though she knew enough never to say this to her father.

Without Elsie's luxuriant moaning and numberless afflictions, life at number 7 Bloomsbury Street felt oddly amputated but it, too, was happier, especially for Daisy, who had always suffered the hard edge of her mother's misery.

While she remained at Bloomsbury Street, Mrs Anderson was drafted in to help out with the domestic chores and Mrs Shaunessy was taken on to do the cooking and watch Franny

when there was no one in the house. The most immediate practical consequence of Elsie's absence was that, with medical bills
to pay, and Mrs Anderson and Mrs Shaunessy to compensate for
their time, and with no income from laundry and flower-making,
the Crommelin family found themselves very short of money.
Joe took on extra shifts, leaving the house before the gas lamp
man had snuffed out the street lights and returning long after
the last lamp had been lit for the night. He no longer brought
treats home on Fridays. Gone, too, were the Saturday afternoons in the park.

In 1915, six months or so after her return from the hop
fields, at the age of twelve, Daisy went out to work on the half-
and-half, spending her mornings at school and her afternoons
at an assortment of factories, sweeping floors and sorting cans.
The arrangement brought in a few shillings but it put an end to
her evenings with Lilly and to the possibility of another summer
visit to Kent.

Notwithstanding the downturn in their own fortunes, the
Crommelins never ceased to count their luck. They had only
to look next door to see what wreckage the war had left in its
wake. Since his return from the front limbless and half blind,
Pat Shaunessy had been reduced to selling kindling on the street
and Mrs Shaunessy had started putting in long days washing
and mending, ironing and darning, cooking and looking after
children in order to try to make ends meet. Even so, they sometimes had to resort to the Relieving Officer, and Mrs Shaunessy
would have to send Billy round to number 7, shamefaced,
clutching bags of linen and tins of corned beef, for the officer
would not issue food coupons to any family who had anything
left to sell.

The Shaunessys' slide into poverty made Billy Shaunessy
meaner and angrier than ever. Now he would lie in wait in a
turning for Daisy and Franny as they walked to school every
morning – from 1916 onwards Franny also attended Culloden

Street School – and spring out, taking a pinch out of the both of them and shouting:

Your ma's as mad as a stick. Yes she is, yes she is. Me ma says so and me dad says so and all.

Billy Shaunessy, you stop that! Daisy would cry, but to no effect. Billy relished the upset he caused and her protests seemed only to encourage him further. For weeks together, he carried on in this vein until, one day, deciding to take things into her own hands, Franny finally turned about and, marching up to him, stood on her tiptoes and flipped him so hard on the nose with her tiny fingers that he froze to the spot in sheer bewilderment, leaving Franny the space she needed to announce that Billy was a fine one to talk, whose so-called dad was a Patty-no-legs what begged in the street for his living.

After that, Billy Shaunessy left the Crommelin girls alone and they saw him only when he slunk in, red-faced and arms full of corned beef tins, in advance of a visit from the Relieving Officer.

The Crommelins' luck – if you could call it that – ran out one morning in 1917, when Joe returned from a visit to the asylum with bad news. Though no one seemed to be able definitively to say what was wrong with Elsie, the doctors had agreed the longer her 'turns' went on, the less likely she would be to make a recovery. This meant that further cutbacks were necessary. Daisy would have to leave school and find paid work the moment she reached fourteen. In the meantime, Joe would have to tell Mrs Shaunessy that the Crommelins could no longer afford her services. He was loath to do it – the Shaunessys had been good neighbours and Mrs Shaunessy had helped out when Elsie had first been taken ill. For weeks he wrestled with himself, struggling to find some way to soften the blow. Until, one afternoon, Mrs Shaunessy did the hard work for him.

She came round as usual at five, carrying a piece of brisket for the Crommelins' tea. While Daisy put on the kettle, Mrs Shaunessy began carving paper-thin slices of meat to make into sandwiches, chattering inconsequentially as she worked. As instructed, she'd bought a sixpenny piece of brisket, which would usually be enough for tea and for Joe Crommelin's sandwiches in the morning. While the girls were eating, Mrs Shaunessy fussed about at the sink for a while before making as if to leave. As she moved towards the door, she hesitated and, in a casual voice, said that brisket had been particularly dear that day and that Daisy was to tell her father that she hadn't been able to buy enough for his morning sandwiches. For a moment she put down her basket and turned to put on her hat, and in that moment the cloth she'd used to cover the basket dislodged itself and both Daisy and Franny saw the unmistakable remains of the brisket wrapped in wax paper wedged beneath.

Daisy didn't want to tell her father that Mrs Shaunessy had stolen the meat, because it was hard enough for the Shaunessys what with Mr Shaunessy having no legs and Billy Shaunessy being the crybaby that he was. She figured that if they just repeated what Mrs Shaunessy had said it couldn't really be called lying, since it was Mrs Shaunessy who'd told the lie. But Franny, who was fast developing into a telltale, ignored her older sister and Joe was barely in the door, taking off his blue serge overcoat, before she was breathlessly relating Mrs Shaunessy's crime.

Wait up, wait up, girl, Joe said, while Daisy unwound the string strapping up the hessian he always tied around his shins to protect his trousers, *your tongue's got caught on the current*, but when he saw there was no meat for his sandwiches the following morning, only a couple of pieces of stale bread, he was very angry and started grumbling about 'interfering'. It was the excuse Joe needed. He told Mrs Shaunessy that very evening not to come any more and asked Mrs Anderson as far as possible to keep to her room, and from then on the Crommelin girls were left to bring themselves up more or less alone.

Low though they might have sunk, though, even the Shaunessys hadn't suffered the worst of it. By the end of the war the same could not be said of all the inhabitants of Bloomsbury Street. One of the Lumin boys at number 47 was killed in action, and Mrs Lumin's young nephew was blown to bits when a bomb dropped on Upper North Street School in June 1917. A French polisher and his cousin, who shared lodgings in The Deep, were both killed at Ypres. Two or three others in the street contracted typhoid or dysentery, one went mad from shell shock, another was gassed and then, if that weren't enough, the Greenbergs lost two children to the influenza epidemic and several elderly men and women in Bloomsbury Street were cut down the same way.

In March 1917, only a week or two after her fourteenth birthday, Daisy left school for good and found work at the Apex Laundry. Lilly's elder sister had worked there for some years and had put in a good word for her younger sister, who had started there a few months before. When the Apex's formidable fore-woman, Mrs Bentley, mentioned that there might be another vacancy for a hard-working, honest and healthy girl direct out of school, Lilly had immediately thought of her best friend. Daisy was not new to laundry work. Like any East End girl, she'd been expected to assist her mother with the weekly wash from a very early age. Elsie Crommelin did her laundry the old-fashioned way. She owned a buck, a wooden washing trough, inherited from her mother, who'd no doubt inherited it from hers. This she kept in the yard, and it was large enough to enable her to earn a few pennies taking in neighbours' washing. On washing day – invariably Monday – she would set a copper of water on to boil, then fill the buck with the water, fold the clothes and linen to be washed into the buck with a scoop of ashes and one of hen dung. She'd turn the lot over with a prosser then finally leave it to soak. This was an old technique to save soap, which, at least when Elsie was a young woman, was an expensive luxury. After an hour or so, she'd drain off the lye and dung through a spigot in the buck, rub each piece of cloth with shavings of pig fat soap and work up a lather on the rubbing board before filling the buck once more with cold water and rinsing the lot in it. It was this washing which was hanging to dry when Franny took it upon herself to raid her mother's sewing box with consequences everyone, except possibly Elsie herself, now knew.

The Apex, which took in sailors' uniforms and the linen from several West End hotels as well as a hospital or two, was rather more up to date. It was situated in a once-red-brick, now blackened building which was part of a huddle of small factories and workshops just off the East India Dock Road. The laundry itself was divided into three principal rooms, each serving several functions. Of these, the washroom was the largest, containing vast copper cauldrons set on gas burners and a state-of-the-art Victress Vowel turner operated by levered wheels, with an area at one side devoted to stain removal and special treatments, and another at the back where the mangles and hanging racks stood. The washroom gave on to a separate ironing room. Beyond that lay the finishing and packing room.

The Apex Laundry hours were from 7 a.m. to 6 p.m. on weekdays and from 7 a.m. to noon on Saturdays. The pay was poor, six shillings a week for a junior girl, and there were no paid holidays or sickness benefits. The laundry seemed to run by a set of rules designed to transfer as much of the weekly wage as possible back to its owners. Any infraction of these rules – which Mrs Bentley was careful never fully to explain – resulted in a docking of the guilty party's pay. Among the infractions included grating the soap too finely, or too thickly, using too much or too little, bleaching or starching any fabric not intended to be bleached or starched or in any other way damaging fabric or fixings, however inadvertently; insufficient mangling, sneezing or coughing on newly ironed laundry, failing to fold correctly, speaking when not required to speak or failing to speak when required to do so, illness, lateness and other assorted malfeasances as and when required.

When the laundry arrived at the Apex, it was first inspected then, if necessary, taken to the soaking and stain-removal area, where it was the responsibility of the stain workers to remove any marks on the fabric with hot flour and water or ground pipeclay, ashes or lime chloride, or salts of lemon and cream of tartar, depending on the stain. The stain-free laundry was then placed in hot water with shredded soap and soda in one of the cauldrons, and turned with a Victress Vowel operated by levered wheels. Every kind of fabric required a different treatment. Coloureds were set with salt and vinegar, prints soaked in liquor boiled from ivy leaves, and blue and black silk fixed with gin. After its wash, the laundry was lifted out with dolly sticks, and, in the case of linens, boiled, then rinsed three times, in warm, cool and blued water respectively, before being moved to the starching area, to be stiffened with rice flour or size made from boiled hoofs and glossed with borax. It was then mangled in huge, multiple-rollered mangles operated by a set of giant wheels and levers, and set on the drying racks. While still moist, linens were transferred to the ironing room, where they were ironed with turps, then polished with glass calenders on a hardboard, and, finally, sent to the packing room to be finished and folded and from there dispatched back to their owners.

Because her sister was a good worker, Lilly was assigned to the packing room, the least arduous area of the laundry, where she had only to fold sleeves and pin shirts and set fancy work in tissue before bundling each customer's order together in brown paper and tying it up with string. Daisy, on the other hand, was put to the mangles. Her job was to fold the newly washed laundry, then feed it through the rollers, turning the levered wheels with one hand, using the other to catch the newly mangled fabric as it appeared at the other end, then transfer it to the drying racks. If the laundry was insufficiently mangled it would drip on to the floor and dry unevenly; if too dry, the ironing room would complain that it was unmanageable. It was, quite literally, grinding labour. At the end of each day, Daisy's shoulders and elbows would throb from turning the wheels. After the first few weeks, the sensitive skin between her fingers opened up, leaving itchy wounds which never healed, then the skin on the back of her hands developed a bloom from exposure to carbolic and soda and the hands themselves throbbed from the constant damp. Several months in, the muscles in her mangling arm began to swell beneath taut, roped veins.

That's more like an elephant's trunk than an arm, Lilly said one day as they were sharing their midday sandwich. *Careful, or they'll think you've escaped from the circus or else* . . . She whispered this with her hand to her mouth so that only Daisy could see. . . . *or they'll think you're one of* them.

Them were the nancy boys who hung around the docks at night dressed in women's garb. Some worked as dockers by day and by night their thickly muscular bodies, granite legs and leather faces looked rather comical dressed in silk skirts and daubed with rouge and beauty powder. They were tolerated, even pandered to so long as they took in good part the jokes made against them, but you wouldn't want to be mistaken for one of them, not for any amount of money, not even if you did have an elephant's trunk for an arm.

Later Lilly apologised, pointing out that her own arms were none too clever, neither, so she had no right to pitch in on anyone else's, and the two girls were as thick as any two girls can be once more.

It didn't occur to Daisy to resent her friend for her easier lot, just as it didn't occur to her to resent her sister for being pretty. Things were as things were. There was nothing to be done about any of it. In any case, Daisy quite liked her work. Her walk to and from the laundry took her past Charrington's and the Anchor Brewery, from whose streaming chimneys forever came the delicious, bitter, spicy scent of hops. There was a certain satisfaction in turning the wheel and seeing wet, sloppy fabric emerge the other side flat, crisp and evenly moist, and the camaraderie between the laundresses made up in part for the laboriousness and monotony of mangle-turning. The East End was full of filthy work in glue factories, meat processing plants and paint and gas works. The laundry at least had the advantage of being clean.

More than anything, though, the twice-daily exposure to the smell of hops kept Daisy going, because it reminded her of the happiest times, during those weeks of late summer and autumn, she'd spent in Kent at the beginning of the war. She looked back on that period as a procession of brilliant, sun-drenched days, each bringing more happiness than the last, and she'd returned to Poplar with a new and uncomfortable perspective on her home patch. The crush of people, which had once seemed so comforting, now grated, and the speed of everything made her anxious. She started to feel penned in and longed to see the thin turban-blue stripe of the sea once more. But she knew that until Franny had left school and was bringing in a wage and could be trusted to look after their father, she would not be returning to Kent.

It pleased her to be able to make a difference to the family economy, though, and by the early 1920s, the Crommelins were once more on an even keel financially, and Daisy was even able to save a shilling or two for entertainments for herself and her sister.

From the mid-1920s, picture houses sprang up across the East End as fast as dandelions through paving stones. By the early 1930s, there were eight around Poplar alone, among the largest of which were the Pavilion, the Hippodrome, the Grand and the Gaiety, each capable of seating thousands. The Troxy, which opened in the early 1930s, seated 3,500 alone. For a while they competed furiously for custom, each decorating its foyer and viewing room more elaborately than the next, with velveteen, crystal chandeliers and gilded gesso. The sisters loved them, but

Franny found their blend of magic and luxury particularly enchanting and would have happily spent every waking minute in one or other picture house had she not had school to attend and a concerned older sister to make sure she went. The picture houses soon became a major part of the sisters' weekend routine. Every Saturday morning after her shift at the laundry, Daisy would walk to Chrisp Street to wait for her sister to emerge from the morning children's show; the two girls would go and do their shopping in the market and as they made their way home Franny would entertain Daisy with descriptions of what she'd seen. In the afternoon they'd head for the matinee at the Gaiety or the Hippodrome and they'd walk home with heads full of stars and stories.

Franny began to become quite obsessed with pictures and stars, and when she wasn't actually watching a film, or talking about it, she'd be memorising lines of dialogue, cast lists and plots, or standing in front of the mantelpiece mirror in the living room, styling her hair and doing her film make-up and talking about becoming a star of the screen. No entreaties by her sister or scolding by her father could make her give up her fantasies. No laundry could contain her, no factory feed her talent. Joe and Daisy would see. She was meant for better things. In a year or two Franny Crommelin intended to be at least as famous as Louise Brooks, as glamorous as Gloria Swanson and as rich as Mary Pickford.

And so, when Franny was finally released from her schooling aged fourteen, the first thing she did was to wave her hair and dab rouge on her cheeks and lips, don her Sunday dress and present herself at the staff entrance of several of the larger picture houses requesting a screen test. Mostly, the picture house managers would say there weren't any openings for picture starlets that week, but a few, noting Franny's lush hair and bonny features, would tip her a wink and tell her to come back after the night's performance and discuss matters over a drink.

Cheeky bleedin' cusses, Daisy would say, *I catch them taking any liberties with my little sister, I'll give 'em a clip round the ear so hard they'll be seeing stars all right.*

Finally, after months of persistence, during which Franny fended off the managers of half the cinemas in East London, with varying degress of success, the manager of the Pavilion, Freddy Ruben, offered her a position as a junior usherette. This she accepted, though not in the best grace, on the assumption that, before the year was out, her true talents would be recognised and rewarded. When, after three months, then six, then nine, she was still sweeping peanut shells and cigarette butts off the floor, with no prospect of advancement, Franny Crommelin decided to change tack. If the world wouldn't come to her, she would have to go out to the world. She began adding face powder and lipstick to her already rouged face and took to curling her hair with rags and irons. When Joe wasn't looking, she would sit in the living room making alterations to her clothes, putting in tucks here and there to accentuate her curves. On her fifteenth birthday she came home sporting a fetching new hat, swearing she'd picked it up for pennies from Flitterman's misfits, even though Daisy could see it had come from somewhere more expensive, like Selwyn's. A few weeks later, a silver-plated filigree brooch appeared on the lapel of her coat, and not long after that, she returned home carrying a new pair of tan kid leather gloves. All of these things, she said, she'd bought from her wages, but Daisy had seen how Freddy Ruben had begun to watch her sister and she sensed trouble ahead.

Trouble there was too, but this time it was out on the streets of Poplar. On 2 May 1926, Joe arrived home from work with the news that a General Strike had been called for the next day.

The bosses had it coming, was all he'd say.

Daisy knew nothing about workers' rights or trade unions. She was vaguely conscious of the fact that, from time to time, Lilly attended union meetings, but Daisy believed it was better not to make a fuss about anything if you didn't have to. Her heart went out to men like Paddy Shaunessy, who'd given their legs for their country only to be abandoned by it, but to her way of thinking men like Paddy were precisely why more fortunate families such as the Crommelins, who really had nothing to complain about, were better off keeping their gripes to themselves. There was something unfair, even unseemly, complaining about working conditions or even about unemployment when there were so many people worse off than herself. Life wasn't fair on anyone, but it had been a good deal fairer on those who still had the legs to march than it had on men like Paddy Shaunessy.

On the other hand, Daisy always obeyed her father, and Joe Crommelin was a union man. If there was a General Strike, Joe said, the Crommelins would stand alongside their fellow workers.

The following morning was the strangest since Daisy had come home to find her mother locked in the understairs cupboard with Mrs Anderson yelling at her. After Joe had left, Franny didn't want to leave the house, but Daisy decided to venture out. It was as though a huge tide had broken during the night and taken away everything familiar. Instead of the usual morning bustle, there were no omnibuses, no wagons or delivery boys on bicycles on the streets, and what few men were making their way along the street in their work clothes kept their own company. Most of the shops along the Commercial and East India Dock Roads had been padlocked and some had even been boarded up, and the routes to the dock gates, which would usually at this time have been aflow with dockers in flat caps and serge suits with neckerchiefs for collars, were oddly empty, as though a strong wind had whistled through and blown them away. The factory gates were padlocked and, along her habitual route to the Apex Laundry, Daisy could no longer smell the rich tang of hops. As for the laundry itself, the door was barred and someone had pasted up a notice, around which a number of laundresses were clustered, gossiping in muted voices.

Daisy returned home past gaggles of men, grouped at the corners of the street, subdued-seeming and anxious. Some of the women had already taken out tea and pieces of bread and dripping to them. Every so often a boy would arrive with a message, which would spread between the groups of men, drifting finally into the houses, where the women passed it on among themselves.

In the afternoon, with Joe still absent, Daisy persuaded Franny to come out with her. The locked shops and barricaded frontages were obscured now behind a phalanx of men and women carrying placards and banners and shouting for jobs and justice. Volunteer policemen, many of them mounted, surrounded the marchers on all sides and the streets were as tense as barrel straps.

I don't suppose no one much will be at the pictures today, Franny said, tossing her hair in a peevish gesture, as if all the shenanigans on the street had been done somehow deliberately to thwart her.

I don't suppose, her sister said.

No point in turning up for me shift, then. I wouldn't mind going to the pictures myself, though, later. If hardly no one comes, they might sell the posh seats for tuppence.

But there won't be no one to buy the tickets off, Daisy pointed out, *nor no one to show people to their seats if you ain't there. Nor no one even to project the picture.*

Oh, said Franny, *I hadn't thought of that.* A man in a suit walked by and Franny followed him with her eyes, adding in a distracted manner, *Closing the docks is one thing, but say what you like, it don't seem right, closing the pictures.*

When they got home, Joe was sitting in his chair, smoking, and there was a smell of beer in the air.

Where you been? he said.

Round and about, said Franny. *It wasn't my idea.*

Well, from now on you're staying in. Ain't no place for a gel out there, all sorts going on, Joe said.

Daisy knew he meant a pretty girl. A girl like Daisy went largely unnoticed. He finished his cigarette then reached into his pocket and, pulling out the lining to find nothing hiding inside, he went to his jacket, which was hanging on a peg in the passageway, and, fishing out a coin, he turned to Daisy and said:

Fetch your old dad a half-ounce of tobaccer. Ain't no one open but old Settle up the road at number seventeen, I seen him selling shag to a docker, so knock on his door. He knows me.

Later, after a tea of leftovers boiled into soup, Joe rolled Settle's tobacco into newspaper and sat smoking and shaking his head.

I ain't saying I'm for that Lansbury cove, nor for socialism neither, but I'll tell you this for free; it ain't right what's happening and that's that.

The strike lasted nine days and the Baldwin government did everything they could to stop it. In the London docks they continued recruiting volunteer militia police, including some pretty disreputable men, and brought in two navy submarines into the Royals to act as generators for the refrigerated warehouses where 750,000 beef and lamb carcasses were going nowhere. On the fifth day, lorries driven by soldiers broke the picket line and on 12 May the Trades Union Congress admitted defeat and called the strike off. Though the action was a failure, it proved to be iron ore to Joe Crommelin's moral compass. From that day in May 1926 on, he was almost always to be found at evening meetings of one kind or another: trade unions, workers' education committees, strike committees, fringe meetings and hustings. Joe didn't talk about these meetings much, though he often brought home pamphlets, which he kept in the locked drawer in the chest into which Elsie had once placed Daisy and Franny when they were babies. Every so often he would unlock the drawer and remove a pile of leaflets, but he never spoke about what became of the leaflets or of his meetings for that matter, and Daisy did not care to quiz him. It was enough for her that for the first time since before the war, Joe Crommelin seemed happy and, for short periods at least, to be able to forget Elsie's absence. Unionism had given him a cause less painful, less puzzling and certainly less hopeless than his wife.

And so months passed and then years and life changed very little. Joe continued to find solace in his meetings, Franny in her dreams of stardom. Neither visited Elsie much any more. Daisy continued to make occasional visits up to Wanstead, but Elsie was so remote now, so disappeared, that her elder daughter looked on each visit with dread, expecting each time to see a little less of the mother she once loved and whose memory she loved still.

Work at the Apex carried on as ever, but Daisy saw Lilly less and less often now. Her friend had married a docker and amateur boxer called Jimmy Blundell, fighting name 'Jimmy the Lip', and they had produced a daughter, Grace. After the birth, Lilly had taken on home work and only came into the laundry now when they were short of hands.

Lilly's marriage separated the friends in other ways. At the age of twenty-six Daisy had yet to be courted and she felt her lack of experience. The women at the Apex Laundry teased her for it, and occasionally made cruel references to her protruding ears or her strongman's arm, but the problem, as Daisy herself realised, was not her looks. Poplar produced few beauties, and most of those who started out beautiful didn't stay that way for long. By thirty, their faces and bodies were usually coarsened by bad diet, poverty and childbirth. No, Daisy's problem was that none of her would-be suitors seemed to measure up to Joe. Most of the women she knew were content to marry a man who managed to keep his fists to himself. Anything more was gravy. She was beginning to realise that men like Joe – dependable, sensitive and good-humoured – were thin on the ground.

Daisy began to think that if she were not to end up a spinster she might have to adjust her expectations.

Though they had lost the habit, now, of spending Saturday afternoons in the park together, from time to time Joe Crommelin would take his daughters for a glass of port and lemonade in the saloon bar of the St Leonard's Arms. On one such evening, when Franny was working at the picture house, Joe and Daisy went alone. They had just sat down, when a thin, pale man walked in and, recognising Joe, came up to greet him. The man's name was Sidney Wells. His voice, nasal and high toned, incorporated a slight stammer, which, coupled with the intensity with which he spoke, lent him the air of a captive animal suddenly released from its cage and not knowing quite what to do with the world. Sidney explained that he'd been at a socialist meeting earlier in the evening and had come into the pub with his comrades. After they'd left, he'd been sitting on his own at the public bar when he had spotted Joe on the other side and, recognising him from union meetings, thought he'd come over and say hello, but now he could see that Joe had company, he was sorry he'd disturbed them.

Company, my arse, Joe said. *She ain't company, she's Daisy. Now, sit down, sonny boy. You're a socialist, ain't you? So, be social.*

From the young man's awkwardness, Daisy could tell that he hadn't anticipated being sat next to a woman and that, outside the rabble-rousing furore of union meetings and socialist groups, he didn't really have much to say and was regretting coming over, but, his escape route blocked by Joe's blustering amiability, he was stuck, at least for now. Daisy watched him gather himself, and after taking a series of short draughts from his pint, begin rattling on about the meeting he'd just attended, which was something to do with cooperation between radical organisations along the river. He was standing for the committee and it was suddenly clear to Daisy that he had approached Joe hoping for his vote when the time came. Not long after he'd finished his drink he clapped his hands on his thighs, stood up and said it was late, and he had better be on his way.

Well, sonny boy, Joe said, sending him off with a cheery nod farewell, *I ain't saying as you got my vote, but I ain't saying as you haven't neither.*

About a week later, Sidney knocked on the door at Bloomsbury Street. He'd been elected on to the committee for cooperation between radical organisations along the river and wanted to thank Joe for what he imagined had been his vote and to talk through some of the ideas he had for furthering cooperation. Daisy made a pot of tea while the men talked animatedly, then shucked peas at the table. At seven, when Sidney made no sign of leaving, Daisy served the men a tea of faggots, peas and potatoes and, her portion taken by Sidney, sat to one side and got on with some darning. Not long afterwards, Franny burst in, flung off her coat and rejigged her curls, complaining that it had started raining outside. Seeing Sidney, she suddenly stopped in her tracks and coughed in a ladylike fashion.

Oh, she said, plumping her hair. *Company.*

Sidney looked up and for an instant they made eye contact. The change in Sidney was immediate. Joe, who did not notice such things, chattered happily on, but both Daisy and Franny were aware of the impact Franny's arrival had on the young socialist. He was no longer listening to Joe. His skin flushed the shade of silk roses and he was alternating between darting quick looks at Franny and long periods of gazing intently at his feet. Always eager for an audience, Joe started on his river stories. From time to time Daisy looked up from her darning and, whenever she did, she saw Sidney gazing slack-jawed at her younger sister and Franny plumping her hair all the while and pretending not to notice.

Over the weeks that followed, Sidney began to be a regular visitor, arriving always on the pretext of needing to discuss something with Joe. If Franny was in, he'd become tongue-tied yet stay for what seemed like hours. If she wasn't, he'd linger only for as long as it took him to down a cup of tea and be on his way. Yet in all this time, the situation between Sidney and Franny never seemed to advance and Daisy began to suspect that Franny had no intention of reciprocating Sidney's feelings but was enjoying the attention too much to do the kind thing and let him go.

It all came to a head one evening, when Franny arrived at the front door to Bloomsbury Street just as Sidney was on the doorstep about to leave. A conversation then took place between Franny and Sidney. Daisy did not hear what was said but the exchange was long enough to be more than a simple *how do you do*, and when Franny came in she was flustered. Joe, of course, noticed none of this, and when Daisy brought it up in the privacy of the sisters' bedroom, Franny batted her question away, saying she had no idea what her sister was talking about and *some* people had to bleedin' graft for their living and *those people* were tired and wanted to go to sleep.

Evidently, something significant had happened between Franny and Sidney on the doorstep that night, because the Crommelins saw no more of Sidney until about three weeks later, when he came round once more at teatime on the pretence of having to speak to Joe about some meeting or other. Now, though, he studiously ignored Franny and instead focused his attentions in a most unexpected direction. This time even Joe noticed. It was unmistakable. Sidney Wells had begun his campaign to win Daisy.

So it had finally happened. Daisy Crommelin had a suitor. Now all she needed was someone to tell her how to act in her new situation. But who? She went to Lilly.

About time, Doze, Lilly said. *Good luck.*

Sidney came round again two days later, at Joe's invitation, Daisy later discovered. Daisy was in the yard hanging out some washing at the time. Sidney, nervous, stationed himself by the table in the living room.

Oi, Daise, get your clobber on, Joe called, *you're going out.*

Twenty minutes later, Daisy Crommelin and Sidney Wells stood by the door in a rictus of humiliation and mortification while Joe manhandled them on to the street.

Do you like the pictures? Daisy ventured once they were alone together.

I-I-I don't go much, said Sidney. *Too busy with meetings and that.*

Oh, I don't suppose you have a favourite picture then? said Daisy.

No, said Sidney.

They walked on in silence for a little while.

Shall we go to the pictures, then? asked Daisy.

All right, said her beau.

He walked her to the Grand. It hadn't occurred to Daisy that her first ever suitor would be as inexperienced as herself. Well, if Sidney wouldn't, she supposed she'd just have to take the lead.

Daisy remembered very little about the film. What she did remember was drinking a glass of sarsaparilla she'd bought from the man in the red booth during the interval while Sidney described in great detail a scheme to provide Poplar's turnings with working gas lamp-posts. She remembered, too, paying for the rissoles they ate at the Lyons Tea Room while Sidney described his job as a clerk at Samuel Cutlers, the gasometer makers, and went into a lengthy explanation about its temporary nature and Sidney's own ambitions to become a local coun-cillor and, eventually, if all went well, the country's first socialist prime minister. After a while, the words drifted over her. Following that, she and Sidney began to see each other regu-larly. It just happened that way. They never went far on their · evenings out. If the weather was fine they might stroll along the Commercial Road, with Daisy surreptitiously window-shopping while Sidney delivered homilies on the evils of capitalistic models of production. If there was a film showing at the Pavilion or the Hippodrome, they might buy tuppenny seats in the gods then stop at Lyons afterwards and order egg mayonnaise, or carry on to Coucha's for saveloys and, if the weather was fine, they'd watch the lighters milling about on the river.

After six months of stepping out, Sidney presented Daisy with a silk rose, not unlike the ones she used to make up with her mother.

That's all very well, Franny said, *but do you love him?*

To this, Daisy had no answer. She knew that she was tired of being on her own and flattered by his attentions. She knew too that she liked Sidney; she must like him, she thought, to be spending so much time with him. But as to loving him, well, how did any woman know whether she loved a man when she had never before had a man to love? It was true that he could be mean with money and sometimes – well, often if she was honest – she found him boring, but there were worse men by far, and women were falling in love with *them* all the time. She had already decided that when he asked her to marry him, which he would surely do quite soon, she would say yes.

To Daisy's surprise, her sister flounced and sulked at the idea of her older sister marrying Sidney. Franny was barely eighteen and had already turned down more marriage proposals than she could remember, but this didn't give Daisy the right to go ahead and marry first. Franny was the pretty one, after all, and if either of them were to steal the limelight by getting hitched, it seemed obvious it should be her. Besides, suppose Elsie's condition improved and she came home? One of them would have to stay at home and look after her, and that someone wasn't going to be Franny, just because her sister had beaten her up the aisle. *She* wasn't going to watch her beauty wither into spinsterhood washing Elsie's backside and slopping up her dribble. It wasn't fair.

It was probably no coincidence, then, that shortly afterwards Franny quit her job at the Pavilion, where Ruben was quite happy to keep her but unwilling to give up his wife in order to marry her, and found work as a waitress in a corner café near the West India Dock. A few weeks later she announced that she was bringing a gentleman friend to tea to meet the family. His name was Jack Baker. He worked as a breaker in the West India and came into the café for faggots and gravy. He was a right bloomin' looker. He had taken her to the dog track at West Ham and treated her to pork pie and pickles at Cardosi's. They'd been to the pictures and once to a dance hall. Franny found his stories of life on the docks hilarious and he was as charming as a singing linnet. He bought her cockles and violets. She was over the moon, she was on cloud nine, she was bursting at the seams. Why, she said, she had never been so happy.

And so a tea was planned, and Daisy made the rock buns and sardine and radish sandwiches because Franny had to make a special effort with her hair. Sidney arrived early. Franny sat at the table. Daisy made a pot of tea. They waited. Sidney finished his tea, bit his nails and launched into a monologue on the subject of the Russian peasantry. Franny yawned. Daisy made a fresh pot of tea and Sidney moved on to the details of a committee meeting he'd attended where the man taking the minutes hadn't been able to spell the word b-o-r-j-w-a-s-i-e. Finally, there was a knock on the door.

Thank God, it's the cavalry, Franny said, springing to the door. There was a murmured greeting and moments later, a tall, burly man with a cocky, street-fighting confidence swept into the living room and, brushing aside Daisy's offer of tea, said:

What are we waiting for, then? Let's get down the pub.

They walked to Charlie Brown's, which was Jack Baker's favourite, sat in the saloon bar and Jack fetched port and lemons for the women, a pint of mild for Sidney and a best bitter for himself. A man with long fingernails started cranking out some old music hall numbers on the piano, and got a sing-song going. Jack disappeared and shortly afterwards the fighting began. Franny spotted Jack in the middle of the fray, arms windmilling about, and shouting blue murder with a great grin on his face. After trying unsuccessfully a couple of times to roust him from the punch-up, Sidney returned to the table and suggested he walk the Crommelin sisters home. Franny protested, saying she wanted to wait for Jack, but once fighting had carried out into the street Franny reluctantly agreed to leave and the three-some began to make their way back east to Poplar. At Pennyfields they had to stop while Sidney was sick on his pig leather shoes. No one mentioned the evening after that, but it was a long time before Franny suggested that Jack come round for tea again.

Christmas arrived and at nine o'clock on Christmas morning, the Crommelins ate a breakfast of boiled eggs and buttered soldiers, then Daisy put a gammon ham on to boil, paid for from the proceeds of the Apex Laundry Christmas savings club, and Franny announced that she'd invited Jack for Christmas dinner. At midday the Crommelins each drank a glass of ginger wine and handed over presents of nuts and knits. At twelve Sidney arrived and they had another toast. By one o'clock, with Jack still nowhere to be seen, Joe decided to begin the gammon ham, which they ate with white sauce and onion pudding, with plum cake and custard for afters. By three, Daisy, Joe and Sidney were all asleep in front of the fire.

When Daisy woke an hour or so later, feeling that it was time for a nice cup of tea, Franny was nowhere to be seen. Daisy assumed that she'd gone to Jack's house and went into the scullery to put the kettle on. She waited for the water to boil, then poured it into a teapot, using new tea leaves since it was Christmas. Through the back door, she could see there was a light flickering in the privy, so she pulled on her coat and boots, walked down the path and knocked on the door.

Franny?

A small and frightened voice answered:

Oh, Daise, don't tell Dad, promise you won't tell no one. I ain't well.

It's that ginger wine, I expect, Daisy said.

I bleedin' wish it was, Daise, I really do, came the small and frightened voice.

Daisy knocked on the door again.

Fran, Fran, she said, *open the door. Shall I fetch a doctor?*

A howl came from behind the door, followed by choking sobs.

I wish you could, Daise, Franny said, *but there ain't no respectable doctor in the world can undo what me and Jack have bleedin' gone and done.*

CHAPTER 5

Harold Baker was not at all surprised by Franny Crommelin's pregnancy, but rather by the news of the wedding to follow. Jack had never had any trouble attracting women. Keeping them off him had always been more of a job. When they were younger, Jack had often sent Harold to the door to make his excuses for him.

Sorry, duck, Harold would say, feeling sorry for the poor girl standing at their door, dressed in her finery, *his nibs ain't in . . . No, I don't know when . . . He's awful busy . . . I don't know if it might not be better jest not to come round again, save you the trouble if he ain't gonna be in and all.*

Harold suspected it was not the first time that Jack had got a woman 'in the family way'. More than once over the years he'd heard his mother muttering about 'fetching the little tart to a woman' and everybody knew what that meant: a back room somewhere and a procedure – Harold did not know the details and couldn't bring himself to think too hard about what they might be.

But with Franny Crommelin things were different. Jack seemed willing to see this one through. Harold felt a surge of pride in his brother and found himself excited by the prospect of becoming an uncle. He was very fond of children, though they often avoided him on account of his caliper and he thought it unlikely that he would produce any children of his own. He was twenty-seven years old now and had never so much as kissed a woman. He was short, lame and, for the last year or two at least, he'd begun losing his hair. None of this was any kind of advantage in romance. He'd lost count of the number of times he had watched some girl's face fall on the doorstep as he trotted out the old lies, his face the colour of rotting strawberries, desperate. He'd always wanted to say:

I'll take you out, instead, if you like.

But he never had. If he hadn't been a cripple, his crippling shyness would have done for him. Besides, he had nothing to offer a woman. He was nothing to look at, he was crippled and though his job as a grocer's assistant paid an adequate wage for a bachelor, it wasn't enough to keep a family and it offered no real prospects for advancement.

Older women seemed to enjoy his company. They thought him sweet and sensitive and he sensed they felt sorry for him, as they might feel sorry for a wounded dog or a starving kitten, but women his own age never seemed so much as to notice his existence.

As it was, he didn't meet many women anyway, other than the wives and spinsters who came into the shop for their weekly bar of laundry soap, or the girls who called for Jack. Knowing he'd look absurd hobbling about on the dance floor, he'd never gone to dance halls as Jack did, and even though he often sat in cafés, no woman had ever asked to share his table and none of the waitresses had ever taken an interest in him.

Over the years he'd grown accustomed to his situation. It was a sadness in his life, but not one he allowed himself to get too worked up about. So long as he did not focus on his loneliness, he was all right. As a bachelor, he was still useful to his parents, running errands, making a financial contribution to the household, tempering Jack's worst excesses. And though there wasn't much affection at home, over the years he had become very fond of the Spicers and they of him. He'd been working in the grocery now for sixteen years, more than half his life, and in some ways he felt more a part of the Spicer family than of his own. Mr and Mrs Spicer had never managed to have children, and now they were too old. As a consequence of this, Spicer had come to treat Harold like a son, albeit a disappointing one. He didn't pay him what a grocer's assistant on the Commercial Road ought to earn, but he was an affectionate employer and Harold returned his affection with more of the same, and with loyalty and hard work. Even Mrs Spicer, who had initially been suspicious of him, eventually came round. Now she was kinder and warmer to Harold than his own mother, fussing over him when he came down with his annual winter bronchitis and forever presenting him with steaming cups of Bovril to keep his blood up. On his birthday and at Christmas she presented him with gifts of socks, scarves and jumpers she'd knitted, and once, in 1928, when women over twenty-one were granted the vote, and she was in a celebratory mood, she grabbed him and planted a kiss on his cheek.

On good days, he was able to persuade himself that it was actually better that he remained unattached. On bad days, he felt that to be alone was no more than he deserved. Another kind of man might think his life a little wasted, but Harold Baker kept himself busy and was content enough. The Spicers had encouraged his bird-breeding enterprises and breeding birds had now become quite an obsession. He had several dozen breeding pairs – canaries, budgerigars and finches – plus two mynah birds and a few linnets someone had given him, and everyone at the bird market in Club Row, formerly Sclater Street, knew him and respected him for the care he took in breeding and his gentle handling of the youngsters.

Most Friday afternoons after work he'd visit the Crown in Church Street for a pint or two. The Crown was where bird fanciers got together to show off their breeders and swap all the latest bird world gossip and scandal. Oh, the stories he heard! Birds whose broken wings had been glued down in the hope no one would notice the break, budgies dyed in expensive colours and, once, an albino pigeon whose owner had built up its beak with plaster of Paris and was trying to pass it off as a cockatiel.

Breeding and talking about birds took up most of Harold's spare time and what little remained he spent helping his father and brother out at the docks. He always reserved Saturday nights for the Railway Tavern, Charlie Brown's, on the East India Dock Road. He was as fond of that pub as his older brother, though for different reasons. Charlie Brown had amassed an extraordinary collection of paraphernalia over the years from visiting sailors: Chinese vases, stuffed exotic animals, African beadwork, wonderfully embroidered hats from faraway places like India, and he put it all out on display. The collection was always changing and Harold could quite cheerfully pass an hour inspecting the new items. But the chief reason he loved the Railway Tavern was for its Saturday night singalongs. Old Charlie Brown was a character and all the old music hall singers wanted to come and sing and play for him. Harold loved those old-time songs – 'Algy', 'The Piccadilly Johnny', 'Who Were You With Last Night?', 'Any Old Iron' and the rest – that he'd sung while selling programmes outside the Queen's as a boy. The tunes reminded him powerfully of his childhood before everything had been spoiled by the war, and there was nothing he liked more than to sit at one of Charlie Brown's tables nursing a pint of mild, listening to some old song thrush banging away on the piano and another clacking away at the spoons and belting out the familiar tunes whose lyrics came as automatically to him as dreaming. The atmosphere in the place was as raw as cats' meat. You could feel the singing coming up from the floorboards, the crowd stirred up by booze and sentiment, and the rent collector, the Relieving Officer, the pawnbroker all blanked out in the great roar of people, his people. And even though the evening almost always ended in fighting, it seemed a small price to pay to be in such triumphant company.

In his more thoughtful moments Harold imagined how his life might have progressed if the accident had never happened. He would have gone into the docks, he supposed, just as his father and brother had done. He might even have made it on to their gang in the West India. What would it have felt like to have been on Henry and Jack's team? Would it have made him more attractive to women? Less shy? Would he have been better loved by his mother? Would it somehow have atoned for the terrible thing he had done as a boy, the thing that Jack had forgiven him for, even though he could not find it in his heart to forgive himself.

Now Jack was about to settle down! He deserved a good woman.

But was Franny a good woman? Harold hoped so. There was no question that she was a beautiful, lively one. That time Jack had first brought her round to meet the family she was wearing a little too much make-up for such a young girl, Harold thought, but what did he know? Such perfect skin, such full hair, such a young and vigorous smile. He had watched her as she chattered away, about the pictures mostly. She'd worked at a picture house – he couldn't remember which one now – but there had been 'artistic differences' with the manager so she'd left and gone to work in the café where Jack had met her, but she intended to *get back into the pictures*. Impressive girl, he had thought. Certainly impressive.

Henry had been a little resistant to her. (This was before Jack had knocked her up, of course.) Didn't want his elder son marrying into the lighter trade. Old enmities between lightermen and dockers, but Franny seemed so light, so full of energy that Henry was soon won over. Only May had remained unconvinced.

Merry dance that one, she muttered.

Just listen to Old Mother Green Eyes there, Henry laughed. He slapped his elder son on the back. *Take no notice of her, Jackie boy*, he said, *she's just a Jealousy Jane*.

May tut-tutted her way towards the scullery. *Merry dance*, she said, *you just wait, you'll see.*

Over the weeks that followed, May tempered her campaign against Franny Crommelin – even she could see that Jack was enchanted with her, and she knew that to criticise the girl openly would only backfire on her – but she did not give up completely, and when her elder son came home a few weeks later and announced that Franny was pregnant and he had asked her to marry him, May sensed her chance had come. She gave Jack a hard look and poured him some tea.

It ain't what you think, Jack said.

Like hell it ain't, said May. She slopped some bacon and barley stew on Jack's plate. *You got yourself regular trapped.*

Jack protested, but May wasn't listening. Getting up from her chair, she went directly over to the mantelpiece. She lifted up a little carriage clock that her father had given her as a wedding present and which had sat there ever since, marking the miserable momentum of her marriage, and pulled out two pound notes. She returned to the table, pushed the money towards Jack and added some more sugar to her tea. Then she placed her hand on Jack's and, patting it, said:

You think you love her now, but it won't last. Fetch her to a woman, Jackie boy.

For a moment all movement at the table ceased. Harold felt the air skin over like wet glue in a wind. It was suddenly very quiet, the only sounds the muffled noises of children playing in the street. Even the carriage clock seemed to have stopped ticking. Jack's eyes rested on their mother's hand for a moment and then, in one violent motion, he leapt back from the table and, leaning in to his mother so close that she squinted in fear, he said in a very calm voice:

Wash your mouth out, you bitter, dried up old woman.

And with that, he pulled his jacket back on and went out into the street, slamming the door behind him. For a moment no one did anything. Then Harold pulled his chair from the table, struggled to his feet, went over to his mother and, grasping both her shoulders, dropped a kiss into her hair. He took the two pound notes, smoothed and folded them and slipped them back under the carriage clock.

I only want what's best, May said, shakily.

I know, Harold said, smiling at his mother. He patted her hand. *Now, why don't you finish your tea?*

For a few days after this incident, Jack kept his distance. By the time he reappeared at the Baker family home the following week, he seemed to have cooled somewhat on the idea of marrying Franny Crommelin. Before the engagement, he had been spending all his spare time with her, but now he reverted to his old ways and spent most of his nights in the pub. As the wedding day drew closer, he seemed to fold inwards, as though he had a vacuum pump inside him, pulling out all the air and forcing the sides together. In public, especially in the company of his mother, he remained determined to go through with the wedding, but Harold wondered whether this was not so much from a sense of duty towards Franny than his older brother not wanting to look like a fool. Maybe it was just the usual cold feet that all men – and maybe even some women – felt. Perhaps his mother was right and Jack was beginning to see that Franny was not all she had at first seemed. Who knew? Like most dockers, like most East End men come to that, Jack Baker only ever kept his own counsel.

Still, in those last days before the wedding, it was hard for Harold to quell the unbearable sense that his brother was about to make one of the biggest mistakes of his life.

CHAPTER 6

Franny Crommelin's wedding to Jack Baker took place on
12 February 1930. It was more fraught than most on account of
the bride suffering a particularly bad bout of morning sickness.
First Franny refused to get out of bed, then she would not touch
the breakfast of fried eggs that Daisy brought up for her, but the
arrival of Mrs Shaunessy with a posy of snowdrops seemed to
perk her spirits and soon she was up and drinking sugary tea while
Daisy, Lilly and Mrs Shaunessy flustered around her, slipping the
buttons of her dress into their keepers, clipping a garland of silk
violets to her honey-coloured curls and making last-minute adjust-
ments to the fitting of her mother's old wedding dress to disguise
the growing mound beneath, and, finally, she was ready.

Joe, who had made himself scarce during these preparations,
appeared back at the house in Bloomsbury Street at eleven and,
since it was a cold day, helped Franny into her overcoat while
Daisy pushed the tan gloves on to her sister's delicate hands and
gave her a little kiss on the forehead.

Don't she look a picture and all, said Joe, with pride and sadness.
If only her mum could see.

Daisy and Joe stood back and admired their lovely charge.
The pregnancy had blushed Franny's skin. Her eyes were a pale
lilac colour, complemented by the violets in her hair, which
shone as brightly as a puddle in the sun. No one could remember
when they had seen such a beautiful bride.

As Franny and Joe walked down the road, with Daisy, Lilly and

87

Mrs Shaunessy making up the rear, women pulled up their window casings and shouted *Good luck, duck* and threw pennies. The only troubling moment came as they were nearing the church when an old crone waved her walking stick and cackled, *Keep your spirits up and your knickers down, ha ha ha!* and for an instant Franny looked as though she might burst into tears. Then Daisy kissed her on the cheek and Joe patted her hand and Mrs Shaunessy, who was in on Franny's secret, said, consolingly:

Take no notice of the old cuss, duck, at least you don't show. Not from the front anyhow, and that's the important thing for the photographs.

And Franny bit back the feeling and set her lips in a gesture of defiance and the wedding party carried on. By the time they were on the approach to the church she was smiling again and looking the picture of happiness and innocence. It was cold and dim in the vestry, but nothing – not the sombre surroundings, the thin turnout, nor even the absence of the groom – could dampen Franny's excitement in getting married, and it was as much as Daisy could do to keep her sister still long enough to arrange her curls and set her veil in a comb beside the garland of violets.

And so they waited for Jack, casting about anxiously for signs of his arrival; except for Franny, who seemed unconcerned by his lateness. After a few minutes, Lilly disappeared outside to see whether she could see him coming. After a few minutes more, Mrs Shaunessy volunteered to pop her head into one or two of the pubs nearby. Still, Jack did not appear. Members of his own family began anxiously whispering among themselves, and with considerable irritation, Franny, who had picked up on the mood, silenced them with a loud *Shhh!*

They need not have worried. Jack pitched up soon enough, looking dishevelled and slightly drunk and steadied periodically by a short clownish figure with a limp who Franny said was his younger brother Harold.

My Jack got all the looks. Oooh, but ain't he handsome! Franny whispered. She watched her conquest loping down the aisle, all thought of his lateness forgotten. The organist hastily started up 'Here Comes the Bride'.

There goes the starter gun, girl, Joe said, taking his daughter's arm, and they set off, Franny reaching out and squeezing her sister's hand as they passed to the top of the aisle and promising that, when the time came, she'd be sure to throw the posy of snowdrops Daisy's way.

On account of Jack being late, the service itself was more hurried than usual and almost before they knew it Jack and Franny had been declared man and wife and the vicar was encouraging the congregation back outside, where the party for the next wedding was already gathering. By now it was cold and rainy, but Joe had booked a photographer who had not yet arrived, so everyone waited, umbrellas aloft and shivering, doing their best to look enchanted by the proceedings. Lilly and Mrs Shaunessy volunteered to head back to Bloomsbury Street, light a nice fire and send Billy out for jugs of beer so that everything would be just so for the party's arrival. Not long after they had left, the photographer raced up, blustering apologies, by which time Franny's garland of silk violets was giving up its colours and everyone said it was as well that the pictures were in black and white so it wouldn't show that the bride was sporting purple-striped hair, nor, so long as the pictures were taken front on, that she was pregnant.

The wedding party walked in bitter, driving sleet to number 7 Bloomsbury Street, where the men helped themselves from the jugs of beer and the women threw back gin and oranges and everyone ate fish paste or ham-and-mustard rolls and Daisy, Lilly and Mrs Shaunessy were kept busy slicing ham to size and scraping on the marge and paste and generally laying out the spread. With everyone warm and fed, the singing began, and by three o'clock in the afternoon the scene had taken a rowdy turn, spilling out into the street, with men and women swaying about, singing and dancing, and the odd drunken skirmish around the edges. There was Pat Shaunessy leading the songs from his Bath chair and Lilly and her Jimmy, arms about each other, belting out the old numbers and Franny, dizzy on gin and adrenalin, rousing them all to song; and in one corner, separate from the party, there was Sidney, drunkenly delivering a lecture on the subject of the working man to a cornered-looking Harold.

By the time Daisy noticed Jack's absence it was dark. She checked the clock on the mantelpiece: just after pub opening time. If she found out her new husband had deserted her for a pint, Franny would be crushed. Scanning about for Lilly, hoping she might go out and look for Jack, Daisy caught Harold in her peripheral vision. Harold Baker seemed to be a dutiful brother and she presumed that he, too, had not yet registered his brother's absence. Most likely Jack had not been gone long. For a moment she considered asking Harold to look for his brother, then she remembered his crippled leg and thought better of it. She slipped out into the passageway alone and grabbed her coat.

The landlord at the St Leonard's Arms said Jack had been in momentarily not fifteen minutes before, then left. He thought he might have gone down to Chin's in Pennyfields for a game of puck-a-poo.

Daisy hurried back to the party and found Sidney, who was by now giving a tuneless rendition of the Internationale to no one but himself:

> So comrades, come rally
> And the last fight let us face.

Sid, whispered Daisy, *I could do with a bit of rallying meself.*

Sidney listened to Daisy relate the situation, shook his head disapprovingly and with some reluctance pulled on his outdoor cap. Together they made their way west in thin rain. They had almost reached Pennyfields when Sidney suddenly wheeled about and in a wild, accusatory tone cried:

He's a bleedin rum lot, that brother-in-law of yours, leaving his own wedding.

For a moment, Daisy felt dazed, as though wrongly convicted of some crime, then, gathering herself, she picked up her pace and said quietly;

It's for Franny we're doing this, Sidney. Besides, whatever you say about Jack Baker, he done right by my sister and there's plenty what wouldn't.

She realised immediately what she had done and cursed herself for it. She had made a pact to keep Franny's condition from everyone but immediate family, Lilly and Mrs Shaunessy, and now she'd let her sister down.

Well oh well, Sidney said, and Daisy thought she detected a note of triumph in his voice. *Well oh well, now ain't that a turn-up.*

They found Jack sitting at a corner table at the back of Chin's café, playing puck-a-poo with his wedding money. Since their night out together the two men had kept an uneasy truce, but it was clear to Daisy that Jack considered Sidney weak and ineffectual, while Sidney looked down on Jack as some kind of ape, unable to see beyond his next pint. She hoped Sidney would let her do the talking, and dreaded him bringing up Franny's pregnancy, but it was too late. Before she could get a word in, Sidney was already addressing Jack in his most condescending voice;

Now then, Jackie, old mate, how's about we all go back to the party, eh?

Daisy watched her brother-in-law absorb the request, and for a moment she thought he might come, but then he raised his arm from the table in a gesture of dismissive contempt. Instead of letting Daisy have her say then, which might have saved the situation, Sidney persisted, *That lovely wife of yours will be missing her Jack*, but this time Jack Baker did not stop to consider what was being said to him but suddenly stood up in a cloud of outraged energy, wheeled round and with his fist raised shouted:

You know what's good for you, you bleedin' leave a man alone. Now sod off!

For an instant Sidney bristled and drew himself erect, but in the next moment he had completely shrivelled, as though someone had let his air out. He turned and went to the front of the café, shaking his head.

They stood outside the café for a moment, thinking what to do next, and it was then that Daisy spotted Jack's brother, Harold, bowling towards them with his odd, broken gait. She waved and saw Harold wave back and quicken his pace. When Daisy told him what had happened, he apologised, insisting that Jack didn't mean anything by his manners; it was just that some people were smooth and others were crunchy, and Jack was one of the crunchy ones.

He's a pup when you know how to handle him, Harold said.

The object of this conversation suddenly appeared at the café door, shot a look first at his brother, then at Sidney, trying to locate some conspiracy between the two men, then, reassured there was none, said:

Don't a man deserve a bit of peace on his wedding day?

Couldn't agree more, Harold said, approaching his brother with a placatory smile and his palms facing up to the stars, if there had been any stars to face. *Only you're missing the free beer, chum.*

Jack sighed and snorted. Ignoring Sidney and Daisy, he patted his brother on the back and said in an affectionate tone:

Saints alive! Who needs a bleedin' wife with a nag like you for a brother?

With that, he pushed past Sidney and began to make his way back towards his wedding, with his brother hobbling along at his side.

The clean-up of the house from the excesses of the wedding,

the settling of bills, the readjustment to normal life and her work in the laundry kept Daisy so busy that it was a week or so before she realised she hadn't heard from Sidney since the wedding day. After two weeks she began to worry, and one evening after work she presented herself at the front door of his house in one of the grid of streets marking the boundary between Poplar and Limehouse. His mother answered the knock and told her Sidney was out, but there was something unusually stiff in her manner, Daisy thought, and she made her way back to Bloomsbury Street full of disquiet.

The following day a letter arrived by way of explanation, informing Daisy that Sidney regretted that his political commitments were such that he would be unable to meet her in the foreseeable future. It was signed *Sidney Wells Esq*, and so amazed was Daisy to receive it that she had to read it three times before she took in its message. It was a clerk's letter, full of highfalutin language and with a silly, bureaucratic tone. All the same, it pained her, the timing suggesting something other than a sudden overwhelming flow of important political matters. What was it that was bothering him so? Figuring it must have had something to do with the wedding, she sat down with a cup of tea and tried to reconstruct the day. It was true that the encounter with Jack at Chin's hadn't gone well, but Daisy couldn't see any reason for Sidney to want to avoid *her* on account of it. She thought back over the past few weeks, then months, trying to remember some inadvertent slight. It occurred to her that her beau was jealous of Jack's conquest of Franny, but it was such a chafing thought that she tried to dismiss it. She read the letter yet another time but she was still unable to get to the bottom of it, so she slotted it under her mother's linen tablecloth in the top drawer of the chest, the same drawer in which, as a baby, her mother had put her down to sleep, and decided not to mention it to anyone. She convinced herself that there had been some temporary misunderstanding. It was too shameful to imagine that she had been dumped, just like that, and over what, she would never know.

For a while, life at Bloomsbury Street felt oddly quiet. In the morning Joe went off to the lighter yard and Daisy to the laundry. In the evenings, she cooked tea for them both, then, when her father left for the pub, she usually sat beside the fire knitting matinee jackets and bootees for her sister's growing baby. Occasionally, when Jimmy was out and Lilly could persuade her mother to sit with the children, they would go to the pictures together. Lilly would ask after Sidney and Daisy would say that he was well. From time to time Franny would come round and gossip about some aspect of married life, but she was too thrilled by her new status and the impending birth of her child to bring Sidney up in conversation or even, Daisy supposed to wonder why Daisy did not mention him. The weeks turned into months and still Sidney did not contact her. When Lilly and then Joe and finally Franny did notice that he no longer seemed to be around, Daisy said he'd been called away for a while, and from her tone her friend and family members judged not to pry.

In May Franny gave birth to a son and called him Richard, after Joe's great-grandfather on his mother's side. Not long after the birth, Franny decided to show Elsie her first grandchild. Only Daisy regularly made the journey to the asylum now. Franny had given up going some time ago. Joe still visited his wife, though only at Christmas and Easter. If a lifetime of working on the river had taught him anything, he said, it was that, once things got lost in the water, they were usually lost for ever. The lighter the object, the more it got bobbed about on the tides, and the lower your chances were of recovering it. There might be a minute or two, perhaps, as it rushed on its way, when you could reach down and, if you were lucky, scoop it up out of the water. But if you failed, there was no point in trying to pursue it. In his experience it was irrecoverable. That was how he saw Elsie – a frail, almost weightless little soul lost to the flow of time. Franny, on the other hand, hadn't given her mother much thought until now, when she needed to be admired.

From the bentwood chair where she had passed the last sixteen years, Elsie Crommelin, her body as thin as an alley cat and her face as raddled as last year's conkers, stared out into the middle distance, refusing to look either at her daughters or her new grandson. When Franny lifted Richie from his pram and placed him in her lap, Elsie seemed at first not to react and then, after a few minutes, she picked up the hem of her skirt and shook it, as if to shake dropped crumbs on to the floor. For the remainder of the visit, she sat perfectly still, her lips moving with some unsaid thought, a lone witness to whatever fragments of her remembered life still remained intact.

I ain't going there again, Franny said, wheeling the old pram back down the road towards the bus stop. *That bloody bitch is as mad as a wasp in a window.*

Though Daisy did not want to believe this of her mother, she had some sympathy with Franny's view. Still, duty was blind to mental incapacity, and it was clear to Daisy that, as the daughter with no family of her own, she should continue to visit her mother until her death. Which, as it turned out, was not long in coming. One day, a few months after this visit, she turned up at the asylum to a grim-faced welcome from the principal. Elsie Crommelin had suffered a stroke, or perhaps a heart attack. It didn't seem to matter much. She was gone.

Joe said it was a good job he'd kept the black suit he'd worn to the funeral of his sons thirty years before, because a black suit was an awful expense at the best of times, and more awful still if you'd only just paid for your daughter's wedding. He walked behind Elsie's coffin on a cloud of naphthalene. Only Franny cried. Joe and Daisy felt more bewildered than anything. A week or so after the funeral, Franny turned up at number 7 Bloomsbury Street and removed what was left of her mother's trousseau – a linen tablecloth, a tortoiseshell vanity set, some napkins and a few other bits and pieces from the chest where they had long lain unused and unregarded – on the grounds that, unlike Daisy, she was a married woman with a home to furnish and could do with the help. When Daisy returned to the chest some time later she found that her letter from Sidney was gone too.

May's dismal predictions swiftly came to pass. After only a few months, and the strains of a new baby, the bloom began to fade from Franny and Jack's romance and the bride began turning up at Bloomsbury Street of an evening, complaining that Jack almost always went out to the pub after tea, and she was lonely at home, cooped up like a brood hen. She loved her little boy, but it was a strain having to mind him all the time. No one had warned her what a strain it would be. And her with no mother to lend a hand either. It wasn't fair. Couldn't Daisy look after the baby sometimes, leastwise until she got her own children?

So Daisy took on the role of surrogate mother. Franny's financial demands were quick to follow. The excuses were various. Richie was ill and needed medicine, she'd had to buy extra meat for him that week and needed to pay the butcher, but Daisy sensed it was Jack's love of puck-a-poo which kept her sister short of money. While Daisy scraped around in her pocketbook for a shilling or two, Franny would wrap Richie up in his blankets and say:

Only I wouldn't ask for nothing for me, but it's for the boy's sake, see.

When whatever small coinage had been handed over, Franny would pass the baby to her sister and head out to the shops, leaving Daisy nestling the boy into the crook of one arm and with her free hand stroking the downy fur on the top of his head and wondering how Poplar could have produced anything so utterly perfect.

Gradually, the demands for money became more frequent and more difficult for Daisy to satisfy. The East End seemed to be in the grip of yet another economic crisis, and if anything this one looked more daunting than that which had preceded the General Strike. By the winter of 1933 an army of the unemployed gathered daily outside the dock gates, desperate for a day or two of paid work. Others meandered aimlessly along the Commercial and East India Dock Roads, hoping to be in the right place the moment some shopkeeper or factory foreman needed a man to put in an hour or two shifting stock or sweeping up or cleaning or hauling coal, but soon the shopkeepers, too, were forced to withdraw credit and call in the tick cards of even their most regular customers, and no longer had the spare cash to employ casuals. Pawnshops ballooned with stacks of unredeemed linen, trays of wedding rings and piles of boots, items no one could afford to buy, and soon notices appeared suggesting that customers with anything to pawn should go elsewhere.

This was no time to be fussy. In Chrisp Street boys in patched jumpers cruised the stalls for fallen fruit and discarded vegetables and there was an epidemic of petty pilfering from the docks. As the Depression bit harder, men began to spend their time out on the south Essex marshes trying to bag rabbits or eels. Back home, women talked seriously about eating their pets, because they could no longer afford to feed them. You had only to walk down the streets to see men, women and particularly children with pinched eyes and gaunt faces, alert to every unattended barrow or van from which, if they were very lucky, they might pinch a few vegetables or a handful of nuts.

During the worst of it, the council set up soup kitchens along the main thoroughfares, but the soup ran out within minutes of the kitchens opening. The Salvation Army pitched in, and from dawn onwards men could be seen queuing outside, shifting from leg to leg to stave off the cold and the boredom so they might stand a chance of getting a cup of soup for themselves at lunchtime and a piece of bread they could take back to their hungry children.

Everyone blamed someone. Posters went up on shop walls,

denouncing bosses, capitalists, foreigners, communists, Jews, politicians. In cafés and dockers' clubs and in the top rooms of pubs throughout the East End men and women gathered to argue and suggest action. There were calls for strikes and demonstrations and even, when the mood grew desperate, for revolution. But there was no cushion, no disaster fund, no stashed savings, no government handouts, no syrup that could sweeten the bitter pill of poverty.

One early evening during these very dark times, Daisy was at home making scrag-end soup for tea when there was a knock on the door and, imagining it to be Mrs Shaunessy come to borrow an egg or a spoon of jam or a half-cup of sugar, she went to answer it in her apron and saw Sidney standing there, with his hands in his pockets.

Hello, Daisy, he said.

She looked at him for a moment, too stunned to speak. At first she just wanted him to go away, then, remembering her manners, she checked herself and asked him in. He seemed pleased that she had, and hurriedly stepped inside the passageway before she could change her mind. She went ahead, flustered, unable to recall whether the living room was clean or full of drying washing, then, remembering that she had already folded the washing and put it in the scullery ready for ironing, she relaxed a little and motioned Sidney to sit. While he was settling himself, she went into the scullery, put the kettle on the range and mashed the tea leaves from breakfast so that they would be ready when the water boiled.

Come straight from work? she said.

He said he had.

Peckish?

He shook his head but she could see that he was. In the two years since she had last seen him he had grown more gaunt, a pale reed swaying in a cold breeze. There was something unpleasant about him too, which had always been there, she realised. It was not physical but, rather, emanated from within. Perhaps it was just that there was less flesh to hide it now, she thought. Or perhaps it was that her own heart had hardened towards him.

She sugared the tea, cut a slice of bread, and layered the marge thickly on the bread, as he liked it. They exchanged small talk for a while. He did not ask after Franny or Jack, or give any indication that he remembered that they had been expecting a child, and she chose not to mention Richie to him. As the minutes ticked by and his voice droned on, she realised she hadn't really heard anything that he'd said, but had been passing the time trying to summon to mind the smell of hops, as she did when she felt a need to be comforted. Often, in moments of stress, she would conjure that smell, which spoke to her now, of sitting with Lilly on the rim of the gravel pit, watching Ship's Cat and Marmalade chasing butterflies, as yet not fully comprehending that she and Franny had lost their mother. Suddenly, she longed for Sidney to get to the point, and he must have noticed it on her face, because he stopped and changed tack.

Look here, he began, his voice finally suggesting his true purpose, *I'm sorry about how things was left. It ain't been easy, the last while.* He sounded both stuffy and whiny, she thought, then checked herself for her lack of generosity. Was this not the man she had once loved? The only man who had ever taken any interest in her? A man she might love again?

But that don't mean I didn't miss you, he said. He blinked his watery eyes and adjusted his hair, then sliced what remained of his bread into even-sized squares and began to chew delicately, like a rabbit.

I've been having a think, see, he said, his Adam's apple dancing about like a conker on a string. *Now, I don't expect you to understand, but I'm a thinking man, Daisy, and I had my reasons for doing what I done.* He looked at her between creased and urgent brows, like a dog sitting next to a bone it has been forbidden to touch. To prevent him venturing any farther down the path he was about to take, to save his pride, Daisy was about to say something comforting but final when he raised his palms to silence her.

Now hang on, he said, *I ain't finished.* Purple blotches moved about on his face, reminiscent of clouds scudding across a sunny sky. *The thing is, Daisy, I got ambitions. In politics. And a politician needs a wife.* He paused for a moment for the impact of his words to sink in. *I ain't going to be nobody for ever.* He had it all worked out and this is what he had decided. They would need to save £200 before they could marry. To that end, he would begin by saving one pound and ten shillings a week and Daisy would save ten shillings. Thus it would take two years, give or take. Until then, they could remain officially engaged. Since they would be saving, there could be no more trips to the Pavilion or to the Lyons Tea Room, but he would make sure she got a decent ring so that everyone would know she was taken. *What say?* He took a handkerchief from his pocket, rolled up one corner and began to use it to pick his teeth.

Daisy Crommelin sat back in her chair and bit her lip so that she would know she was awake and wouldn't be tempted to talk. She'd been twenty-six when she'd first met Sidney. Now she was thirty, virtually an old maid. How much time he'd wasted. She wondered why she didn't just grab the nearest broom and chase him from her house, but it wasn't her style. She took a sip or two of tea and tried to gather herself. She thanked Sidney for his visit and said she'd think about his proposal. She waited until he had left before she began to cry.

Over the following days, she felt a surge of anger, humiliated that he had simply assumed he could slot himself back into her life, but after a few days, she began to calm down and take stock of her situation. Here she was, a woman already, by the standards of her times quite some way past her prime, with a much younger sister already married and with no other offers in the wings, and the thought of spending the rest of her days working in the laundry and her evenings sitting on her own knitting bootees for other people's children chilled her to the marrow. She saw what happened to spinsters. They became everyone else's favourite objects of pity. She didn't love Sidney, exactly, but she was fond of him, she didn't despise him. She could do worse. Worse was no one.

In the weeks that followed, Daisy didn't mention Sidney's visit to Lilly. She knew her friend well enough to appreciate exactly what she would say. Lilly had always been wary of the man. Ne'er Do Wells, she called him, because he never asked Daisy for her hand. Well, now he had and it really didn't take long for Daisy to decide that she'd be better off married to Ne'er Do Wells than sitting on the shelf waiting for a man who measured up to Joe. So, a month or so after his visit, she agreed to Sidney's terms, and the moment the word yes passed her lips, it was as though she had dropped a twig in a fast-flowing river, and the speed at which it would travel and the distance it would go were no longer matters over which she had any control. She felt relieved and very grown up. Daisy Crommelin would be no more; in her place would rise Mrs Sidney Wells.

The couple announced their engagement. Joe did not try to sway his daughter from her course of action. Franny offered no guidance either, commenting only that she'd never thought her sister would have much use for a husband. Only Lilly protested, but Daisy ignored her. It was all right for Lilly. She was married and now with two daughters. No one was ever going to think of Lilly as a sorry spinster, a woman whom the world had chosen to leave behind.

And so the twig continued to bowl along on the current, and soon the women at the Apex Laundry were putting their coppers in a jar in preparation for 'the event' and Daisy could barely walk down to the shops without being stopped and asked about 'the Big Day'. The attention was dizzying. So this was what it was like to be a bride. No wonder Franny had been so keen to get married.

She began to save for the wedding. In six months, by eating only bread and marge and a bit of barley soup and tripe, by taking in mending and spending the evenings of Sidney's meetings playing with her nephew, babysitting him at weekends instead of going to the pictures, Daisy managed to accumulate fifteen pounds, which she kept under a liner of violet-sprigged paper in the chest drawer, and was feeling very pleased with herself. In addition to saving the money, she had managed to spend so much time with Richie that he called her Mummy Daisy and assumed that he had as much claim on her as he had on his mother, which was sometimes a source of frustration to Franny and sometimes a relief. What a joy it had been coming to know him, in the knowledge that she would continue to know him, all her life.

A year passed, but by Christmas 1934 Sidney still seemed to want to push the wedding farther into the future. In the spring he was needed for a local election campaign, he said, and then in the autumn he had to go all out to raise funds; winter was a bad time to get married and the following spring the committee would be meeting to put together a new manifesto. Once that had been drafted, he promised, they would set a proper date, and Daisy began to allow herself to imagine that, in two years from now, by Christmas 1936, she might be sitting beside the fire in her own home, with her husband beside her and a baby growing in her belly.

On Christmas Eve, she was soaking a gammon ham of its salt to ready it for cooking the next day, and looking forward to the celebrations, when Franny unexpectedly turned up and asked whether she would mind looking after Richie for a while as she and Jack needed to visit an elderly distant relative of Jack's and thought the old man might frighten the child, who was turning out to be a sensitive little thing. She promised to be back on Christmas Day in the morning to fetch him and give him his Christmas presents. Then, depositing a drawstring bag on the table containing a few of Richie's things, Franny kissed Richie goodbye and was gone. For the remainder of the evening, Richie played happily with his spinning top, seeming not to have noticed his mother's absence. He was used to spending much of his time with his aunt and was content to sleep beside Daisy in the bed she had once shared with his mother.

As a pale light opened Christmas morning, Daisy rose, set the fire and put the Christmas pud and the gammon on to boil. Once Richie had had his breakfast, she handed him oranges, nuts and cough candy from Father Christmas and a small tin car from herself. Joe gave his grandson a ship he'd made up from fruit crates, then Franny packed the little boy's things back in the drawstring bag so he would be ready to go when his mother came.

At lunchtime Sidney showed up. They didn't wait for Franny but ate the gammon ham and Christmas pudding, and Daisy saw to it that Richie found a sixpence in his bowl. Afterwards, Sidney slept beside the fire, while Richie and Joe passed the afternoon racing the tin car along imaginary roads. Still, though, Franny did not appear. In the evening, Joe volunteered to go over to their house, but there was no one at home and the neighbours didn't seem to know anything or weren't saying if they did, so he left a note stuck under the door. Boxing Day passed with no news, and on the following day, Daisy had to leave Richie with Mrs Shaunessy while she went back to her job at the laundry. And so the days passed, and still there was no word, nor any sign that Franny or Jack had been home. On New Year's Eve Daisy found herself sitting beside the window in the front room, watching her nephew's sleeping face in the moonlight, her thoughts clumped together like dumplings in boiling soup. What if Franny and Jack had bought tickets on the Christmas packet and emigrated, to South Africa, perhaps, or Canada? It seemed far fetched, yet not impossible. Franny loved Richie – would she leave her own son? Daisy thought about it and realised that she wasn't completely sure Franny wouldn't. What a terrible thing to think of your own sister, and over Christmas too. She decided to make it her New Year's resolution not to think unkind things.

Midnight arrived and the docks exploded with the sounds of ships' sirens and with the clatter of pans on dustbin lids banged by the neighbours along Bloomsbury Street, down St Leonard's Road and across the drab grids of Poplar. Richie woke briefly, then drifted back to sleep with Daisy's hand stroking his hair. Once his breathing had lengthened and slowed, Daisy picked up a perfect hand and licked it. His skin tasted warm and briny, like the air around the hop gardens, and there was some bitterness there, from the smuts, she supposed. Her thoughts turned once more to Franny's absence, and with a shameful surge she realised not only that she hadn't worried about her sister but that she had been quite glad to have Richie all to herself.

On New Year's Day, Franny reappeared, flustered and tearful. She told the whole story over a cup of tea and one of Daisy's rock buns. In the lead-up to Christmas Jack had been caught hefting crates of Jamaican rum from the dockside and spiriting them out on the backs of lorries filled with bananas. The Port of London Authority police had arrested one of the lorry drivers and this man had given Jack and a number of others away. Jack had lain low for a while, avoiding home and the usual haunts, hoping a Christmas spirit would prevail, or at least that the PLA police would be too drunk to bother with him. He wanted Franny with him because he didn't trust her not to blab if questioned, so it had been he who had sent her to drop off Richie with Daisy until things had calmed down. He and Franny had then both gone to stay with a relative of his in Hackney, but the police had eventually tracked him down and he was currently clapped in a cell at the PLA police headquarters in Wapping. An understanding sergeant had agreed to overlook his role in the contraband operation and let him out in exchange for a fifty-pound donation to the police hardship fund. Harold had stumped up fifteen pounds, Henry another ten, and Franny couldn't bring herself to ask Joe, it was too humiliating, so she was hoping Daisy might be able make up the rest.

The request was so unexpected and, at the same time, so predictable that for a moment Daisy did not know what to say. She watched Richie pushing his car across the linoleum, un-hampered by traffic or crossroads or sudden turns. She pictured him at the gravel pits in Kent, watching the cats hunting butter-flies. For a brief moment she saw herself as a girl standing on the platform at Selling station, smiling and waving at a departing train, then the image faded. Poor mite, she thought, dad in prison, what hope was there? She went into the scullery and put the kettle on, and while it was boiling, she opened the chest drawer and was hit by the smell of dry, ageing dust. Carefully she took her roll of savings and peeled off twenty-five pounds. Then she went back into the living room.

She decided to tell Sidney one rainy evening not long after-wards, as they were walking along Commercial Road. It would be a test of his resolve. She asked whether they could break their walk with a cup of tea. He took her by the elbow, led her down a nearby side street to a poorly painted Maltese café and opened the door. The place was tiny, a half-dozen small tables lined up along cucumber-green walls. At one of these tables, a group of four coloured men were playing dominoes. At another a white woman was in deep conversation with a Lascar. Daisy began unbuttoning her coat, wondering how Sidney knew such a place. A small, round Maltese man with oiled hair showed them to a table then brought them a pot of tea, and a plate of tiny, sweet pastries in the shape of stars.

She poured the tea then began, casually she thought, wondering whether he'd recently put his mind to their wedding. The instant she said the word he stiffened and, taking a long swig of tea, which was too hot for long swigs, and swallowing it with a pained look, he said that yes, as a matter of fact he had. She was going to tell it all then, the fact of Jack being in prison, and having to give Franny a part of her wedding savings, but the moment she opened her mouth to speak she saw that Sidney had something pressing of his own to say, something that she had inadvertently given him permission to tell her and that would not be kept back a moment longer.

He began by reminding her of the Depression. It had left a long wake in the East End. There were men, he said, who were having to watch their children walk to school barefoot because they hadn't the money for the rent, let alone a pair of boots. Daisy finished her first cup of tea and poured a second. He went on and Daisy did not interrupt. A twinge of impatience crossed her face. It wasn't that she was unsympathetic, but it was hard to keep up sometimes and she wished he'd stop talking. She didn't understand why he was bringing all this up now. It wasn't as though she hadn't already heard it a thousand times.

The white woman got up from her table and left. A couple came in. The man embraced the Maltese owner and they exchanged words in their own language. It was odd to see two men hold each other, Daisy thought. Among Englishmen you didn't even see that at funerals. Her thoughts meandered from funerals to weddings and she was suddenly conscious that Sidney had stopped talking and was looking at her.

Well?

She smiled sheepishly.

So you won't make no trouble for me, Daisy? Sidney said.

She shook her head. Trouble? What was he talking about? He reached out for her left hand and patted it. There was an expression of concern on his face but there was also something else; ruthlessness perhaps. He was holding her hand, now, rather too hard, bending the fingers so that her engagement ring was facing him.

No hard feelings, then, Daise, he said. She nodded. A well of feeling rose up from her belly, but it had nowhere to go.

I don't like to ask, but you won't mind giving me ring back? Sidney was looking hopeful now.

She looked at the ring and then at him and understood what he was saying.

No, she said at last. She felt a great rush of feeling and recognised it to be relief.

She walked home alone, ringless.

A few months afterwards, a letter arrived from him, full of carefully measured recriminations. She had no idea why he sent it. A pointless exercise. She folded the envelope and tucked it away to act as a reminder, should one ever be needed, of what she had not lost.

Later, she heard that he'd met someone else a while before he had broken off his engagement with her, but the woman was a Jew and there had been family problems. In the end, though, love had prevailed and he had asked the Jewess to marry him.

CHAPTER 7

In early August 1935 the first of the hop letters and cards began dropping into postboxes across Poplar, and Lilly suggested to Daisy that she come hopping, to get over a grief which, in all honesty, she did not feel. The manner of Sidney's betrayal still clung to her like a stubborn stain, and there were residual affections which she did her best to ignore, but what Daisy most missed about her life with Sidney, she realised with some sense of shame, was the opportunity to get out of the house. Here was that opportunity. There were risks attached to saying yes. Having a family connection to the Apex, Lilly could be sure of her job back when she returned, but for Daisy things were more uncertain. On the other hand she knew she was valued at the laundry, and there had never been a better time to take a risk. Elsie was dead, Sidney was gone, and Franny was now more settled than she had been the Christmas before. Old Mrs Shaunessy would be happy to look after Joe for a few shillings. With Paddy the way he was, she hadn't been able to go hopping for years. So Daisy saw Lilly's invitation as the blessing it was, and gratefully accepted.

As the time drew closer, the event began to take up space in her imagination. She'd be standing at the mangles, when some long-forgotten detail would suddenly spring to mind, but that first trip seemed so remote now that she had no confidence in her memories, only in her feelings, which told her still, outrageously after all these years, that some part of her belonged in Kent. The nearer the departure day, the more these feelings began to intrude on Daisy's peace of mind. Every time she thought about that one perfect summer of her childhood, she was filled with almost unbearable longing. It was as though the whole of her subsequent life was measured by that feeling. But it was a lonely feeling. She had no one with whom she could share it. The country held no magic for Joe or Franny or Jack. Only Richie, she thought, had shown signs of interest in her stories. She began to want to take him there and show him the bright streak of the sea, the pond and the mists hanging over the gardens. He would love it, she was sure, and the fresh air of Kent might do him some good. He was a fragile child and had to be wrapped in goose fat and brown paper every winter to stave off bronchitis. The East End was an unhealthy place to grow up in, surrounded by so many belching factories. Lilly's children – nine-year-old Minnie, seven-year-old Susan and three-year-old Grace – were much more robust than Richie and they had been hopping every year of their lives.

She brought up with Franny the possibility of taking Richie with her but, after having virtually ignored him for most of his short life, her younger sister suddenly wouldn't hear of being separated from her son. She and Jack had drifted so far apart by now that Richie was the only mooring for their marriage, and Daisy thought her sister was afraid of what might happen if he went away. At the same time she often seemed hardly to notice the boy. Daisy routinely bathed him, washed his hair, kept him properly fed and mended his clothes. It was ironic. To Franny he seemed more like a treasured doll than a human being, a comforter to which she clung in times of need.

From time to time Daisy wished she had children of her own, but she was afraid that if she did, she would not love them as she loved Richie. Other fears piled in too. She still recalled the incident with the silk flowers so many years before. They said madness ran in families. There was some hint of it in Franny,

Daisy thought. Perhaps some as yet unnoticed intimations of it in herself. What if having children tipped her over the edge, as it had her mother? Who would look after Franny and Joe then? Who would see to Richie?

In the hours before dawn on the morning of the leaving day, 25 August 1935, Daisy laid all these troubles to one side. Dragging her little hopping box behind her, she met Lilly, Minnie, Susan and Grace at the top of Bloomsbury Street and the party set off together on the long walk to Borough. The annual exodus had begun, and the streets were crammed with women and children like themselves, towing old prams, dragging cardboard suitcases or pushing carts nailed up from boards. There were babies in arms and toddlers perched atop the carts with their older siblings skipping alongside. Nervous-looking dogs slunk behind their owners and here and there a cat peeked out from inside a wicker basket at the canaries swinging from their cages. An onlooker might observe that this was nothing more than an annual migration of cheap labour, but to the hoppers it didn't feel that way. Despite the hour there was an atmosphere of celebration. Hopping was in these women's blood. Their mothers had been hoppers and their mothers before them, and to the women and children heading for the station, what they were doing was part of an honoured tradition, a collective adventure, greater and longer lasting than themselves.

At London Bridge, they crossed the river to Borough Market, edging west in a thickened crowd of mostly women and children until they arrived finally at their destination; the grand, colonnaded sweep of the Hop Exchange building in Southwark Street. All about now there was a tremendous cacophony of shouting and engine noise. Lilly and her family had secured places on one of the lorries hired for the occasion – they were cheaper than the hoppers' trains and left at a more civilised hour, and places on them were so prized that fighting often broke out over seats. They made their way towards a man holding

up a sign and shouting *Selling here, here for Selling.* He stopped
to speak to Lilly for a couple of minutes, then directed them to
a lorry parked beside the pavement. The driver was checking
the air in the tyres, but they had yet to begin loading and a small
crowd had gathered around with their bags, anxious to make
sure of their places. Lilly waved to a large woman with a face
the colour of stale pastry and grey, wiry hair, who seemed to
be marshalling the crowd. The woman waved back and began
directing a group of men hauling the hopping boxes and carts
on to the back of the lorry. When that was done, everyone began
to clamber on board, reserving spaces on the nailed-down
benches for their friends and children, and the large woman,
whose name was Maffie, went round collecting tickets. A cloud
of filthy-smelling fumes rose from the lorry. When everyone
was settled, the Selling lorry began to move off into the road
and Maffie stood and shouted:

Three cheers for the good old hops! And everyone at the back of
the lorry roared:

Hop hop hooray! Hop hop hooray! Hop hop hooray! and laughed
like mad things.

The lorry rumbled southwards towards Elephant and Castle,
accompanied by cheers and clapping, then turned east along
the Kent Road in the direction of the coming sunrise, and by
the time they reached New Cross a caravan of hopping lorries
stretched out in front and behind them, and it seemed as
though all the world was going hopping, which in a way it
was, for it was all their world. On the other side of Blackheath,
the lorries became separated by the more usual early morning
traffic of milk carts, brewers' drays and buses, and they gradually lost sight of their comrades. A while later they passed an
old cart filled with thin ragged men and worn women, and
someone on the lorry offered to sell a hopping card to anyone
on the cart who could pay tuppence. There was a brief scrum
as the men and women scrabbled in their pockets, but the

lorry soon moved out in front and left the cart behind. The air became brittle and odourless. For a while Daisy watched the progress of the lorry beneath the stars, then, as the last thick remnants of the night bore down on her, her eyelids began to droop and she slept.

She was woken some time later by the sounds of children sniffling and crying. It was cold. Lilly was already awake.

Where are we? she said.

Dunno, Chatham, maybe, Lilly replied. *We ain't got that far now before the lorry stops for breakfast.*

Half an hour went by, then the lorry shuddered to a halt, the driver's help jumped down from the cabin and Maffie ordered everyone to clamber off. Before long a couple appeared through the flat early morning light, leading a donkey loaded with several billycans of tea and a basket of bread rolls, and the passengers ate and drank in silence, their breath pooling into the steam rising from the tea, while, all around them, the sun rose on a new world and they could see that the huddle of houses, factories and shops had given way to trees and gently folding hills. Birds rose up like scattered beads. The air smelled of earth and animal shit, and, from time to time, the breeze brought an odour of honey and bruised leaves.

Here, said Lilly, as they finished up the last of their breakfast, *do you remember when we went blackberrying? And you got red juice all over your face and Franny thought you was the Sandeman! Ha!* She dug her friend in the ribs. *I'll bet you ain't given a thought to the Sandeman in years.*

They laughed, though Lilly laughed harder than Daisy. How much time had passed, Daisy thought, and how little there seemed to be to show for it.

The two friends took Lilly's children off along a dirt track, now thinly illuminated in the new day, to relieve themselves. They passed women squatting, lightly hidden in a brush of nettles and hawthorn, enjoying the feel of the breeze on skin they rarely exposed. Daisy found herself a spot and pulled down her bloomers. An instant later she sprung up, yelping.

Saints a-bloody-live! Something bit me on the hoola.

She heard Lilly's laughter coming from somewhere nearby.

It's the nettles, you great boneache.

They began to make their way back. Grace toddled on ahead, reappearing moments later clutching a circular object woven from wheat, the ears pointing to the four points of the compass, and immediately, with a sudden rush of protective energy, Lilly launched herself at her daughter, shouting, *Drop it, drop it now!* She swept the little girl into her arms and started turning circles with her. After a while she put her down, gathered her children about and told them all never, under any circumstances, to pick up such a thing again, because it was a Gypsy thing and Gypsy things had magic in them, and the magic wasn't always good magic but the kind of magic that could do you harm.

The lorry took off once more, winding past hedgerows hung with green berries. The whitewashed cowls of oasts began to appear against what was by now a pale summer sky. On the ridges clambering up from the hedgerows, dark copses of trees pulled at thin, braided clouds, and in the dips and gulleys there were orchards of fruit trees and deep green hop gardens strung about with coir. Finally, someone cried out:

The sea!

And there, far away across the fields, a thin stripe of peacock blue sparkled for an instant and was gone, as the lorry turned its back to the coast and began to sway along a thin, unpaved lane breached by crests of Queen Anne's lace and hogweed. The route opened out and they found themselves sailing past softly folded hills speckled with farmhouses and oasts. On the slopes between them sheep grazed. Then the air filled with a heavy tannic tang, and Daisy was gripped by the sensation that everything that had happened in the intervening years had happened to someone else. The real, most important part of her had remained behind here, waiting to be rediscovered.

The lorry slowed before a large field which sloped gently upward to two rows of low huts standing before a wood. A red-faced fellow jumped down from the lorry and ran beside it and, following his cue, the older children began jumping from the flatbed and scrambling away and up the hill. The scene before Daisy was almost unbearably familiar: Pheasant Field, where as a little girl she had watched the bobtails of rabbits and the flickering flight of bats, where she had washed her hands of hop tar and eaten potatoes straight from the fire and gone to bed on piles of sticks. A surge of feeling rose up. Why had she left it so long before returning?

Lilly had been down a few weeks before to clean hut number 21 and make it ready. A line of hooks drew Daisy's eyes towards the side walls, which were three-quarter height, filled in with wire mesh at the top. The earth floor had been covered with rough board and there were old linoleum tiles nailed unevenly to it. She breathed in the smells of old wood and creosote and whitewash and smiled. Lilly stuck her head around the door.

Remember the old place?

A cousin of Lilly's, a tall, dark woman by the name of Iris, came by with tea. Her son, Tommy, a soft-set boy with bruised-looking features, had brought over a pile of faggots and they got to work laying the faggots neatly inside the hut, one against each side wall, while Tommy knelt down in the grass outside, stuffing the palliasses with straw. From time to time, women approached, neighbours from Poplar, mostly, to gossip and catch up on the news. Had they heard Old Nell had died and her daughter had scattered her ashes on Old Ground? Billy Shaunessy's new wife, Dot, had had a baby and his uncle, wall-eyed Alfie, was down with his wife Joan and a few of their grandchildren. By the time the news had been exhausted, it was that evanescent hour just before twilight when the light pushes its way low across the land, outlining the shapes of things and dimming their interiors.

Come for a walk with me, Daise, Lilly said. Leaving her children in the care of Iris, she took her friend's arm and they wandered down to the chalk road heading towards Vicarage Lane. Life felt simple, and with the dust rising from their boots and the sun rosying the hedgerows, they could almost have been ten years old again. On they walked, past banks deep in goosegrass and hogweed and alongside copses of oak and ash where birds were already beginning to roost, past Big Kit, Little Field, Brook Meadow, Old Ground and the great green factories of the hop gardens. In the distance, cows bellowed, and everywhere there was the thick, rooty smell, that unmistakable, acidic, tarry tang of hops.

It's awful the way you got done, Daise, Lilly said, *but that Sidney, he was, well, he was . . .* She glanced at Daisy and, judging it safe to say what was on her mind, she added, *. . . he was right pleased with hisself, that one.*

Daisy giggled.

Didn't you never find him a bit stuffed up, Daise?

Daisy looked at her friend and felt suddenly very free.

As a bleedin' Christmas goose, Lil, she said.

The two friends laughed.

Mind you, Lilly said, *even the best of 'em gets awful dull after a bit. Mending their clothes, cooking their teas, having their babies. Matrimonial ain't all it's cracked up to be, Daise.*

Close though they were, Lilly had never confided in her friend about her marriage before. The women at the laundry made lewd jokes about men all the time, but the rules were plain: you could gossip all you liked about other people's marriages, but you revealed as little as you could about your own. You put up and shut up and if he didn't hit you, you were grateful.

All I'm saying is a bit of variety never hurt no one. Lilly squeezed Daisy's waist and said, *Let's get back.*

Pheasant Field glowed now in the light of a dozen small fires. Snatches of conversation rose in the air. Beside the huts, kerosene-dipped bulrushes illuminated in blue and orange the tired, happy faces of women relieved for a few weeks from the grinding routine of their lives.

They ate a tea of pork knuckle and roast apples and the children went to bed. At nine, or thereabouts – no factory whistle sounded and most did not have watches – the adults followed them. For a while Daisy lay awake watching the splints of moonlight playing against the wire at the top of the partition and listening first to the gentle sounds of sleep in the hut, then to the coughs of children. An owl called. She pulled the blanket over her head and closed her eyes. She was woken some time later by a bell and guessed it was very early because it was still almost dark and the air was as damp as a flannel. Beside her, Iris stirred. Outside, a horse snorted and there were the sounds of a man moving about. Maffie was already up and tending a fire. A kettle hung over the flames; beside it a loaf of bread was balanced on a sawn-off log and next to that a bit of dripping or lard or perhaps margarine twisted up in greaseproof paper.

The garden appeared denser and more mysterious than she'd remembered it. Inside the leafy walls, dew hung from every hop bud and the corridors between the bines were strung with shining cobwebs. The air was soft green and humid. Last night's conversation with Lilly came back to her, but she didn't want to think about it too hard. Old feelings floated to the surface, but Daisy could not place them. The smell of the hops reached her and for once she wanted to give herself completely to the day.

The hop cutter appeared carrying a hop dog and a bine knife on a pole and began pulling and cutting bines from the coir strings overhead, then he blew the pickers on. For two hours they worked without a break, lifting each bine in turn, shaking it lightly, drawing their hands along in the direction of the hairs, snatching buds from their keepers with the forefinger and the pad of muscle beside the thumb. Every so often the bine cutter came round to clip down more bines. He was a tall, strong-looking man, Daisy noticed, with a ridged face reminiscent of tree bark, and eyes an uncertain blue, the colour of the spring sky when rain is brewing. He never stayed any longer than it took to clip down the bines, but his presence seemed to unsettle Lilly, and Daisy noticed that when he was around her friend, Lilly's body softened somehow and an odd, almost impercept-ible energy crept into her features.

It seemed by mid-morning that they had been picking for a lifetime. A few dozen older children, girls mostly, started making their way back to the huts, returning a while later carrying jars of tea, and at midday the tallyman blew his whistle and several hundred hoppers began spilling from the quiet of their drifts to sit on the grass, unwrap their packages of faggots and corned beef and cheese sandwiches and drink jars full of hot sweet tea, singing, joking, the children diving in and out of the bines, playing hide-and-seek or grandmother's footsteps. A noisy kind of peace swept across the garden. Everything was where it should be, and for the half-hour that followed, nothing – not the early start or the thick dew or the insects or the stinging of the hop acid – could threaten Daisy's strong sense that she had discovered some small corner of paradise that belonged forever to East Enders.

Around three in the afternoon it began to rain. The drops thrummed on the leafy ceiling above them and the buds became heavy and reluctant to quit their bines. Beneath them, the ground churned to a thin clay slip criss-crossed by the trails of slugs. A few of the pickers took to stripping their bines under umbrellas but most, including Daisy, slung old hop pockets over their heads and hoped for the best. Someone from the farmhouse brought round milk churns full of hot tea, and the hoppers carried on picking, shivering in their sodden outfits. Still it rained, the water first collecting in the leaves then running down the bines in liquid ropes, leaving their picking arms drenched and raw, but now that the oast kilns were lit, the farmer needed a steady supply of hops to feed into them and the hoppers needed the money. Eventually, the sun returned, raising the air between the rows into a tarry steam and bringing out all the insects, and for the next few hours they were plagued by flies. At five, the tallyman cried *Pick no more bines!* and sounds of whooping came from the drifts. It had been a hard, hard day.

A woman burst through a wall of bines, followed closely by Maffie, screaming, *Come here, you bleedin' scratcher*. An arm appeared then was pulled back across the vegetation and Daisy ran to the top of the row to see Maffie and the woman scuffling in the wet clay with the cutter and the tallyman making half-hearted attempts to separate them. The woman had ignored the tallyman's call and carried on picking, putting herself at some tiny, forbidden advantage.

After it was all over, they walked back through the gate in the hawthorn hedge and up the slope into Pheasant Field, dappled now in the late afternoon sun, clutching their lower backs and aching shoulders, wringing out their sodden clothes. Gathering her children about her, Lilly said:

Don't you never be a scratcher, little 'uns. Don't you never pick nothing after the bell. Don't you never try to get one over on your own.

Outside hut number 21, Daisy scrubbed her hands with carbolic and scraped and rinsed the mud from her boots and washed out her shin rags and looked forward to her tea. A man came around, offering hens and rabbits, and Iris put on some young hop shoots to boil in the kettle over the fire. Gradually the light dimmed and once more the field glowed from the hoppers' fires and the bulrushes picked out faces in blue and orange. Maffie lit her pipe and told the story of the scratcher.

They should kick her out, Maffie said, but Iris disagreed.

The scratcher had children to feed and you couldn't blame her, she said.

We all got nippers, Maffie snorted, then, remembering Daisy, checked herself. *Most of us, anyways. And some of us even got nippers what belong to our husbands. Ain't you looked at them brats? Two's the spit of the hop dryer, that gingernut cove. He brung 'em into this world, why don't he bleeding feed 'em?*

And so the conversation went on, back through hop years gone and forward and into the far distant future of the weekend when they would have Sunday roast with their menfolk and there would be singing and dancing and later, in the privacy of the woods and fields, more hop nippers would come into being, and likely quite a few would look nothing like the men they would regard in later life as their fathers.

Next morning the sun was already breaking through the early morning clouds and the trees seemed less close than they had appeared the day before. The grass beneath Daisy's feet was dry and warm. Maffie was standing before a fire, stirring cocoa in a pot.

All right, duck? Lilly still asleep, I'll bet? She gave a sly wink. *Busy night.*

She poured cocoa into a jam jar, spilled some on her hand and shook the burn out, talking about the old times, before the hop huts had been built, when they had lived in old army tents and in cowsheds and slept on piles of hop bines. One year, she thought it was 1909, a storm had blown away the tents and stoved in the roofs of the cowsheds and ruined the hops. A few hoppers were able to afford the train journey back to London but the storm had happened so early in the season that most had not made enough money for a ticket. Some without children or elderly relatives managed to walk back but the majority were stuck. People began stealing potatoes, apples, snaring rabbits, then farm cats, and the parish council had to give them all free beer to reduce the risk of cholera. In the end, the police were sent to help the hoppers get to the workhouse in Maidstone, which is where they stayed until friends or family could send money for the return journey.

It was only after she'd finished her story that Daisy was struck by what Maffie had said about Lilly. Last night her friend had gone off directly after tea, and when Daisy asked her whether she wanted company she'd been offhand and awkward, saying that she needed some air to clear her head and was planning on going for a long walk, so not to wait up for her. When Daisy had woken, her friend was in a deep sleep beside her. Daisy thought about the bine cutter, but no, she couldn't imagine it. Rather, she didn't want to imagine it. She wouldn't give the matter another thought, she decided. It was the strategy she had employed when Sidney left her and, with the exception of a few brief instants when some kindness of his sprang unwelcome into her mind, the strategy had worked. She never again wanted to relive the agonies she'd suffered recalling the day when she'd failed to protect the Christmas flowers from Franny's attentions, and in the years that had passed she had actively cultivated a technique of wilful forgetting. She forgot her father's favouritism and her sister's meanness. She forgot that they didn't have much money. Most of the time she had even managed to forget that she had no husband or children, though she also forgot sometimes that Richie was not hers. Now she would choose to forget that Lilly had ever spoken to her about her marriage and she'd forget her friend's shiftiness and she'd tell herself that what she'd seen in her friend's eyes when the bine cutter had come around had been nothing more than an effect of the light.

And so the day passed, and another, then another, all of them sunny and warm and the gardens lush and spicy with the aroma of hops. At lunchtimes the children took off blackberrying and in the evenings they roasted potatoes and apples in the embers, while their mothers sang and gossiped and a few disappeared arm in arm with some local man, and an atmosphere of such friendliness, such neighbourly amiability and familial solidarity spread around that everyone forgot their sore hands, their leaden legs and aching backs and the hop-eye itch of sulphur and felt as though they had been born only for this and that their lives in London were just shadows of a past to which they would never have to return.

Perhaps because she sensed Daisy's efforts not to get involved, Lilly did not mention her marriage again, and though she went for long lone walks every other night and returned after everyone had already gone to bed, she said nothing more to Daisy and Daisy did not ask. The bine cutter, Michael, still came around the drift, and Daisy was polite but distant, turning from him the moment she could so that she might not catch the play of his lips or the widening of his gaze that happened whenever he looked at Lilly.

And so the days came and went, and each day Daisy woke with the fulsome, heady feeling of happiness which comes only from living outside and eating food cooked on a fire and waking after a dreamless sleep to the first warm rays of sun. At lunchtime Hennage, the farm manager, would be advancing money on the week's pickings and the women would be sending their children to buy a bit of bacon, some pig's trotters or a roll of brisket from the butcher's at Hogben's Hill or Perry Wood House, and two ounces of margarine from File's, and by the time the tallyman shouted *Pick no more bines!* that evening there would be water on the boil for the weekly bath and a thick porky smell would already be rising up from the cookhouse and the pickers would rinse off their best blouses and take the stains out of their aprons, washing their hair and tying it in rags so they would look their best when their men arrived.

On Saturday morning at around nine men in flat hats and gabardine suits and their Sunday braces began to appear off the London train to take over the picking while their wives cooked lamb hotpot, bacon pud and faggot stew for their lunch. At midday the men came up from the gardens to eat, relay the news from home and trade insults.

Old Squint here, can't take him nowhere without he's shivving up some scheme. Sell hoppers back their crabs he thought there was margin in it.

I dare say you was always a better man than me, Jimmy, giving out yer crabs for free.

And so it went on until the meal was over and the men took off in time for last orders at the Sonde Arms and the women drifted into a luscious, empty sleep in the grass, while their children played around them or took themselves to Ghost Hole Pond to fish or to the orchards to scrump for apples. At closing time the men returned, drowsy with drink, and joined their sleeping women, and at six they ate the remains of the faggot gravy with slices of bread and margarine.

A Dover man arrived, and set up a rough stall selling eels and whelks, and a group of Gypsy children turned up, the boys in breeches, girls in flaring, raggedy skirts, hawking clothes pegs, plums and rabbits in their broken English, peppered as it was with strange, exotic words and phrases.

At the pub that night Jimmy leaned into Daisy and said in a kindly voice, *Shall you be havin' the same as the old lady, then?* and Daisy felt bad both for knowing what she knew and for wilfully trying to forget it. Jimmy wasn't a bad man. On the contrary, he never beat Lilly or kept her short of housekeeping money, and in the East End these two facts alone were enough for him to be considered a good man. Daisy hoped Lilly would come to her senses, but you never knew with Lilly. Her unpredictability was one of the qualities Daisy most appreciated in her, and, by the looks of things, Daisy wasn't the only one. Her old friend seemed to have quite a following.

A lorry drove up, with a man and his piano on the flatbed. In good time the man struck up a tune, and the hoppers either ignored him or listened in polite silence. It grew dark and an autumn breeze blew in from the north. From the darkness a woman's voice suddenly shouted:

There's cats down the farm what can caterwaul better than that. For Gawd's sakes give us some real music.

And Maffie's deep, velvety voice began belting out:

She was only a bird in a gilded cage . . .

and the piano player was soon forgotten.

That night Daisy slept with four children so that Lilly and Iris might have a night alone with their husbands. When Lilly and Jimmy emerged the next morning looking happy, and went off into the fields together to look for mushrooms, she felt a great sense of relief. It was all right, she thought. Lilly had come to her senses.

On Monday morning at eight o'clock another week of picking began, families moving from one drift to another, clearing Big Kit and Old Ground and moving gradually north towards Boughton. Everyone had an opinion on which of this year's Goldings or Fuggles bore the plumper cone, which clung more tenaciously to the bine, which gardens were naturally drier and which dank and humid. On Tuesday, the Gypsy children turned up again, bringing clothes pegs, fresh eggs, weasel and rabbit pelts and sorrel, and a little later the cake man arrived with parkin and lemon sponge. On Wednesday a doctor and nurse set up a mobile surgery, shouting *Bring out your dead!*, the nurse dispensing syrup of figs, plus lice and nit lotion, while the doctor tapped lungs and depressed tongues, looking for the telltale signs of tuberculosis and diphtheria. On Thursday the Sally Army dropped off bottles of milk for the children and held an impromptu concert in the Drawing Room by the crossroads. On Friday evening, long after the children had gone to bed and the owls had begun hooting and the vixens were beginning to screech, an old man with a humpback appeared on a bicycle and set up as a temporary swag shop, selling an assortment of trinkets, needles, thread, lurid glass beads and small wooden toys, as well as women's bloomers, socks and a few other pieces of second-hand clothing. On Friday, too, the shellfish seller arrived from Faversham with fresh eels in jelly and whelks and vinegar. A while later the local vicar came around to remind everyone that the hoppers were God's children and had a duty to God not to drink, and everyone nodded and looked solemn until his bicycle disappeared over the horizon and it was safe to have a good laugh at his coarse red nose, his broken veins and promises.

Another week passed, then a third. The oasts were working flat out now, and the smoke from their kilns settled across the hop huts like a London fog. The morning dew was heavier, the dawn grew colder and the picking days seemed longer, though that might only have been an illusion brought on by the closing of the light. Daisy's hands ached and her back throbbed and her eyes streamed, but she felt herself to be in a kind of happy daze. Hennage announced that at the end of the week the pick would be over, and on Saturday everyone would be paid and all pickers would be welcome at the usual hop-end feast at which a Miss Hop Queen would be appointed to mark the end of this year's hopping season, and the day was suddenly taken up with discussions of how much everyone thought they were owed and what they would spend it on when they got it.

The morning before the feast, Hennage and the tallyman set themselves up on a trestle table and chair outside the huts to reckon the accounts and settle up. The routine complaints followed over the rate per bushel, the credit docked off, the extra strain put on the hoppers by the unbearable weather, the impossibly housey hops and the unspeakable meanness of the farmer, but no one took them particularly seriously, and by nine in the morning most families were already heading into Faversham to grab the best pick of boots and winter coats for their children before their menfolk arrived in the afternoon and took possession of whatever remained of their earnings. By the time they returned, the Sonde Arms was full of Londoners and the air was scented with the unmistakable and delicious aroma of roasting pig. The women spent their time comparing their purchases and packing their few belongings back into their hop boxes and lighting their fires and arranging apples and damsons in the hot coals.

Daisy was eagerly anticipating a family visit. She had written to her sister, sending her a postal order to cover the cost of the train tickets and begging her to come for the end-of-hopping feast, secretly hoping that Franny might enjoy herself enough to agree to bring Richie down for a week or two the following year.

She was outside hut number 21 washing tea towels and hanging them on a makeshift line to dry, when she heard a familiar voice shouting: *Auntie Daisy! Auntie Daisy!* and Richie appeared, rushing up the hill. She opened her arms and held him close. He hugged her back and pressed a bunch of daisies into her apron and she told herself to remember this moment in all its detail as one of the few in her life so far of complete, uncompromising happiness.

How he'd grown in the month since she'd last seen him, she thought, knowing that he almost certainly hadn't. How much more handsome he was, and how cleverly he had picked the daisies! She ruffled his hair, deposited a little kiss on the top of that perfect head and promised him baked apples and the biggest piece of spit-roast pork that a boy could fit inside his stomach.

He smiled back and she saw that he had a bruise on his face. He was fragile, but he was growing up tough. She knew that, and it made her at once both proud and melancholy.

Franny followed behind, looking as lovely as ever, wanting to know whether Daisy has a cardigan to spare because it wasn't half nippy in the country, and look at her, as tanned as tarpaper, and had she picked them any blackberries? Jack and Harold brought up the rear. They kissed her once, lightly on the cheek, Jack asking, only half jokingly, what kind of welcome this was, when there was no beer waiting for a thirsty man, and Harold saying he's only joking, you know, and a nice cup of tea would be just the thing – look, they'd all chipped in and bought some flapjacks and a pot of cream to dunk them in and if there were no blackberries, then why didn't he go out into the lane straight away and bag a few?

Then the farmer's wagon appeared loaded with home-made cider, and the women dispatched their children with jugs and injunctions not to spill a drop or there'd be a clumping and a clouting so hard it would send them all flying through the sky and into the next parish.

And it was a rare evening that followed, an evening full of grand food and limitless cider, with singing and Miss Hop Queen elected, and the women all teary eyed and declarations of undying loyalty and friendship and *Till death do us part until next year*, and *Don't do nothing I wouldn't do* and *Keep those children tight to you*, and baked plums and sugared apples and more cider and porky crackling and sobs, and at the end of the evening, before taking himself off to sleep in the barn by the oast with some of the other men, Harold brought Daisy a bunch of red campions. Daisy sat them in a jam jar by her palliasse and once or twice in the night she woke and smelled their perfume.

The following morning, the cart came by to carry their boxes and carts and they staggered, bleary eyed and thick headed, along the road past the Drawing Room, past the great grey stone house whose grounds gave on to views of the sea, between dank green hedgerows now daubed with clusters of hazelnuts and cobs, their leaves lit the colour of old marmalade. On they walked, past naked hopping wires and emptied gardens, past the orchards on which, a month before, the hard little fists of apples hung, which were now full of Gypsies, picking. Soon they were heaving their bags and cases on to the lorries waiting beside the station and trundling back through Sittingbourne and Chatham and into the still-leafy suburbs of Bromley, the villages of Lea Green and Hither Green and St John's.

At the Woolwich Free Ferry they met London in a rush of powdery air, part chemical, part dirt. No one talked much, no one sung. Across the river they went, winding along North Woolwich Way, tangling in the dock traffic coming in and out of the Royal Victoria and the King George VI docks, stopping every so often to unload another family. As their numbers dwindled they waved and made their promises to stay in touch, but already the month's shimmery magic was losing its lustre, fading into the bellowing grey bustle of the city.

Daisy returned to her mangling at the Apex Laundry, visiting Richie on her way home, and passing her evenings cooking Joe's tea and trying to forget the bunch of red campions she'd read far too much into. Until, one autumn evening, much like any other, there was a knock on the door and when she went to open it, she found Harold Baker standing on the step holding something in his right hand.

Hello, Daisy. Mind if I come in for a cup of tea? He lifted up the thing he was carrying and with his left hand swept off its fabric covering. And there, inside a cage, there was a bright, buttercup-yellow canary.

He's a right little singer, this one, Daisy, I thought you and him might get along famous.

CHAPTER 8

Richie Baker grew up an only child at a time when being an only child was a rare and pitiable condition, akin to having some chronic, life-diminishing disease. His earliest memories were of women looming over him when he was out shopping with his mother, cooing at his pretty, curly hair and sky-blue eyes, then invariably demanding to know where his brothers and sisters were.

Ain't got none, Franny would say, *and ain't getting none neither.*

The women would blanch a little and smile frail smiles, then disappear as fast as they could, as though Richie and his situation might contaminate them.

From time to time Richie would bring the topic of a sibling up with his mother, and would always get the same response:

As if you ain't all the trouble I need right there.

Like many other only children, Richie learned to be self-reliant. Other children seemed puzzling, and he was credulous to the point of eccentricity. The neighbouring children could – and did – spin all manner of lies to see whether Richie would swallow them: glue was made from dead people, a lion was an overfed cat, a Chinaman's braid was a tail left over from his days as a monkey. Richie never failed to believe whatever he was told. His credulity only set him up for further teasing. By the time he was five barely a day went by without one or other of the neighbouring children playing a trick on him. It wasn't long before the tricks became kicks, then punches.

His parents were unsympathetic. When boys gathered outside the small house his family shared with the Wilson family in Gaselee Street, waiting for Richie to appear, Franny would tell him to go and stand up for himself, open the front door and push him out on to the street, and Richie would stand there on the doorstep with his eyes closed, waiting for whatever was to come. He quickly realised that if he stood still and did nothing, the boys would see no sport in him and, after a few punches and kicks, they'd grow bored and move on. He'd let them have their fun, then, when they were done, he'd go back into the house and his mother would wipe his cuts with iodine and put calamine lotion on his bruises. Later, they'd tell Jack that he fell over.

Or he'll blame me for bringing a son into this world what never stood up for hisself, Franny would say.

Sometimes, in the privacy of his bed at night, Richie would cry, but mostly he wouldn't.

In order to minimise encounters with women demanding to know the whereabouts of his siblings or with murderous boys, Richie passed much of his early childhood at his Aunt Daisy and Grandad Joe's house in Bloomsbury Street. His own home seemed chaotic and made him anxious, but he found his aunt and grandad reassuring and their rooms warm and comforting.

Grandad Joe would set him on his lap and tell him salty tales of the monsters and mermaids he'd encountered on his travels. Occasionally, he would walk him down to the docks and list all the names of the ships in dock and the places they'd come from. Auntie Daisy would plop kisses on his head and bake him little treats; a rock bun or two or a bit of shortbread wrapped in brown paper. Unlike his mother, she took an interest in the details of his life. Sometimes she'd reciprocate his stories with some of her own, and though she always said there weren't many stories to tell because nothing much had really happened to her,

Richie never ceased to delight in her tales of the place where people ate whole pigs and you could pick apples and pears from trees, no matter how many times they were repeated. He loved his aunt so much he liked to call her Ma Daisy, but his mother put a stop to it.

Richie saw his Uncle Harold less often because he lived with Nanny May and Grandad Henry. Grandma May was a wicked old witch who spent her time making brushes which were actually broomsticks and Grandad Henry was always telling you to *put 'em up* and trying to punch you. Still, Uncle Harold was kind and he kept margarine-coloured birds that sang better than penny whistles. Richie loved them almost as much as he loved his uncle.

At Gaselee Street, Richie liked to play in the backyard the house shared with next door. The Wilson family, who rented the upper floor of the house, kept a dozen or so hens in the yard, and Richie would amuse himself picking dandelion leaves and digging up worms for them. The Wilsons allowed him to collect the eggs and he loved that too.

On Friday and Saturday nights his father was in the habit of heading down to the Resolute or Charlie Brown's or Chin's to spend his wages. From the age of four, when Richie was deemed old enough to go out on his own at night, his mother would dispatch him to stand at the door at whichever establishment her husband had chosen that evening as a reminder of his family responsibilities. Many of her neighbours did the same. Few men were so heartless or so casual as to be able to ignore the sight of their children standing in the rain at nine o'clock at night awaiting their return home, and whatever Jack Baker might have been, he was not heartless.

All right, all right, he would say, conjuring an arrowroot biscuit from his pocket. *You eat this and I'll be out presently.*

So Richie would wait, standing in the cold, while inside in the warm men laughed and sang songs then came spilling out on to the street in frightening states of rage or sentiment. Richie didn't know which he dreaded more, the fighting or the tearful adult intimacies whispered in his ear.

For the first five years of his life, aside from the occasional trip to the park or the pictures with his aunt and grandpa, and an annual jaunt with his uncle to the summer circus in Victoria Park, Richie went nowhere. Then, in the summer of his fifth year, his Aunt Daisy went hopping again. A week after she'd left, he received a postcard from her. The card gave him a tremendous amount of pleasure, and he spent hours looking at it. The photograph was of an enormous building, a church, perhaps, and some smaller, higgledy-piggeldy buildings with black stripes running up and down them. The odd thing about the buildings, he thought, was, with the exception of the black stripes, how light in colour they were. Everything in Poplar was dark and sooty. But when, not long afterwards, his mother announced that they would get on a train and go down to visit his aunt, it wasn't those light-coloured buildings he thought about, it was the idea of going on a real train to a place where people ate whole pigs and apples hung from trees.

When the day came, the train was so overwhelming that Richie thought he might lose control of himself and start to cry, and it was only the pat-a-cake games his Uncle Harold played with him which stopped him. The Baker party arrived in Selling before lunch. Richie followed his parents and his uncle along the chalky road to Pheasant Field. His father seemed keen to get to the pub, but his mother said it would be rude not to say hello to Aunt Daisy first and, besides, she wanted her lunch. They left the road and began the scramble up the field. Dandelion clocks rose up in sprays before him as he walked and he held out his hands to catch them. At home there were hardly any daisies and not that many dandelions. He scanned the scene up ahead, looking for his aunt, and finally saw her up by the little street of tiny houses. Too excited to wait for the others, he went running up the hill towards her, snatching up fistfuls of daisies, shouting:

Auntie Daisy, Auntie Daisy!

She swept him up and dotted his head with kisses, and he felt as happy as he ever had. Pretty soon they were joined by the others. Daisy had made cheese sandwiches, which they ate sitting on the grass, surrounded by other men and women, laughing and singing and eating *their* sandwiches. An older boy called Tommy said he was going egg collecting and he didn't suppose that Richie would like to come, and Richie said that he *did* suppose, very much, if that was all right, because he knew all about egg collecting and he liked chickens very much, and his Aunt Daisy gave him a little parcel of fried flapjacks and told him to go off and have fun and not to worry because Tommy would look after him.

Normally it would be too late for eggs, Tommy said, *but it's warm still so we might get a few second-clutchers.*

Richie didn't know what second-clutchers were, or first-clutchers for that matter, but everything before him – the pea-green hills, the clear, untroubled sky, the thick furze of wood – was so new and dazzling that he didn't really care, and trotted after his new companion with a Christmassy feeling of wonder. Before long, when they reached the deep shade of a copse, it was as dark as night and quite frightening, but Tommy bounced oddly from side to side as he walked, and reminded Richie of his Uncle Harold, and this he found reassuring. Richie said, *Where are the chickens?*, hoping that Tommy would not detect the fear in his voice, but the older boy was busy looking up into the web of branches and didn't answer him. They carried on like this for a while, then Tommy stopped and said he'd seen one and would Richie do the climbing because he, Tommy, couldn't get very far on account of having had the polio. For a moment Richie stood, uncomprehending. He understood that he was required to climb the tree but didn't see what this had to do with anything; then it struck him that maybe country chickens lived in trees and laid their eggs there. He stepped towards the trunk and felt the bark. Looking up, he saw a black clot of twigs which he assumed must be the nest. He had never climbed a tree but knew how to climb drainpipes and street lights all right, and he figured they must be more or less the same. Tommy gave him a leg up and he found himself standing in the elbow of a branch a few feet off the ground. The nest was resting quietly on a high branch, partly obscured by leaves. It looked rather small for a chicken's nest, but perhaps country chickens *were* smaller. Inside were six perfect eggs, but tiny. He wondered whether this could be right, but Tommy was standing beneath him now, urging him to take them, so he reached in, placed each egg in its turn into the bag Tommy had given him and began to lower it very gingerly towards his new friend's outstretched hands. He climbed down on to the lowest branch then jumped to the ground and ran across to where Tommy was inspecting the haul. One of the eggs had broken on its journey, but the five remaining sat on the palm of Tommy's hand. Tiny, perfect things they were, still warm, their shells the colour of old putty.

Tommy held one up to his ear, then, tapping it on a stone, began peeling off the shell. Inside there was a tiny, writhing thing topped by a diamond of gaping pink which twirled upwards like a malevolent arm. Tommy stared at it a moment then, laughing, opened his hand and the thing landed with a soft thump on the leaf mould.

Richie watched the thing move for a while. It occurred to him in a rush that whatever had come out of the egg was alive. He remembered his mother telling him that eggs were just food, like bread or dripping, but here was an egg like the eggs he knew, only smaller, inside which something living moved and breathed. But bread didn't move and dripping didn't breathe. The anomaly puzzled him, but the evidence was there before his eyes and the more he thought about it the more convinced he became that his mother had lied.

Richie passed the afternoon playing with dandelion clocks and picking early cobnuts with his Uncle Harold. In the evening he ate slabs of pig, as his aunt had promised, and everyone talked about what money they'd made and how much of it they were taking home and sang a great deal. Then he slept on a straw mattress with Tommy and some other children in a tiny house with a tin roof through which the wind blew, but not at all like the thick, stinking draughts that crept in through the windows at home. In the morning, when Auntie Daisy fried eggs for sandwiches, he was disappointed to see that his aunt's eggs were the routine ones, full of transparent and yellow slime. He went home on the train that afternoon changed, though he couldn't say how, only that he felt different. Even back in Poplar he felt different.

He began taking an interest in his Uncle Harold's bird-breeding activities. Now that he'd seen it first hand, the transformation from egg to chick was fascinating. Uncle Harold kept most of his birds in the backyard at Spicer's now, and Richie would often go down there after school to help his uncle with the feeding routine. Pretty soon, Uncle Harold was allowing him to handle the birds, and before long he was regularly helping his uncle take the young birds to the bird market. On a weekend, he could often be found sitting outside the Crown in Church Street nursing a lemonade, watching deals being struck and singing competitions won and lost through the window of the public bar. The miraculous nature of the living egg no longer threw him in the way it had when he first discovered it, but no matter how many times he witnessed the little beak appearing through a hole in the shell, chipping its way to freedom, then wresting itself from its case, stretching itself out into the world, his chest never failed to swell.

When Jack caught wind of his son's new interest, he decided that the boy had too much time on his hands. Richie was already familiar with the routes between his home and the West India,

Spicer's and the Resolute and Charlie Brown's, and Jack quickly worked out how he could put his son's knowledge to use. So at seven years old, Richie began to run messages between the Bakers and their customers. It was perfect. No one would be likely to suspect a seven-year-old boy of running orders for contraband. Even if they did, Richie was unlikely to give the game away since he had no real idea what he was doing. His credulousness, too, proved a handy ally. Jack could send his boy out to collect his money and at the end of it hand him a tuppenny bit for his trouble and, shaking his head, announce that takings had been very poor that day, knowing that the moment the boy walked in the door at Gaselee Street and Franny started quizzing him, he would unquestioningly repeat his father's line.

Richie took to the work immediately. To him, it was simply an extension of what he already did, following his father about from pub to pub. Though he could not read any but the simplest road signs, he found it easy to get about by memorising shop windows, rows of buildings and the configurations of bus and tram stops. His routes were mostly regular ones, and by asking strangers when he was stuck, he soon built up a network of familiar sights and sounds as his guide through the maze of streets.

On one of his riverside expeditions one winter's afternoon in 1937, just as he was passing the church where his mother and father had married, something moved in Richie's peripheral vision. Thinking it was a rat, he carried on, until, realising that what he'd seen was too big to be any kind of rat he'd ever come across, and he'd come across a few, he retraced his steps and, moving closer to the corner, he spotted a small sack, tied at the top by a loop of string. He bent down and, very gingerly, picked it up, and was about to undo the string when the bag gave a violent twist and began squirming and whining. Alarmed, he let go and the package thumped back on to pavement. For an instant nothing moved. Frantically now, his heart scudding, Richie bent down and tore at the knot in the string around the mouth of the bag and inside the sack saw a small black creature with gooey eyes and ears crusted with dark matter. At first he thought that it was a cat, or a ferret, then he realised it was a small dog. It had been injured but he could now see that the wound was not fresh. He felt a sense of relief. He had not hurt the creature. He looked about but there was nobody around. He remembered that his mother had a brooch in the shape of a dog and decided to take the puppy back home as a present for her.

When he arrived at the house in Gaselee Street, Franny was on the front step three doors down talking to an elderly neighbour, and he was able to sneak the sack through the passageway and into the scullery without her noticing. He decided to take the bag into the privy and clean up the dog to make it presentable. Reaching for a match, he lit the paraffin lamp so that he could take a better look. It was small but healthy looking, except for its ears, which had been cut right back to its head, the whorls of congealed blood still damp around the edges closest to the wounds. How odd, he thought, but how sweet it was, wagging its tail. He opened the privy door, crept outside, picked up the stick his father used to threaten the neighbourhood cats and pinned it under the door knob so the dog couldn't get out. Then he took a deep breath and headed for the scullery, his heart dizzy with the anticipation of his mother's pleasure.

When she saw the dog, Franny screamed:

Lord bleedin' save me! Look at them scabby ears! Get it out before yer dad gets home. He'll go bleedin' mad and I'll get the blame. She shook her head and snorted. *This is all your Uncle Harold's doing, I suppose. Whatever possessed you? I hate all them dirty things, birds, dogs, cats, they're all the same. Filthy! Take it away or I'll have to get your father to drown it in the river.*

Richie left the house, pulling the dog behind him on a string. He was crushed. How had he got everything so wrong? Only

half an hour ago he was still warming himself with the notion
– illusory, as it turned out – that his mother would be pleased.
He remembered her saying that the one thing she most wanted
was a mink or a beaver, like the ones the film stars had. Wasn't
a dog the next best thing? He felt devastated to have been so
mistaken. Now he was landed with the dog. He thought about
taking it back to the churchyard, but it looked so happy to be
out of its bag that he couldn't bring himself to. He thought
about taking it to his Uncle Harold, but knew that his
Grandmother May would make a terrible fuss. Ten minutes later
he was at number 7 Bloomsbury Street. His aunt opened the
door.

Come in, duck, she said, looked at the dog and added, *Oh, he
yours? We'll put him out in the yard. Poor mite, what's gone on with
them lugs of his?*

Inside, the house was pristine, as always. Daisy had just done
some laundry and hung it on a clothes horse in front of the fire,
and the room smelled of soap suds and order. His aunt's friend
Lilly was sitting at the table drinking a cup of tea.

Well, well, said Lilly, *I don't know who's the more handsome
chap!* Aunt Daisy's friend Lilly was always saying things like
this, but she meant well and Richie liked her, not least because
she had never once asked him where his brothers and sisters
were.

You got a name for him? Daisy asked. She opened the back door
and Richie tied the dog to the drainpipe outside. *Even a dog
deserves a name.*

Richie thought about this and realised his aunt was right.

Bird, he said, eventually. He didn't know why the word had
come to him. It sounded good.

Lilly opened her mouth and he saw his aunt purse her lips
and very subtly shake her head. She bent down and ruffled his
hair.

Your mum seen him yet, duck?

Richie nodded and looked at the floor.

Well, anyway, Aunt Daisy said, *you can keep him here if you like. Your grandad will fix him up a kennel in the yard.*

And so it was settled. Bird would live in Bloomsbury Street with Aunt Daisy and Grandad Joe.

With the dog as his companion, Richie began to venture out beyond his usual haunts, to the bascule bridge to watch the ships in the West India or along the walkway that ran beside Blackwall, from where you could see the A boats bringing timber in from Scandinavia to the Surrey Docks and splash about in the water beside the old tar pier. From there boy and dog might turn back towards Poplar past the Coloured Seamen's Mission to Chin's, or wander down to Enderby Wharf, along the narrow lanes, imprisoned by walls, where the gas lamps left pools of light in which tiny mosses grew. Once his ears healed, Bird proved himself a devoted companion, and in the care of Daisy and Richie he grew into a lanky creature with a boundless appetite for adventure. So long as Richie delivered his messages on time, Jack didn't seem to care where he was. His mother sometimes complained, but only when he wasn't there to act as a buffer against his father.

Soon, the pair were venturing farther out, across the Lea River at Glengall Road Bridge, from where you could see the glitter of ships' funnels in mid-stream, and in the thick ochre flow of the river, lighters pulling out to the long ladders of the ships moored on either side of the roadway. As the weather improved, they walked farther still, over the Lea into the city of belching chimneys and dark turnings that was Chequerboard Town, where black men sat in the cafés with white women, not caring about the rumpus they were causing. Sometimes they would reach as far as the Connaught Inn alongside the Albert Dock, where big-knuckled sailors with budgie-blue eyes and skin as pale as flour gathered in groups, laughing and joking in foreign languages.

One summer evening, Richie and Bird were wandering along

the riverside in Cyprus, a good three or four miles from their home patch, on the Beckton marshland, Bird barking at a couple of cormorants sitting on the river buoys stretching their wings. Richie loved it here. The marshes were broad, and though there were houses and roads and the odd pub, and the outfall sewer and the giant gasworks at Bugsby's Reach, there remained on the marshes a sense of quiet and space completely absent from the bustle of life to the west. Here, instead of the roar of trains and the ticking of trams and the hooting of lorries and factories, all you could hear was the wind and the honks of passing Canada geese and the excited whining of a dog in the full flush of his youth.

So absorbed was Richie in his enjoyment of the scene that he didn't notice the Gypsy boy with tousled hair and a sly limp sidling up behind him, until the boy began shouting:

Oi, that's my dog.

Richie called Bird in and held on to the string that served as his collar.

He felt his stomach shrink into a little knot. His first inclination was to believe the boy. Then he remembered. If mothers told lies, he was sure boys did too. And even if the boy had not lied, even if Bird *had* belonged to the Gypsy boy like he said, then it must have been the Gypsy boy who cut the animal's ears. He felt a sudden, unusual surge of anger.

Buzz off, he said. *He ain't yours no more.*

You've stole my dog! the Gypsy boy cried, coming towards Richie with raised fists, and before Richie really knew what was happening, the two boys were going at it in a fury, Bird circling around them, snapping and barking. For the first time in his life, Richie felt a tidal rush that gathered up all his strength and brought it crashing down on the Gypsy boy. The boy felt it too and lost his appetite for a fight his opponent was so unwilling to lose. He backed off, and for a while both boys stood panting in a companionable silence between equals. Drawing a small metal canteen of poteen from his pocket, the Gypsy handed it to Richie. Richie put the bottle to his lips and drank. The liquid burned and rankled. The Gypsy boy sat down in the grass and Richie sat beside him. He felt his head and eyes begin to swim.

Here, what'll you give me for four rabbits' feet? the Gypsy boy said.

A toffee apple?

Done, the boy said. *Come back tomorrow.* And with that he stood up, brushed himself down and wandered off along the marsh.

Richie stayed for a while, taking in the events. He felt that he had crossed a threshold. He didn't know why it had taken him so long to see it. The East End had no room for boys like his former self, sissy boys who would rather be left alone than fight, boys who just believed things. Just as the episode with the egg had woken him up to the idea that people lied, and often for no other reason than because they could, the event with the Gypsy boy taught him that he couldn't afford not to fight any more. The East End belonged to fighters. And for now, at least, Richie Baker belonged to the East End.

Noticing his son's bruises the next day, his father said:

Not that again, when are you going to learn to stand up for yerself?

Richie smiled. *You should have seen the vardo boy. I give 'im a right bashing,* he said. He mimed a thump.

That right? His father looked surprised and happy. *Well, well, miracles never cease.*

Richie did return to the marsh with Bird a week later, his delivery work having kept him away till then, but the Gypsy boy was nowhere to be found. He went down to the riverbank where London sounded as distant as a dream and there was a wide vista of sky and water, and, across the water, the blue hills of the Weald in the far distance. There he sat for a while, watching arrows of ducks swishing by and the odd pair of geese coming in to land on the foreshore, until, in the distance, he caught sight of the Gypsy boy, carrying a stick and a bucket and hunting for something along the shoreline. Eventually the boy drew close, and, recognising Richie and Bird, he wandered up and asked whether he had brought the toffee apple, but Richie hadn't and the boy did not have his rabbits' feet either. The boy squatted beside Bird and patted him. *He was eel fishing*, he said. He'd show Richie how if Richie had something to offer in return.

They bandied about for a while and settled on the promise of an amount of Lascar toffee, some carob beans and marbles, in return for which the Gypsy boy would show Richie how to catapult ducks and build a hide and a seagull trap, and how to hunt for eels and make crab pots from hazel switches. He'd also show him how to shoplift, steal milk both from doorsteps and from the cows tethered out on the marshes and trick house-holders into giving him treats. Best of all, he'd teach Richie how to mudlark. Not mudlark like the East End boys mudlarked, with no real understanding of the tides, or of the treasure available to the careful mudlarker, but in the Gypsy way, with profit foremost in mind.

And so began another instalment in Richie Baker's education, at the hands of this Gypsy boy whose name, years later, Richie could not recall, but who brought him closer to what he wanted from life than anyone had ever done before.

Among the skills the boy taught Richie, none was so useful to him in those days as mudlarking. In the bored mob of chil-dren hanging outside the pubs hoping to prevent their fathers from spending all their money, Richie discovered a ready market for the old marbles, bones, old pawn tickets, boots and other tradables he'd picked up from the Thames beach. For the first time in his life, he had money. Not much, but enough to know he liked how powerful having money made him feel.

It was a small stretch from mudlarking to more straight-forward pilfering, and this, too, the Gypsy boy taught him. With Bird as his watch, he began to saunter down to where the lighters tied up at Blackwall wharf to wait for the shift change at nine. If there were no uniformed beetles on patrol, he'd leave Bird up on the quay and, leaping from the jetty, creep about from lighter to lighter, feeling for sacks of peanuts, locust beans, tins of golden syrup and corned beef or fruit, anything he could sell to the children waiting outside the pubs.

He didn't think about whether what he was doing was right or wrong, and he might not have cared if he had. His encounter with the Gypsy boy had given him confidence. He knew the other children considered him odd, but he saw himself as a young man now, learning to make his way in the world, without the help of his parents, two people who, in any case, didn't seem to be able to help themselves.

Time flew by; 1937 rolled into 1938 and the boys on the street selling the evening papers started shouting headlines about the approach of war. Most of the talk between his parents and at his Aunt Daisy and Grandad Joe's house about Chamberlain and Hitler went directly over Richie's head, but all about him he saw that Poplar was readying itself. Posters appeared on the walls of factory buildings exorting men to volunteer, red post-boxes were repainted in yellow gas-sensitive paint. Sandbags appeared and overground shelters were built. In Victoria Park trenches were dug and workers began hanging blackout curtains across factory windows criss-crossed with blast tape. Grandad Joe gave him a collection of ARP cigarette cards that had come free with his Woodbines. With their menacing pictures of bombs and burning buildings, they seemed to exist outside Richie's own reality. He saw them only as colourful pictures.

In May 1939, his mother came home with gas masks and Aunt Daisy said she wouldn't let him in the door to feed Bird unless he was carrying his; the situation was serious and everyone needed to be prepared. In early August 1939 he joined in Bloomsbury Street's blackout practice and was not afraid like some of the children because he knew that if he was ever caught outside and unable to see, Bird would be able to sniff the way home. In general, he still couldn't really see what the fuss was all about. It wasn't as though anything had actually happened. On 28 August, school was suspended for an evacuation rehearsal and children paraded along the street carrying their gas masks and with labels around their necks. The idea of being evacuated and living away from Gaselee Street was very appealing to Richie. His parents shouted at one another all the time now, and he was virtually living at his aunt's in any case. After the rehearsal the teacher asked whether there were any questions, and Richie said, yes, he had one: when would dogs be having their evacuation rehearsal? His teacher only laughed at him and replied that there were no spaces on the trains to evacuate dogs, so he went back to Gaselee Street that afternoon and announced to his mother that he had decided not to be evacuated but wished to stay at home. His mother asked him why and he said because there was no space on the trains to evacuate dogs and he was not prepared to be separated from Bird, and his mother looked crushed for a moment and he realised he had said the wrong thing.

A day or so later Richie let himself into the house at Bloomsbury Street. His aunt had gone hopping the week before and already Joe's cigarettes and newspapers lay all over the place and the house was beginning to look unkempt. He went to the yard and fed Bird and, in the absence of school, took himself to the docks to run errands for his father and Grandfather Henry. In the afternoon his mother, who was sewing uniforms, asked him to deliver some completed sleeves and cuffs and pick up some more fabric cut-outs from the tailor. By the time he was done it was growing dark and he wanted to see Bird, so he walked back to Bloomsbury Street. Joe was not in, so he let himself in with the key that Daisy kept on a piece of string through the letterbox, and went to the yard. Bird was not in the makeshift kennel his Grandad Joe had built for him. He was not in the yard itself, nor in the house. The lodgers living upstairs said they had not seen or heard him the whole day. Richie went out into the street and called, but the dog did not come. He walked along the street, whistling and shouting, but still Bird was nowhere to be seen. Returning to number 7, he went through every room, though he knew already from the flat, empty air that the dog was not there. He checked the privy and in the understairs cupboard. He wondered if his Grandad Joe had taken the dog. He'd never known Joe take Bird anywhere before, but you never knew. He went back out on to the street and knocked on the door of number 9. Getting no reply, he then knocked at number 5. He knocked again. Just then the door opened and Billy Shaunessy appeared. He said he knew nothing about any dog but Richie didn't trust Billy Shaunessy because he was mean. Just then, Mrs Shaunessy came to the door, looking frail and sombre. Mrs Shaunessy had the world's cares on her chest, but she was not mean and he'd not known her to lie, except to save money or make people feel better.

Did you see my grandad with my dog, Mrs Shaunessy?

No, dear. The dog was with your father.

Richie thanked her, then he ran all the way from Bloomsbury Street to the house at Gaselee Street, where he found his mother sitting in the chair in front of the fire, dozing. A guilty look stole across her face when he told her what Mrs Shaunessy had said, and he knew she was going to find a way to lie to him. He took off across the broken cobbles of Gaselee Street, over the heaps of sandbags, past the criss-crossed windows and the outdoor shelters. He ran till his muscles had taken every last bubble of oxygen from his body and his chest was gasping. He reached the Resolute and burst through the doors. A few drinkers wheeled round to look, then, seeing it was only a boy, they turned back to their drinks. Jack Baker wasn't there. He ran back along the pavements until he reached Charlie Brown's, and there was Jack, standing at the bar, swaying and with a look of attention on his face, as though it was all he could do to stay upright.

Where's he gone? Richie said, watching his father, steeling himself for the lies that he thought would come. *Where have you taken him?*

Calm down, now, son, Jack said. He turned to his drinking companion, a large man with a ruddy face. *He thinks that's all he's got to worry about,* he said, winking, then, turning back to his son, he took him by the shoulders and said: *Look, sonny, there's about to be a war on and this ain't no place for a dog. Once the war's over, you can have the bleedin' dog back, all right?*

Richie looked into Jack's eyes. His fingers grasped his father's jacket sleeve.

You're lying, he said. He had never dared say such a thing before and he didn't know what he meant by it, he just wanted his father to tell him everything was all right. But Jack only raised his arm and shook his son off.

Get going.

A while later, Richie managed to extract the truth from Billy Shaunessy. A man had been going around the streets encouragng people to kill their dogs, saying there wouldn't be any dog food once the war started and that for every dog that had to be found meat for, a soldier would go hungry. For a couple of shillings a man had taken a club and knocked Bird on the head.

Richie never confronted his father about the lie. He was old enough by then to know that it wouldn't have made any difference. His father would continue to lie to him. That was how his father was.

CHAPTER 9

The war lay far distant on that sleeting, comfortless day in February 1930 when, at the wedding of his brother to Franny Crommelin, Harold Baker had first been struck – and struck very forcefully – by Daisy Crommelin.

It had been a difficult morning. The night before Jack had drunk until he'd blacked out and for a while there seemed to be no waking him. When he did, finally, open his eyes, they were so red and puffed you could have made beetroot soup with them, and no one would have known the difference. He was in a foul temper, too, so foul, in fact, that only Harold could handle him. It had taken every wheedle, every plea, every threat that he could muster to rouse Jack from his bed and take the day for what it was: his wedding day. And then they'd been late for the church itself because Jack would insist on dropping into Mr Chin's just as someone delivered a barrel of poteen and it had been almost impossible to extract him. They'd stumbled in, Jack leaning heavily on Harold's bad leg, and there was Daisy, standing beside her sister, with such grace, such a generous and quiet kindness in her eyes, that Harold was astonished Jack did not know he'd picked the wrong sister.

Later, at the reception, everyone was admiring the bride, because that is what is expected at weddings, and because there was no denying that this particular bride was a dazzler, but Harold was thinking only of Daisy. Daisy, Daisy, with her uneven arms, her protruding ears. Daisy in all her loveliness.

But what did Harold have to offer a woman like Daisy? She'd already got a beau, in any case, a man called Sidney, who'd cornered him at the reception and boasted about his intention to become the first East End prime minister. How could he compete with that? A cripple with a humdrum job in a grocer's and no ambitions beyond breeding the best little bird singer in Poplar.

Over the years, he and Daisy rubbed shoulders from time to time, digging one or other of their siblings out of whatever trouble they'd got themselves into, and his esteem for Daisy only increased until, though it was hard for him to admit this to himself, he realised that he loved her and he could see that, for all his political pretensions, Sidney Wells wasn't making her happy. Lilly, he knew, had nicknamed him Ne'er Do Wells, but still Daisy seemed determined to stick with him, and who was he, Harold, to interfere? In any case, she was his sister-in-law's sister. It didn't seem quite right.

It was only when she and Sidney parted and she went away hopping that Harold realised he no longer wanted to live unless it was by Daisy's side. From then on, every day, every hour and every minute of every day, he planned on how best to win her over, finally alighting on the idea of the canary.

By then he knew her well enough to appreciate that his best strategy was to hold back a little, certainly not to tell her how he felt, to persist and, most of all, to be patient. It was a skill he'd learned from his bird breeding. Look how long it had taken him to understand the finer nuances of the art, to be able to predict colour, type and temperament, all the while refining breeding technique. A healthy young male canary such as the one he'd brought round for Daisy could live for ten years, and that was how long, he reckoned, it might take to win its new owner. Well, never mind. He'd already waited eight. What were another few more?

He began by using the canary as an excuse, inventing reasons why he had to come round to check on it. He guessed that Daisy would not suspect his motives and he was right. Daisy expected everyone to be as open-hearted and guileless as she. From his earliest acquaintance with her, he knew he could trust her. The issue was whether or not he could trust himself. He needed time to become familiar with her habits, to understand her make-up. He was wary of upsetting her, of getting it wrong.

He graduated from dropping in to see the canary to coming round to see her more quickly than he'd imagined. Soon, they were seeing one another twice a week. On Wednesdays and Saturdays, he would put on his best brown serge suit and, at precisely six thirty in the evening, present himself at the door of number 7 Bloomsbury Street. Daisy would wave him into the passageway, where he would take off his brown serge jacket, shaking out the creases and folding it prior to hanging. At first she would stand with her hands clutched together, as though fending him off. Later, she allowed him a small kiss, initially on the cheek, then later, when they knew one another better, on the lips, and they'd move into the living room. If Joe was in, Harold would greet him with a smile.

Bearing up, Mr C?

Joe would nod and offer Harold a Woodbine from a crush pack. Harold soon realised this was a test. He himself smoked Capstans, but on the days he came round to Daisy's house, he was expected to take his cues from Joe.

Thank you, Mr C, don't mind if I do. He'd draw a cigarette from Joe's packet.

Well, don't stand there looking like a sailor with the Jolly Roger up his arse, sonny, sit down.

The two men would smoke in companionable silence for a while.

So how's the river trade this week, Mr C?

It's fair to say that it's in and out with the tides, sonny.

Glad to hear that, Mr C, very glad. Canary still singing sweet, is he?

Oh, that, Joe would sigh, in mock desperation, then he'd tell his joke, the one about having to put up with too much twittering.

One twitterer was enough. Why d'you have to bring in another?

Then he'd say he hoped that Harold would take at least one of the twitterers off his hands and Harold would laugh and look at his shoes.

About then, Daisy would usually appear with a teapot. Harold discovered early on that lingering only encouraged Joe to crank up one of his long, salty tales from which there would be no escape for an hour or more, so tea would be a hasty affair, then the couple would pull on their coats and head out into the street where they could be alone.

When the weather was good, they wandered along the Commercial Road, stopping in front of Spicer's to admire Harold's work on the window display. On market days they gravitated to Salmon Lane, where, by light of the naphthalene flares, they picked at vinegary winkles and spooned up gristly stew from cones of newspaper. Sometimes they would watch the street entertainers. They were particularly fond of two men in drag who went about with a barrel organ and a little dog which would howl along to the music. If their meanderings took them as far as Stepney or Whitechapel, they might stop off at one of the Maltese cafés there and drink a cup of cocoa laced with brandy.

When rain cut short their walks, Harold would buy two tuppenny seats at the Troxy or the Palladium for whatever was showing. Later, once they'd become an established couple, Lilly might join them, when she could get her mother to look after the children. Very occasionally Jimmy would show up too, but there was a coolness between husband and wife now that made Harold and Daisy, in the first flush of their romance, uneasy, and the two couples would usually go their separate ways once the film had ended. Afterwards, Harold might treat Daisy to a port and lemon at the Resolute, or to a Fry's Chocolate Creme from the deaf mute at the confectionery store nearby.

These outings were never punctuated by much in the way of chit-chat, not because Harold had nothing to say, nor Daisy either, but because there was such a singular sense of recognition between them that talking seemed unnecessary. It was enough simply to be in one another's company.

A year passed and they began to spend more evenings together. Reluctant to go home after an evening out, they would stroll into Tunnel Park, and watch the ships' lights glinting on the thick water of the Thames, and the lighters clanking gently at anchor in the clearway.

We should have done this years ago, Harold would say, squeezing Daisy's hand.

Better late than never.

Finally, when they could put it off no longer, Harold would walk Daisy home. On the doorstep they would kiss chastely, then, squeezing her hand, Harold would turn and toddle back down the street. It was hard to leave her and go back to the little box room he'd lived in most of his life. He already knew that he wanted to be with her all the time, for the two of them to be husband and wife, but he also knew that he could not expect her to commit herself to him unless she knew his secret, and right now he was too frightened of losing her to risk divulging it.

The signs were good, though. She began to want to see more of him, hurrying home after work in the laundry so that she could be back in time to change, before rushing along to Spicer's. Mr Spicer discouraged wooing during work hours but Daisy liked to be waiting for him when he got off work. She didn't seem to mind waiting at all, sometimes standing under the awning, other times, if it was raining, nursing a cup of tea at the nearby Lyons. On the occasions when Spicer was out or in the back room and Daisy was early, she would venture inside the shop, running her eyes along the conker-coloured shelves in an effort to pick out something she could find an excuse to buy – Zebra blacking, Cross Brand tinned milk, flypapers, Sunlight soap – in case Spicer suddenly reappeared. Harold began to get the strong sense that she was waiting for his proposal.

All he had to do now was tell her. But he was afraid of what he might lose if he did.

He met his brother at the Resolute and told him of his intention. His parents, he knew, had never spoken about the accident, nor, he supposed, had Jack. His brother had always been protective of him, and even in his darkest, most booze-fuelled moments Jack had never once let slip to any outsider anything about what had happened. If anyone asked about his younger brother's leg he told them what he and Harold had agreed, that Harold had fallen down the stairs. This was not a lie, nor was it all of the truth. As to the rest, Harold had always assumed that Jack had never mentioned it. But no, as it turned out, Jack too had lied to him. He was sorry about it, he said, but he was telling his younger brother now. A few weeks back, in the midst of one of their frequent fights, Franny had been going on to Jack about being nicer to her. She was always pressing Jack to be nicer. *Why do you have to be such a cuss?* she'd say. *Why can't you be more like your brother?* He'd told her then. Everything. The whole story. He'd been drunk and he was ashamed of it, but a man could have his younger brother's character dangled over him for only so long before he cracked.

So far as he knew, Franny hadn't told anyone, but you never knew with Franny. She was unreliable.

That was it. Harold knew he had to act. He went round to number 7 Bloomsbury Street the following evening. Daisy opened the door and ushered him in. He could feel himself shaking and his forehead was sweaty. In the passageway she helped him off with his jacket. He strained to see whether she was behaving any differently towards him, whether there was any new cool-ness, any twitch of disappointment. He went into the living room and politely ummed and aahed his way through one of Joe's interminable stories, and everything might have seemed perfectly normal except for the fact that he knew it wasn't.

They agreed to see whatever was on at the Troxy. On the way, she did not ask him what was on his mind. He paid for their seats, they sat down, he lit a Capstan, his anxiety swooping all about him. The newsreel preceding the picture made things worse. The situation in Germany was terrible. Hooligans roaming the streets destroying Jewish shops. There was never any excuse to destroy shops, Harold thought. But that's how they were, those blackshirt types. He'd seen all he needed to see of them in the East End, among Oswald Mosley's gang. A bunch of villains.

He couldn't concentrate on the main picture. Afterwards, looking for some excuse to lead her somewhere quiet where he could tell her, he suggested they get saveloys from Culcha's and, since it was a mild night, wander down the little path that wove down from Salmon Lane and sit on the retaining wall over-looking the river. He loved the view there, he said, it reminded him of good times in his childhood, helping his brother and father. They walked in silence until they reached the place, then they sat and ate their saveloys. Tugs and lighters arrowed past them in the dark water. As they were finishing their saveloys Daisy turned to him and said:

Whatever it is, spit it out.

And so he did. He began with Archie Baker, the youngest of the three Baker brothers. Harold couldn't remember much about him and he felt bad about that, but the years had washed away the sharpness of his memories. He knew he was dark, like Jack and Henry. He had a passion for treacle toffee and Jack had once told him that it was made in the tar distillery across the road. He was the sort of little boy who believed things his brothers told him, and for days he had gone and stood by the gates until finally he'd got up the courage to ask the guard whether he could have some some treacle toffee. He'd come back in tears, saying the guard had laughed at him, but the man had come round the next day with a little jar of treacle he'd brought from home and let Archie have a spoonful of it. That was how Archie was. He delighted people. It was difficult to say no to Archie.

It was odd that he remembered so little about his brother. Of the day of the accident itself, he had forgotten nothing. Each moment remained like an icicle in his mind; crisp, hard and immaculately transparent.

At that time the Baker family rented rooms in Broomfield Street, between the tar distillery and a chemical works. May and Henry lived in the front room, May's mother slept in the living room and the three brothers shared a mattress upstairs in what had once been a corridor connecting two bedrooms. A fight of sorts had broken out that morning between Harold and Jack when Jack took Harold's breakfast and May had clobbered both of them for causing a ruckus, so it was in bad humour that the two older boys readied themselves for school, adjusting the card inserts in their boots to cover the holes, pulling up their socks, buttoning their jackets and winding scarves made from socks around their necks. It was a still, matt sort of day, and the two boys kicked their way through kerb mud to the corner of Brabazon Street where Freddie Green lived with his slop-jowled cur Mungo. Sometimes Freddie waited for them, but not that day, so they continued on, crossing Upper North Street and heading towards Northumberland Street and school. They had reached the urinal at the top of the street, opposite the sawmills, when Jack said:

What say we go larkin'?

Jack often skipped school and spent the day mudlarking on the Thames beach. Mostly he went with his cousin, Jonah, who was the same age, but Jonah had recently been taken ill with tuberculosis. There was no point in going alone because Jack was colour-blind and he found it hard to distinguish between similarly coloured objects. Though he had never found anything more spectacular on the beach than the usual midden of old crockery, bones, clay pipes, reading glasses and bottles worn smooth by the tides, and never would, it was in Jack's nature always to focus on the next big thing. What drove Jack always was the fantasy, the possibility of magic just up ahead. He and Harold were different that way, as in so many others. Harold clung to things already around him – a bird in the hand, and better the devil you knew – but Jack was a gambler. Back then, he had convinced himself that it was his destiny to find a piece of pirate treasure or perhaps some rich woman's jewels on the beach, and thereby make his fortune, and he was keen to get back to the foreshore, but he needed a spotter to tell him whether what he saw was a gemstone or a piece of brown bottle glass rubbed smooth by the water.

Harold was desperate not to go with his brother. At that stage he'd yet to hear the name Albie Bluston and he was still enjoying school. But he wanted to do right by Jack. After all, how many times had Jack promised him that when they were dockers together, he would look out for Harold and see to it that he came to no harm? How many times had he sworn that he would make sure Harold got a decent job and didn't have to work out an apprenticeship being lowered into pitch-dark cargo holds on freezing mornings with a mop and a bucket as he had, and Henry before him. So he said he would come.

The two boys headed off towards Wapping, where a set of ancient, rocky steps gave on to the beach, and began methodically kicking over muddy driftwood caked in oil. After an hour or two, when they had found nothing of any value, and the tide was beginning to creep up, they began to make their way back to the steps, kicking pebbles as they went, and it was then that Harold stumbled on a small canvas bag, half soused by filthy river water, wedged in the slime between a piece of driftwood and some long-discarded oyster shells. He reached for it and, as it came into his grasp, his fingers made out the shape of coins inside. He held the bag up to his ear and shook it, then called out to his brother, who looked up and came running across the soft mud and spoil.

Jack opened the bag and tipped out its contents on to his hand. Set in the river mud, but otherwise undamaged, were twelve penny pieces. Twelve pennies. To the boys it was a fortune.

Bleedin' Nora, said Jack. He fingered the coins. *Don't tell Mum.*

They set off home via the horse trough on Poplar High Street, where they washed the coins and their boots, and reached the house in Broomfield Street at the usual time so their mother would not suspect anything amiss. They ate their lunch of barley soup and at the usual hour left, but instead of going to school, they took a tram to Victoria Park where there was a fair on, and they bought plates of chips and waited in the rain until the fair opened then dizzied themselves throwing balls at coconuts and shooting targets. They drank sarsaparilla and made themselves sick on candyfloss. At the gate on the way out, Jack bought each of them a bag of treacle toffee for the journey home and made Harold promise to eat all of his so that May wouldn't find the remains and ask them where they got the money. Harold readily agreed – when it came to treacle toffee he was as greedy as the next boy – but halfway home he began feeling sick and so he rolled the remainder of his toffee up in its bag and shoved it down the sleeve of his jacket, where neither Jack nor his mother would see it, deciding he would hide it under a loose corner of linoleum in an obscure corner at the top of the stairs when no one else was looking and return to it later.

At home, he just managed to force down his tea of bread and dripping then, saying he was going out to play football, he stole up the stairs past his mother's basket of now mostly completed hairbrushes, which now sat on the top landing, and placed his bag of toffee under the linoleum. Then he went out into the street and kicked around a rag ball with Stanley Goldman, whose footwork was that of a genius even though he was actually a Jew. He didn't know what Archie and Jack were doing then, only that they remained indoors.

At bedtime the three brothers clambered up the rickety stairs to their room, and slid between the blankets in their usual positions, with Jack taking up the whole of the left side of the bed and the two younger boys crammed in top to toe on the right. May had already retired to her bed at the front, Henry was out and a soft quiet had settled through the house, broken only by the nightly ritual of farting and belching, which always accompanied Jack's blowing out the candle and helped drown out the sounds of mice and cockroaches emerging from their daytime hiding places. Harold turned away from his younger brother and was already adrift on dreams when he felt Jack's foot tapping at his face. Half waking, he shook it off, only to have it return, more insistently this time, accompanied by a sharp dig in the ribs. After a minute or so he heard his brother's voice, saying:

I know where you put that toffee.

So he was discovered. Yet, even now, something prevented Harold from opening his mouth. He felt he was teetering on the edge of a trap from which only adult life, impossibly distant, would liberate him. Why hadn't Jack simply taken the toffee if he knew where it was? What kind of game was he playing?

Jack, ever careless of consequences, reached over and shook Archie, and when the youngest boy grunted and turned back towards sleep, he rolled him over and said:

Harold hid a bag of treacle toffee under the lino at the top of the stairs. It was supposed to be for you, but Harold hid it 'cause he don't want you to have it.

Harold recalled each part of what happened next with such an unnerving clarity that it was almost as though he was watching the individual frames of a film. Archie shot from the bed followed closely by Jack. He found himself following them in a flash, stumbling over the bed and out into the dark hallway, so close to the others that he could feel the air expanding and contracting between them. Why hadn't he given the toffee to Archie anyway? He knew how much Archie loved it. Well, never mind, he'd give it to his brother now. He was nearly at the top of the stairs, with Archie and Jack just ahead of him, and in his desperation to save his toffee so that he could give it to Archie and right the wrong he had already convinced himself that he had committed, he reached out and grabbed at whatever first came his way. His fist got a purchase on Archie's nightshirt, which had once served as his own and as his brother's before him. It was patched and threadbare and no longer very strong, and as he grasped it, he felt it give. Then he slipped and suddenly he felt his whole body shudder backwards. With his hand somehow still attached to Archie he felt himself lurch through the banister with a terrible splintering sound and he reached out, grabbing at the dark, his stomach tensing then and his head thudding like a tug engine. Something rushed through his blood and he felt a shocking thump. He heard himself gasp, then he heard nothing.

He woke to a surging sensation in his left leg and hip and was conscious of the lodger, whose name he could no longer remember, pulling on his arm and his mother in her hairnet and rags, shrieking. Someone had lit a lamp. Directly above he saw Jack standing on the landing and between his older brother and the floor below an unfamiliar arrangement of banisters and wooden planks, and he realised he was on his back somehow, or almost on his back, for there was something beneath him. Then he felt himself being dragged, and through a sudden surge of what he guessed was pain, he heard his mother's voice screaming:

Get him off, get him off!

Some time must have passed during which he fell unconscious, for when he came to, he was aware that he had been moved and was lying fully on his back and there was a warm stickiness on his hand. An unbearable heat blazed through his leg and punched his groins and he gasped and felt his mouth full of something and realised it was blood and loose teeth. His mother and the lodger were a way away and his mother was making odd, animal noises, and he realised that his eyes or his neck must be injured because it hurt to move his head. Everything was warped. There seemed to be a woman standing in the front doorway. He had the impression that she was talking but for reasons he could not understand, he could not hear what she was saying. He suddenly remembered he didn't know where Archie was, but trying to move his head intensified his pain and made him feel nauseous. He tried to speak but he couldn't get his tongue to move. Someone was now kneeling beside him, wiping his face with a twist of cloth, and he remembered wishing she would find a softer cloth. Then he lost consciousness.

It was only later, when Jack related his version of the incident, that Harold knew what happened next. A passing rag-and-bone man had loaded him and Archie in the back of his cart and taken them both to Poplar Hospital for Accidents. He had lain in the hospital, Jack later told him, for three days, while doctors splinted his broken leg and strapped his pelvis to prevent him moving it and stitched up his lip where he had bitten it open. A passing surgeon removed what remained of a broken tooth and nurses cleared away the splintered bits and pieces of another two. He remembered his mother visiting, but she did not touch him, and when he tried to speak to her she put her finger to her mouth.

Archie had lingered on for some days and for a while there had been hope but in the end the internal injuries he sustained from the impact of his brother's body landing on him proved irreparable and he died two days after the accident. It turned out that the banister was very rotten and that the nails attaching the stairs to their frame had moved.

Harold was not well enough to attend Archie's funeral,

and afterwards neither May nor Henry had ever mentioned the accident again. A few days later, May attempted to patch her dead son's nightshirt so that it might be handed on to her sister, Alice, who had a boy about the same age, but the fabric had been too torn and after many fruitless hours darning and stitching she gave up, cut the garment into pieces and used the pieces as dusters.

When the landlord began demanding compensation for his damaged staircase, the Bakers packed up their things and fled to the rooms in Gaselee Street, at the other end of Poplar. Some time afterwards, Harold went back to Poplar Hospital to have his leg plaster cut off with hoof clippers. Beneath the plaster sat a blue-white peg, as skinny as salsify but not noticeably shorter than the other until Harold attempted to stand on it and found that it hovered above the ground. The doctor seemed to think that a limp was the least of Harold's worries and told him he was lucky to be able to walk at all, given the number and type of bone breakages. It was just as well, for his sake, that he'd had a soft landing on the body of his brother. The doctor set him some exercises and discharged him into the care of May.

In those early days and weeks, disjointed, momentary memories of the events before the accident came to Harold at the oddest times. Going about some ordinary chore, he would suddenly and vividly recall the pull of the sheet as his little brother leapt from the bed or the shape of Jack's mouth moving in the light from the gas lamp outside. On the other hand, though, he could no longer clearly remember his younger brother's face. Sleep became a torment. When it came at all, he would be plagued by dreams of falling. He fell backwards over bridges, fell forwards into dark ravines, stepped into open manholes, sank into quagmire, slipped through thin ice and disappeared under waves. When he woke he felt exhausted. For a month or two, his waking hours passed in a kind of blankness. His mind seemed locked away behind a door to which he had no key. Every so often he would peer through the keyhole and see colours and shapes, but none of it connected up.

He was meticulous with his exercises, and six months after the accident he was able to walk on the flat with the aid of a pair of wooden crutches his father fashioned for him from the wood from a cooper's yard. He still had trouble with staircases but Poplar itself was so flat that he could get about, if not with ease, then at least with a clumsy sort of swinging motion. For a while, a certain kind of glamour attached to him, on account of the crutches, but once he no longer needed them he became a ripe target for the taunts of neighbouring boys, who would follow him as he hobbled down the street, shouting:

Spassie Baker squashed his brother.

But it didn't last long. The boys got used to it and, until the arrival of Albie Bluston in 1916, Harold was left alone.

Oddly, at least Harold thought it rather odd, the more his physical health improved, the worse he felt mentally. It was as though the door that had remained shut for so long finally opened but that, instead of shedding some light on his situation, what lay beyond only served to confuse. The disparate images and sounds he had witnessed through the keyhole were not parts of some greater whole at all, but a vast, terrifying jangle, and he shrank, powerless and fearful before the confusion, realising the depths of his withdrawal from the world only when his mother took him aside one evening and asked him why it was that he hadn't spoken in a month.

Elective muteness, the doctor called it. No impairment of his intelligence. He hadn't become a cretin. It was the shock, and it would get better eventually of its own accord. In the meantime shouting at him would only make it worse. So Henry and May stopped. Instead, they ignored him. It was embarrassing having a boy with a perfectly good tongue who wouldn't use it. Elective muteness! Who'd ever heard of such a silly thing.

And so it went on, until Henry won a mynah bird in a bare-knuckle bet and brought it home, thinking it might encourage his boy to talk. Harold named the creature Minnie and he sat by it for months. It grew attached to him and would squawk when he came in the room, but both boy and bird remained resolutely wordless. Eventually, on a warm day in the summer, the situation changed. Opening its beak, Minnie suddenly shrieked:

Peg leg peg leg!

Jack, who was in the room with Harold when it happened, wept and shook so hard with laughter that his brother couldn't help but join in. For months Jack had been teaching Minnie on the side, and finally the bird had come good.

After that, Harold's speech slowly came back, and though the memory of what he'd done to his younger brother still left him winded, he knew his older brother had forgiven him and for that, Harold said, he would forever be in Jack's debt.

And so Harold finished his story. It felt good to have rid himself of it at last. When he was done he took Daisy's hand.

If you got stage fright after that, I wouldn't blame yer.

Daisy squeezed the hand in hers and said:

Don't be so bleedin' daft, you rusty ha'porth.

Not long afterwards, Harold Baker bought a bunch of pink carnations and walked to number 7 Bloomsbury Street and, over egg mayonnaise at Lyons Tea Room, he asked Daisy Crommelin to marry him and Daisy Crommelin said yes. There was no talk of saving or waiting, both parties having done quite enough of that. They celebrated their engagement with crab sandwiches and were married on Daisy's thirty-sixth birthday, 17 March 1939, at St Stephen's, Poplar.

In some respects the event was the opposite of Franny and Jack's wedding nine years before. Harold Baker turned up far too early and bit his nails to the quick waiting for his bride. Daisy wore her mother's dress and carried a bunch of primroses. The two matrons of honour, Lilly and Franny, fell out on the way to the church and Daisy had to separate them. After the ceremony the wedding party went back to Bloomsbury Street, drank beer and ate meat paste rolls and Dundee cake. When the beer was all drunk and the rolls were all eaten the party took themselves off to the St Leonard Arms where the best man, Jack Baker, and the matron of honour, Franny Baker, both drank themselves into a soup, and Lilly started up a version of 'Daisy, Daisy, give me your answer do'.

The following day, Daisy packed up her dress and put it in the drawer where Elsie had once kept her trousseau. The primroses she put in water. They lasted out a week. On the same day, Harold moved from Gaselee Street to number 7 Bloomsbury Street, bringing with him several canaries and budgerigars. He and Joe spend a weekend fashioning an aviary from orange boxes and the remains of a roll of wire.

For a while life was a dream gone right. Daisy carried on at the laundry and Harold worked at Spicer's. Harold applied for – and got – an allotment, and began growing vegetables. Richie helped him dig it out and plant seedlings. In the evenings, Lilly would sometimes come over, often with bruises on her arms, and she and Daisy would sit in front of the fire and do their darning or their knitting or their crochet while Harold read his bird-fancier books and Joe went to the pub or to one of his meetings, or churned out his stories. Often at night Harold would put his arms about his new wife and squeeze her and plant kisses on her cheeks. At weekends they visited the family or went to Lilly's house for tea. From time to time they treated themselves to a paper cone of whelks or to tickets at the Troxy.

Whenever they talked about their future, which wasn't often, the feeling was that they had left it too late for children. If Daisy minded that, she didn't say. Their plans were modest. They hoped to continue in employment, and, one day, perhaps, to be able to put aside a week once a year for a holiday in the country or at the seaside. In the meantime, Harold would continue to breed his birds and grow vegetables on his allotment and Daisy would continue to go hopping. The years would pass as peaceably and uneventfully as possible. Richie would get married and have children and they would be grandparents of a sort and that would be enough.

But of course, life didn't turn out that way.

CHAPTER 10

In August 1939, five months after she'd married, and despite all the talk of war, or perhaps because of it, Daisy Baker née Crommelin went hopping. Lilly had already been down to scrub the walls and fix the curtains in hop hut number 21, so there wasn't much to do. They cleared away and swept the little patch of concrete beside the hut, stuffed their palliasses with straw and laid them on the piles of faggots inside and arranged their things on the set of makeshift shelves and rows of little hooks. Then they set a fire and put on a kettle of water.

Things had not been going well between Lilly and Jimmy this past year and Lilly's husband was now threatening to volunteer for the army.

He can join the bleedin' circus for all I care, Lilly said. But then there were moments when she'd wipe a tear from her eye and remember the old days.

While they were preparing the hut, Michael the cutter appeared, bringing late raspberries and a jug of cream. Lilly put on a fragile smile. Daisy wondered whether her friend was growing bored of her fancy man. Michael was a nervous, reedy thing, not at all like Jimmy, but, perhaps, in the beginning at least, that had been the point. Now it seemed the point was blunted.

Ever since she'd guessed what was going on between the pair, Daisy thought that no good would come of her friend's liaison, but no good came of all manner of things and no one put a stop to *them*. *Ask no questions, hear no lies*, Elsie used to say, and gradually over the years it had become the code Daisy lived by. She was like those little figurines the Chinese kept at the doorways to their laundries and on the threshold of their cafés. *See no evil, hear no evil, speak no evil.* That was Daisy. Seeing, hearing nothing, never truly speaking her mind.

They didn't see Michael again that day. When the sun went down, they lit a a fire and sat around it with Iris, Maffie and old Nell's daughter Ann, catching up on all the events of the previous year and speculating on the pick to come. Would the cones be housey or loose? Who would take a fancy to the farmer's chickens? Or his hop dryer? Would the publican at the Red Lion continue to water his beer? Would the weather hold out as it had the year before? No one mentioned the war that was almost upon them. They knew perfectly well that all Hitler's might would be heading the East End's way if war broke out – they were living around the largest port in the world, the road to empire – but here, now, they didn't want to think about it.

August 1939 turned out to be an idyllic month. The weather was balmy and dry and in the late afternoons the sun drenched the air in honeysuckle perfume. Hennage, the old farm manager, brought milk and the first apples to their doors, a man came from Dover with mackerel and herrings and others brought hares and rabbits they'd snared. For a while the approach of war ceased to have any bearing on their lives. Then a letter arrived for Daisy from Harold. After Jack had had Bird destroyed Richie had gone to the evacuation officer himself, asking to leave. He'd been billeted with an elderly couple in Essex, but had been caught pilfering from the village shop and the couple had refused to accommodate him. Franny had taken all this very badly, and with the war imminent she had suddenly demanded that Richie stay at home with her. They would take their chances with the bombs. Harold couldn't rouse his brother on the matter. He was preoccupied with his business and seemed to have lost interest in his wife and son. Still, Harold didn't think it was right to keep Richie in Poplar when an attack might come at any time. If Daisy could find a space for him in the hop huts he would try to persuade Franny to let her son leave.

Daisy wrote back: *Please send him.*

The day war broke out started cool and dewy, the early morning clouds gradually dissipated until by nine spears of sunlight began piercing through the drifts, bringing with them the shy warmth of the late summer sun. Daisy, Iris, Ann and Lilly stripped bines while Lilly's daughter Millie picked up the orphaned cones and tossed them into baskets and hovered nearby when the tallyman came to measure and the cart appeared to carry the pockets of cones off to the oasts for drying.

Around midday a man in a soldier's uniform unexpectedly appeared, strode into a drift, grabbed his sweetheart and, kissing her full on the lips in front of the gathering crowd, clutched both her hands to his breast and asked her to marry him. In the cheering and badinage that followed nobody thought to ask who the man was, or what his uniform was for, or how or why this unusual event had come about; and so it came as a tremendous shock to the hop pickers assembled for their lunchtime sandwiches when Farmer Berry strode into the garden, held up his hands for quiet and announced to everyone that Chamberlain had not long since gone on the radio and that, as from now, Britain was at war with Germany. For a few moments there was silence; no one seemed to know what to do or say or to whom to turn. Some gasped, others began to cry. Then Maffie's deep, coarse voice rang out along the green drifts.

Gawd bleedin' bless us!

And someone else said:

Hear hear to that.

And gradually, one by one, the pickers stood and joined in, shouting *Hear hear!* until Maffie, calling for silence, began to sing 'God Save the King', and from drift to drift along the length and breadth of the hop garden, women and children joined in, holding hands, some with tears running down their faces, others trembling with the sense of what was to come, and when they were done, everyone stood in silence and took it all in, the green walls, the dappled light, the families, the long line of generations. Then they began to melt back to their drifts and the afternoon pick began.

It was not a normal afternoon. How could it be? In the drifts, the adults were silent and even the children picked quietly, without the usual horseplay and runaround. There was no singing, not even for an instant, and the silence was broken only every so often when someone gave voice to what everyone else was thinking.

What'll happen to our men?

Who'll protect our children?

What if the bastards start bombing this afternoon?

At four o'clock a local woman came round with cherry cakes and anxious mothers ran to buy one, to offer crumbs of comfort to their children.

Eat up, duck, never you mind.

Not long afterwards, they heard engine noise in the distance, and readied themselves to run – but where to? There were no underground shelters in the countryside, no wardens or helpful policemen ready to shout instructions through their loudspeakers. Some drew their children to them, others pushed them under hop baskets. In the event, whatever it was came no closer. A few women began to mumble about going back home, and when the tallyman called *No more bines*, most did not wait to finish their work, but, dropping their baskets in the drift, they grabbed their children and ran to the huts. Once there, they stood in anxious groups, considering the next step. A rumour had started that German bombers were planning to machine-gun hoppers as they flew by on their way to London, and some, not wanting to take their chances, packed their things and made their way to Selling station. By the end of the day, though, the vast majority were sweeping their huts and scrubbing their laundry and putting on the tea to cook and reminding themselves that they had lives to get on with. They may have felt lost in the enormity of what had happened, but there was a spirit of defiance too. Hitler could do what he liked, but he would never stop them feeding their children and keeping their homes clean.

Don't you worry, Maffie said, echoing the sentiments of most around the fire. *That Hitler don't know what he's taken on.*

But no grand expressions of defiance or hand-wringing sentiment could alter the fact that many hoppers went to bed that night and shook and sobbed themselves to sleep.

The next morning, those who had decided to stay prepared their huts for the blackout and reorganised the cookhouse. Mid-morning half a dozen labourers arrived to paint the huts in drab and scatter branches on their roofs. From now on, there would be no more cheerful whitewash, no more laughing evenings surrounded by the smell of baking potatoes, no more singing by the light of bulrush torches. They spent the afternoon picking and at the end of it a handful more took the money owed them and made their way to Selling station.

For those who remained, there was a sense that the real preparations were going on without them. Sandbags appeared in Selling. Someone reported seeing soldiers on the train. In the mid-afternoon of the following day they heard the distant sounds of aircraft engines and two days later, when the cloud had finally cleared, they saw a lozenge-shaped speck hanging in the sky, which those who had been through the first war immediately recognised as a barrage balloon. One woman, returning from Canterbury, brought back the news that tents had gone up in a field just outside the city and she had seen ditches being dug and barbed wire laid down. A woman and her children arrived back from London on her husband's insistence. Things were very tense there, she said. Anyone going back would already find the place considerably altered. There were soldiers every-where and the blackout made going about after dark peculiarly dangerous. Already people had fallen into the Thames and drowned. Go? Stay? No one knew what to do for the best.

For most, the decision was made for them. Call-up papers began to arrive, mothers received evacuation notices, there were ration books to be collected. Everything pointed towards going home. The end-of-hopping feast was a muted affair. No one felt much like celebrating. A few of the men came down to elect Miss Hop Queen but as the poor girl was being garlanded, she burst into tears and begged to go home.

Daisy and Lilly decided to stay on in the country. Now that young men were being called up in large numbers, many of the farms around Selling needed apple, plum and pear pickers. The work was tiring, requiring, as it did, an endless trudge up and down ladders, and by the end of a day picking pears or apples, Daisy's arms were like weights and her buttocks like nuggets of hot flint, but it was work, and it was paid, and while it was just about warm enough to stay in the hop huts, it was all right.

Harold wrote regularly with news from home. The new war administration made everything complicated and bureaucratic. Already they'd been forced to revise their blackout rules, and the plans for rationing were little short of chaotic. Not much had actually happened as yet. There had been a few air raids was all. He and Billy Shaunessy had built a Morrison shelter next door for Paddy and old Mrs Shaunessy and they were thinking of digging out an Anderson in the backyard. He'd even sent the birds to a cousin in Essex for safe keeping. He had taken up new duties as a munitions inspector and was on the air-raid rota, so he was seldom at home and didn't need cooking or cleaning for. He didn't want Daisy to worry. He had been to see Franny to try to persuade her to leave, he said, but he hadn't been able to get her to agree to anything. Of the women and children who had left in the early evacuation of August, some had returned to London, disillusioned with their billets, missing family and friends or homesick, and this Franny took to be proof that evacuation would be a mistake. He thought the idea of the war had hit her hard, even though the reality had yet to bite. She was crying a great deal, complaining of feeling alone and repeating over and over that Richie, in whom she'd taken virtually no interest for years, was her only comfort.

In Selling, the war remained physically remote throughout the month of September. From time to time, planes passed over and soldiers marched by. There were occasional sirens and even the sound of anti-aircraft fire, but all of this seemed abstract and unreal. Letters from London only reinforced the feeling. Daisy had to wait until October before she saw Harold. He and Jimmy travelled down to Kent together. They both looked drawn. Jimmy had volunteered for duty in the engineer corps and was waiting to report for basic training. Harold's skin had turned a canary colour from handling TNT. On Saturday night they all went down to the Sonde Arms and Jimmy picked a fight with a local man and left early on Sunday morning. Harold stayed. He was putting on a brave face, but Daisy could see he was afraid. Her lovely, quiet, trustworthy Harold. How much she wanted him here in Selling, where the days passed like the turnings of a mangle and nothing ever changed. She knew how unpatriotic this was, she told him, because he had important work to do in London, but she could not help herself from wanting it, and when the time came for him to leave she felt panicky and had to stop herself from crying. The visit unsettled her terribly. The war had already brought out all kinds of un-familiar feelings, she realised, not all of them honourable. In the days that followed she found herself thinking not just about Harold, but about Joe too and, most of all, about Richie. The thought of losing her nephew sent an ache through her bones. How could Franny be so selfish? Daisy laughed at herself for asking such a question. How could her sister not be selfish? Hadn't she always been everyone's darling? Hadn't Daisy herself treated her sister that way?

She tried to compensate for her feelings by keeping busy. A small community of evacuees – women, children and the elderly – had moved into the huts. In the mornings, the children among them attended a makeshift school in Boughton. In the afternoons they helped plant potatoes or collect firewood. For many of the children it was a great adventure. But there were those among them who had left their families and were homesick and frightened. For these children night-times were particularly bad and Daisy would go to them and read bedtime stories and sit beside them until they slept. Later, she and Lilly would sit on the makeshift beds in hop hut number 21 and by the light of the paraffin lamp they'd knit blankets for the troops.

In front of her children, Lilly remained cheerful, but the moment they were sleeping she became morose and tearful. She was worried about Jimmy and convinced of her responsibility in his decision to volunteer. Jimmy had never confronted his wife about her affair, but she was sure that he knew, and she became preoccupied by the idea that, if he was killed fighting, then his death would be her fault.

One day in October, Lilly announced that she was feeling unwell and wouldn't be able to work that day, but when Daisy returned from her labours that afternoon, Lilly was gone. She did not appear to help peel the potatoes for their tea nor even for the meal itself.

Best left alone, Maffie said, tapping her finger to her nose.

That night Daisy drew the blackout across the window and sat for a while in the light of the paraffin lamp, knitting blankets and worrying about her friend. She thought about the little Chinese figurines and felt a bolt of shame. After a while, when she could tolerate the feeling no longer, she threw off the blanket that she'd put across her knees, pulled on her boots and crept out of the hut. In dim moonlight, she made her way slowly down Pheasant Field and along Selling Road, past the giant grey house with its view of the sea, past the Drawing Room and towards the neat row of red-brick cottages. It was the first time she had been out in the countryside alone at night. The darkness expanded the space around. Everything was utterly still, almost as though it was holding its breath. Her fearlessness surprised her. She carried along the road as far as the pair of red-brick cottages, then turned along the compacted mud path that ran up a slope and into woods. Halfway up the path, she stopped, realising that she was heading for Michael's cottage, where he lived with his sullen wife and their four children. She stood on the path for a moment. Silly woman, what was she doing? If Lilly and Michael were together, they certainly weren't at his cottage. Did she think she was going to burst in and break the news of her husband's betrayal to his wife, to his four children? What was she thinking? She began to make her way back along the lane, angry at herself. Finally, she had managed to act and this limp, useless gesture was the result. She felt more ashamed of herself than ever. Heading back, she reached the junction with the chalk road when she heard a whispered voice behind her.

Daisy, Daisy. Lilly's face bloomed through the darkness. *Don't ask no questions, just help me get to bed, I'll be right as rain tomorrow.*

A thought went through her head. *Here*, she said, her voice sounding panicky, *you never went up Michael's, did yer?*

Daisy shook her head.

Oh, Daise, what a mess, what a bleedin' mess. She staggered slightly, then grabbed for Daisy's shoulder. In the moonlight Daisy could see that her face was shiny, as if she'd been crying.

I saw to it, Daisy, I saw to it the Gypsy way. But I ain't going to

say nothing to Michael, Daise, it ain't his fault, he don't need to know.
She took her friend's hand.

Christ Almighty, if it don't hurt like bloody hell, Daisy. But I fixed it. I fixed it. She grimaced. *Take me back to the hut.*

For a moment Daisy's mind froze. Then she opened her mouth to speak but nothing came out. After all her resolve, it seemed she'd missed her chance. It was too late to speak out after all. As they walked and stumbled along the lane, past the Drawing Room and the great house, pewter in the moonlight, Lilly still clutched her belly but her breathing grew more moderate. Delicately, so as not to wake them, Daisy moved Grace and Susan on to Maffie's bed. Waking Millie, she told her to go and sleep with Iris as her mother was unwell and needed a palliasse on her own. Then, pinning a spare blanket as a divider so the children would not see their mother if they woke in the night, she found a scrap of towel to place between her friend's legs and laid her down. By now Lilly was sweating and doubled up, her face a knot of eels, long, ropy tears running down her cheeks, lips bleeding, hair matted with anxiety and heat, her fist in her mouth to keep her from crying out. Daisy bundled some tea towels in a bag and gave them to her friend as a comforter, as she had once seen a nurse do for Elsie, then she lay down beside her and stroked her hair. In the coldest, emptiest part of the night, just before dawn, Lilly whispered:

Fetch us a bucket, Daise.

When Daisy returned Lilly was up and dressed in an old housecoat and carrying the lantern, not yet lit.

They went out into the moonlight and into the soft darkness of the woods behind the field. Lilly dropped to her hands and knees and, grabbing the bucket, held it between her legs. For the longest time neither of them said anything, then, out of the blue, Lilly began sobbing and gasping, rocking from side to side like a cat waiting to pounce on a mouse.

For Gawd's sake, Daise, put your hand on my head.

Daisy did what her friend asked, and for a while they remained unmoving, except for the tiny rocking motion Lilly was making. Then, in the low light of the lantern, Daisy saw dark trickles of blood making their way down her friend's thighs. A spicy, sour smell drifted up on the air. Lilly coughed and barked as though she were turning inside out, and all of a sudden something solid slapped the bottom of the bucket and, half sighing, half sobbing, Lilly fell back on to her knees and put her hands over her face. After a while, she reached for the scrap of towel and began frantically to wipe between her legs. Daisy closed her eyes, wanting not to give in to the horror, the feelings of disgust and helplessness that bounced around her head like drunken bees.

Fetch some water, Daise.

At the tap by the cookhouse, Daisy reached down and splashed her face, then she went back into the wood and the two friends began the process of cleaning up. When that was done, Lilly said:

I want to bury it in the gardens, among the hops.

The moon had faded now, and in the first glimmerings of dawn they slipped along the edges of the fields where the branches formed a veil, past Little Kel, then Big Kel to the hop garden at the most remote end of the farm. It had long been stripped of its bines and in the half-light it wore a melancholy and slightly sinister air, its wires shifting slightly in a new breeze. No one would come here again until winter fertilising. They walked around the edge and, finding a spot that would not be disturbed by hoes or tractors, began to dig a small deep hole. When the hole was done, they poured in the contents of the bucket, covered it over, then Lilly asked Daisy to say the Lord's Prayer. The words sounded unused, useless. They returned to Pheasant Field, rinsed out the bucket at the tap, and hung it on the nail outside the hut where it belonged, and agreed to say that Lilly had a fever. Then they fell asleep, exhausted, on the palliasse until, what seemed like only moments later, they were woken by the ringing of the morning bell.

At work that day, Daisy's hands moved across the branches of the apple trees like the levers of a machine. At lunchtime tongues flapped. At the hut that afternoon, the air smelled tense and rancid.

It seemed to Daisy to take a great long time for darkness to fall that night, and when it did it brought no softness or mellowing. The moonlight seemed accusatory and the hooting of the owls sounded like judgements. When Daisy woke the following morning, she knew she would never be able to see her friend again without hearing that dreadful sound at the bottom of the bucket, without feeling once more the listing, light-headed nausea she had felt as she poured its contents away. She felt floored by her passiveness. So many times she could have spoken out in the matter between Michael and Lilly, but she hadn't, and this was the result. In the whole of her life so far, the only times she had really stood up for what she believed, had stuck her neck out, had actually *done* anything to change the course of events, had been to do with Richie. She was stronger in her resolve to help him escape – the war, yes, but not just the war; the whole condition of his life, trapped between love-less parents in a place where everything seemed gauged and measured to drag a person down.

At the end of November, after the fruit and nut picking, after the mulching and preparations for winter, Daisy and Lilly returned to Poplar and the Apex Laundry. In the evenings, Daisy found work making artillery casings. Poplar was lonelier then than she had remembered it before. She barely saw her husband or her family; everyone was so busy with war duties. The phoney war, as they were now calling it, ground on all through the winter, leaving everyone in a constant state of nervous antici-pation. The feeling of foreboding, of a wave about to break, continued into the spring and came to an unexpected head when

Joe was taken ill and it became clear that he would not recover. Borrowing the delivery cart and bicycle from Spicer's, Harold pedalled Joe down to Blackwall so that he could take one last look at his beloved river, but the tank traps and barbed wire made it impossible to get through to the riverbank and it was not clear, in any case, how much Joe now understood of what was happening, or even whether he any longer knew where he was. All the same, Daisy felt, it was a happy occasion, and Joe seemed contented with his lot. A few days later Harold went into the front room to give his father-in-law his morning tea and, finding him dead, he gently broke the news to Daisy, and she pressed her face into his chest and sobbed loud, animal sounds, and her body juddered like an old engine.

Of necessity, this being wartime, it was a perfunctory funeral.

For Daisy, Joe's death came as a call as clear as a ship's horn through the fog. She knew that Harold would not leave London, but she was determined, now, to get Richie out. If only she could secure employment and a place to stay in the country she could apply for leave to be released from the munitions factory. There would be forms to sign and permission to obtain, but there was no reason why the authorities would say no. When she was settled, Richie could come and join her. Once the bombs began to fall in earnest, as they surely must, no mother, not even one as capricious as Franny, would prevent her child leaving for a place of safety. With this in mind, Daisy wrote to every farm around Selling she could think of, asking whether she could exchange a place in the hop huts for fieldwork. She didn't have much experience but she was a good worker and she'd work harder still now that the country's future was at stake. Much to her relief, she received a letter from Gushmere Court inviting her to come down in May to help to prune and train the hop bines. She could stay in the hop hut for as long as she liked. And so Daisy Baker arrived at Selling station on 1 May 1940. In the six months she'd been away the place had changed. Every straight road and strip of field had been filled with heaps of junk – old cartwheels, barbed wire, scatterings of this and that – to prevent German planes landing, and she suddenly had the sense that here was frontier country, a sense confirmed a few days later on 10 May, when the Germans attacked the Low Countries. The invasion was an extraordinary success, and by the end of the month the Germans had driven the Allied troops to the north-western fringe of France.

On 29 May, the evacuation from Dunkirk began. Daisy and the other women working on farms about were drafted in to provide tea and sandwiches for the weary-looking soldiers rumbling in on the trains from Dover. Just three days later, lying in her hut, Daisy heard the terrifying sounds of the Luftwaffe's bombardment of Dunkirk. For a while, though no one said it, everything seemed lost. The Germans were advancing.

Pretty soon, the Luftwaffe were sending Junkers out to attack shipping convoys in the Channel, and for the next two months life in Kent became if anything more perilous than it was in London. Phalanxes of Hurricanes and Spitfires daily buzzed east to confront the enemy. German dive-bombers continued to attack merchant ships, and on 31 July a party of Messerschmidts managed to dislodge the Dover balloon barrage, sending runaway balloons scudding across the Kentish hills. From the hop gardens, as she worked curling the new tendrils around their wires, Daisy witnessed ferocious dogfights, often ending in a scattering of burning metal and human flesh as one aircraft or another fell to earth. In these conditions, there was no question of Richie coming to live in Selling. Kent was far too dangerous.

The German raids continued through the summer. If Daisy wandered along towards Danebridge she could see the vapour trails of downed planes strung along the horizon like streamers. Standing on the platform in Perry Wood known as the Pulpit, from where the Earl of Sondes had once surveyed his estates, she could see plainly the glow in the sky from artillery fire in

France. From Telegraph Hill the view was clearer still, so clear in fact as to be almost unbearable. Night after night and day by day, she could hear the booming and shaking of the guns. The noise was almost continuous now. The Junkers were gone, but she quickly learned to distinguish between the engines of the Spitfires and Hurricanes and those of the Dorniers, particularly after the Dorniers began their low-level raids. On 15 August more than 500 German bombers escorted by 1,250 fighters attacked Kentish airfields, and yet she felt calmer than she had in Poplar during the phoney war months before.

Towards the end of August she received a letter from Harold begging her to return to London. Despite their agreement that she should stay in the countryside, things now seemed safer in London. She wrote back to him to say that she would come once the hops were picked and they would consider what to do next.

On 1 September, night raids began. London was hit, accidentally as it turned out, and civilians, including children, killed. The RAF retaliated with attacks on Berlin. In Kent, country roads were closed and road bridges demolished, and across the North Downs church bells rang to signal the start of an invasion. But no such invasion came. On 7 September, just after 4.30 p.m., while East Enders were watching West Ham play Spurs at Upton Park, 150 Heinkel and Dornier bombers, protected by Messerschmidts, began their assault on the London docks, Hitler's Target A.

A few days later, Daisy received a letter from Harold. Things were getting worse. First it had been parachute bombs, now it was heavy explosives and incendiaries. Night after night the bombs were falling. The North Quay of the West India import dock, where Jack often worked, had been very heavily damaged. Rum barrels had exploded and a gin factory had burst open, the gin burning with a blue flame. At Woolwich Reach, Tate & Lyle suffered a hit and burning liquid sugar spilled out across the Thames. People had to wear handkerchiefs around their faces to protect them from the smell. So many mines had fallen that the river had been partly closed for sweeping. No one talked about how many Londoners were being killed, but the casualties must be high. Among the dead was Billy Shaunessy, who had been hit by flying debris making his way home from work. The news had nearly slain old Mrs Shaunessy, who had not long been widowed to boot.

Everybody who could was leaving or being called up. Poplar was emptying out. The emergency schools had all but closed, their buildings requisitioned as stores and ARP posts. After the first weekend of the bombing, Harold had gone to Gaselee Street and begged Jack and Franny to allow Richie to leave, and they had finally agreed. If Daisy thought she could persuade the farmer to let Richie stay, they would put him on the next available train to Selling. He could be with her by the end of the week.

CHAPTER II

There was no sign on the platform to indicate that the little brick-and-fretwork building was Selling station, but when Richie saw Aunt Daisy on the platform, waving, he knew he had reached his destination. He clambered down from the train, dragging his cardboard suitcase, and waited for his aunt to come to him. She'd never been beautiful, but the country air had given Aunt Daisy the kind of bloom that he'd never seen on his mother. She seemed taller, but perhaps that was just the way she walked towards him, the energy in her step, and she was wearing a new apron, he noticed. It made her look more confident, as though by wearing it she was saying that, even in the midst of war, not everything in life was dirty.

She bent down and kissed the top of his head and he felt himself return her smile. It had been a long time since he'd smiled. He didn't know what to think of this. The past few months had been so bewildering. He felt small and for a moment he wanted to bury his head in his aunt's chest and cry but, collecting himself, he slunk back and wiped the place where her lips had been with his hand. For all he loved his Aunt Daisy, he wanted her to understand that, at ten and a half, he was no longer a little boy. There was a war on, he had already lost his dog and his grandad and all this made him a man.

He took his case back from her so that he would have something to hold on to and followed her down a flinty path that led from the station, his mind sending up brief, bright flares of memory; picking daisies and collecting eggs. They stopped briefly at a crossroads beside a red-brick pub, and he noticed with surprise that only two of the roads had houses on them, and not many at that. He couldn't recall whether this was the same as the time before. When he tried to remember what the place had looked like before the war, when he had visited with his mother and father, all he saw was the postcard his aunt had sent. He wondered what all the spaces were for. Had the other houses been bombed? There was debris everywhere in the fields, but it looked deliberately placed. Perhaps Selling had some special exemption from the war, and this was why he was being sent there? He remembered his Uncle Harold talking about German planes making day raids on the RAF bases along the Kentish coast. Was that nearby, or somewhere else altogether? It was hard trying to be a man in the face of so many unanswered questions.

They were walking along a road running between two hedges, away from the houses now. The road was the colour of the old newspapers his Grandfather Joe collected to light the fire, and Richie could feel the flints embedded in it gnawing through his tatty shoe leather. A gust of wind made his eyes water and the smell of it reminded him of the river. Beyond the confinement of the hedges he could see only empty ground now, some green and the rest a kind of pale brown. Scattered here and there below a broad sky there were buildings, mostly red brick, and the occasional white-capped cone which he took to be a factory chimney, but they were awfully few and far between. He felt suddenly relieved to be away from his mother, then guilty at the thought. He said:

When I'm old enough I'm going to join up.

His aunt just smiled at him.

One thing at a time, Richie, son, one thing at a time.

They walked on through a second crossroads. He heard the voices of other children behind him, but he did not feel like turning around to look at them. A great grey bird with a long neck bent like factory piping swooped by. It was very low and its wings pressed the air towards him like a train approaching a tunnel. He'd seen similar birds out at Beckton, the Gypsy boy had had a word for them, but he'd forgotten it. The dog had been very agitated by them, by their size. But it was too upsetting to think about Bird. Not wanting to cry, he diverted his attention. On one side now, trees obliterated the view. On the other, he could see a large house surrounded by smaller buildings, a school or maybe an old workhouse. He couldn't detect the river smell any more, but the air was full of the kind of thick perfume he associated with funeral processions. Reminded of death, he went back to thinking about Bird and his eyes began to fill with tears. In the distance he caught sight of something familiar: a barrage balloon. In an instant he pulled himself together, remembering what Uncle Harold had said, that Aunt Daisy needed his help.

They stopped before a wooden gate, beyond which rose a broad slope of grass, which at the top gave on to two rows of huts. For a moment he stood in the field, trying to take in the enormity of his change in circumstances. If his Aunt Daisy had brought him here to live when he was very young, before his father's business, before Bird, he would have run straight back to Selling station to wait for the next London train. He was soft then, he'd never been out of the little grid of streets where he was born. Now he was older, he'd learned things from the Gypsy boy and he knew that people lied and bombed one another. His aunt had gone on ahead and he did not try to catch her up. The aroma of cooking meat breezed into his nostrils. How glorious it was! The air in the East End was stinking and exhausted. If you smelled meat, you had to wonder where the nearest bomb site was.

The inside of Aunt Daisy's hut was surprisingly spacious. Two largish beds took up each side and were divided at the back by a home-made chest on whose shelves sat a couple of paraffin lamps, a bowl and some cutlery. Enamel mugs, pots, pans and cooking utensils hung from hooks along the back wall, and one or two pieces of clothing were draped over pegs under the window at the front. Richie laid his bag on one of the mattresses and, clambering on to the other, tested it by springing up and down. He felt happy. Happy to be away from the bombing, from Poplar and the loss of his dog and his grandfather, and happy to be with his aunt.

The door swung wide open and a boy's face appeared, a little older than his, and brown as a nut. The boy looked Richie up and down with deep-set, restless eyes.

Your mother says as your dinner's ready, the boy said.

She ain't me mother.

The boy shrugged. *All right, your sweetheart, then*, he said. *See if I care.* Richie stood for an instant, but then he heard his mother's voice telling him to go out and defend himself, and he rushed at the boy with all the thrust of his new-found manliness, but the boy just laughed and pushed him away.

You bugcrushers are all the same, the boy said. *Why would I want to fight with you? You ain't even the same age as me.*

The boy turned his back and began to stroll away, leaving Richie feeling that his legs had been kicked from under him. The boy could have beaten him easily, he was much taller and more powerful than Richie, but he chose to walk away. He chose to walk away as Richie himself had done for years, before his mother and father said he was a nancy boy, bringing shame on them.

When it got dark, he lay on the palliasse, divided from his aunt by a makeshift curtain, listening to the roar of the silence, punctuated from time to time by other noises less familiar; screeches and croaks and yelping; sounds like mocking laughter. All around him there were living things, but no sirens sounded, nothing thudded or splintered, no engines throbbed or incendiaries clattered. He thought about the boy.

The next day, his aunt took him to the hop gardens and set him to picking up the cones that had fallen to the ground when the bines were cut. It was hard work, and the cones left a sticky residue on his hands, but it was all a novelty to him and he didn't mind. Towards the end of the afternoon, Aunt Daisy told him to go and play while she made the tea, and so he returned to the hut and looked for something to play with, but he realised that, though he could amuse himself for hours around the docks, or even in the marshes, he didn't really know how to play in the countryside. He'd never done anything there except egg collecting, and he wasn't confident enough to go and do that on his own, so he sat on a log outside the hut and watched other children romping in the grass. He must have drifted off, because when he opened his eyes, the boy was standing beside him with his hands on his hips.

What's your name, bugcrusher? asked the boy.

Who wants to know?

Colin Swayne, esquire, of Hammersmith way, up London Town. Call me Col. The boy paused to admire the sound of his voice. *Here,* he said, *you can come with me to a pond where there's a dead body if you like.*

The boy's solemn face suggested he wasn't joking. A dead body! Richie imagined a Jerry floating face up, bayoneted through the heart. He suddenly felt extremely grown up, almost adult.

Col strode down the field and over the gate, then along the white path back towards the station. After five minutes or so, he pointed to a small oval of green water, set back a little amid hanging trees. The water was still, and even from a distance Richie could see there was nothing floating in it. He felt he'd been had. Despite his unwillingness to fight, Col Swayne was clearly no different from the rest.

Where's the body? Richie said.

Col gave a shrug.

Well, is there or isn't there, since you know all about it? Richie felt suddenly demoralised. What was the point of being here, in this empty place, when he could have stayed in London and faced the bombs? Wasn't it enough to have taken away his dog? Who was this boy anyway, to refuse to fight and be disrespectful towards his aunt? He'd really wanted to believe there was a body in the pond. He turned to walk away, but Col caught up with him and touched his arm.

Aw, don't be like that, Richie Baker. There's a body all right, but it's a ghost body, a girl, a bugcrushing cockney like you, what came hopping and got drowned. She's still down there, that girl. This pond here, they call it Ghost Hole Pond.

Richie sat with this thought for a moment. He picked up a stone and threw it into the water.

You got brothers and sisters? Richie studied Col's face for a moment. It was a wide, shallow face, with knowing eyes.

Nah, Col said. *Me mum says I had a sister once but I don't know nothing about her. She got the measles or the mumps or something. You?*

Nah.

Didn't think so.

Richie and Col began to hang around together. Each afternoon after hop picking they would set off along the road to Ghost Hole Pond to check on the dead bugcrusher girl, then head south to Perry Wood and up to Telegraph Hill. From the hill you could sometimes see the faint bloom of artillery fire across the Channel. If there had been a fight between German bombers and British fighters, they would scoot about looking for cannon shells and artillery cases, which they would find in the oddest places, buried in dirt or sitting still smoking on the roofs of pigsties and chicken coops. Once, Col took them past Downwell Cottages to a Gypsy camp in a clearing, but he wouldn't approach. He said it was all right to approach country Gypsies in the orchards picking early apples and plums, but you couldn't walk into their camp unless they asked you to or they would put a hex on you.

In 1940 Colin Swayne was twelve years old and had come to Selling six months before the war broke out on the instructions of a doctor to stay with relatives in the hope of curing his rheumy lungs. When his great-uncle and aunt had come down to the hop huts to get away from the war, he'd moved out of his relatives' house and into the huts to be out in the open air. He'd had six months to explore the countryside and knew Selling and the surrounding area quite well, but in all the time he'd been in Selling he had yet to make a friend. He was still a Londoner and most of the country boys despised him.

For the most part, the Londoners were grudgingly received. The country folk considered them aggressive, untrustworthy and pest-ridden. There were signs in the windows of the shops and pubs reading *Londoners no pilfering!*, which half the Londoners couldn't in any case read.

Emboldened by their friendship, Col and Richie quickly agreed that they might as well live up to their reputation and started pilfering from the grocer's shop and from the couple who ran the temporary store in the old chicken shed down by the Drawing Room.

They ain't very friendly, considering there's a war on . . . Richie said once, emptying his pockets of stolen sugar cubes and eggs. . . . *and we're only thieving stuff what we can't buy.*

Stands to reason, don't it, Col replied, lifting his shirt to reveal two rashers of bacon squeezed between the waistband of his trousers and his skinny stomach. *Why would you nick anything if you could get it for free?*

You had to take your hat off to Col, Richie thought. He might not be a bona fide East End bugcrusher but there were no flies on him.

And so another day would end and Richie would lie awake in the hut at night thinking about dogfights and Gypsies and the poor ghost bugcrusher girl. And he'd fall asleep only to wake again to the distant burr of engines on their way to London, and he'd think about his parents in Gaselee Street and he'd feel a sharp spike of anxiety, and though he missed his uncle, and his old haunts down by the docks, the anxiety would soon give way to relief that he was no longer among them.

And so the weeks passed and the hop pickers stripped another few gardens and London life began to seem a distant and unwelcome memory. Night after night, as he listened to the drone of German planes and the ack-ack of anti-aircraft fire, he wondered when the war would end and, when it did, what kind of London it would have left behind.

After the hop harvest, the evacuee children were expected to begin school. A makeshift emergency school had been set up for them about a twenty-minute walk away across unfamiliar countryside. The school had a single class which evacuee children of all ages were expected to attend. The teacher, Mrs Nuttall, a freckle-faced, amiable socialist with hair the colour of oxtail soup, was herself an evacuee and keen to see to it that, for the duration of the evacuation, London children should get the most from country living.

You may not think so now, children, Mrs Nuttall would say, *but this time in the countryside may well be the making of you all.*

Nutty Nuttall, as she became known, turned out to be quite a nature lover, as a consequence of which the class rarely spent much time inside the makeshift classroom but wandered about the lanes, with Nutty pointing out the various species of birds, the different kinds of trees and clouds and how to know whether it was going to rain. Sometimes Nutty would borrow a radio so the children could listen to the *Nature Study* programme at 11.35, before going out once more into the lanes and fields to put into practice what the class had learned.

Their afternoons were taken up with what Nutty Nuttall referred to as patriotic duties, which included collecting firewood, hoeing, potato planting and cobnut picking.

Once a week, the children would be bundled down to the

rectory, where the vicar's wife would serve them sweet drink and cake. At five o'clock, she would switch on the radio and they'd hear Uncle Mac chirping 'Hello, children everywhere' as *Children's Hour* began. It was during these visits that Richie and Col were first introduced to the antics of Mr Badger, Mole and Toad in *The Wind in the Willows*. He and Col both considered the stories to be silly, but they were very taken with the notion of 'messing about in boats', and from then on the two friends spent a great deal of their time, though never very successfully, tying willow branches together in the hope of launching a raft on Ghost Hole Pond.

Not long after school began, Nutty's father, Old Mr Nutty, came to live with his daughter and he soon took it upon himself to organise an elite squad of aircraft and fire spotters from among the country and bugcrusher boys. He would appear at the hop huts very early each morning with the country boys, pick up the bugcrushers and they would do drills together. Later Old Mr Nutty would bring bottles of sweet drink and test his squad, as he called them, on aeroplane identification and weather patterns, then he'd send them out spotting to all corners of Selling and the surrounding countryside. Aircraft would pass by most days and the boys would record them in their notebooks. Sometimes they would see trails of anti-aircraft fire. Old Mr Nutty had been in the trenches, he'd fought at Ypres and he knew that war was a time to put petty differences aside. The squad must be unified at all times, he said, and threatened any boys caught fighting with his own variant of court martial. Richie and Col got fit on Old Mr Nutty's drills and Col's lungs improved. Under Old Mr Nutty's tutelage, the war seemed like the best kind of game, a serious one, and Richie and Col were happy to keep playing.

And so the weeks passed and the winter came on until, rising one day stiff from the cold, Richie pulled open the door of the hut to find his whole world had frozen. He'd seen ice and snow before, in Poplar, but never as pure and white and icy as this.

The trees were furred, their branches as plump as pillows and lined with slowly dripping icicles. Below them the hedges tinkled in the breeze. The grass crunched under his feet. Here was the iciest snow and the snowiest ice.

Lodgings were found for Richie and his aunt in the Wentworths' cottage, a plain, red-brick building in a row of similar dwellings sitting on a mud turn just shy of the Drawing Room. The Wentworths were an ancient and, from Richie's point of view, slightly frightening couple. Having no teeth of his own, Mr Wentworth chewed tobacco with his gums, spat a great deal and mumbled when he spoke. Mrs Wentworth was so tiny and brown she looked like a doll left out in the sun. They were originally from somewhere Richie had never heard of, but had moved to Kent more than half a century ago when Mr Wentworth was offered work as a dryer in the oasts. The work was highly skilled – the hop dryer having to sleep inside the oast in order not to miss the optimum moment to turn the hops so that they would be neither too wet nor too dry – but it was also seasonal, and when the season was over, Wentworth took on more general agricultural labouring. He had given up working as a drier some years ago – all those years spent inside dusty kilns had given him farmer's lung – and the couple now scraped by with the proceeds from a smallholding. They were not altogether taken with the idea of having evacuees billeted on them, but they had no choice.

By usual standards, their cottage was cramped and it smelled of neglect, but by the standards of the hop huts – and of the houses in Poplar, come to that – it seemed enormous. Richie and his aunt dragged their bags into the passageway and still had room to follow Mrs Wentworth into the kitchen beyond. The kitchen itself was dominated by an old iron range, which faced a scrubbed pine table and four rickety-looking pine-and-rush chairs. Beyond it, through a door beside the range, there was a gloomy scullery, bathed in shadow, into which Mrs Wentworth disappeared, reappearing a moment later carrying a teapot.

While they were drinking their tea, Mrs Wentworth went to the back door and shouted:

Oi, you, boy, help these people take their things up.

And Col Swayne appeared. Richie was startled, but his aunt winked at him. Of course, these were the relatives Col had mentioned. Clever Aunt Daisy. She'd found them lodgings with Richie's friend.

The two boys grabbed some bags and went up a set of narrow, damp-stained stairs, and Col showed Richie to the tiny room with its rickety bed which the boys would be sharing with Mr Wentworth in the winter months to come.

Richie looked about the room.

It ain't so bad, he said. *Leastwise, if I'm sharing it with you.*

The two boys allowed this small show of affection to settle for a moment then, heading back down the stairs, Col said:

The old boy's as deaf as a brick. We can talk all we like in the room at night, it won't bother him. Now, I suppose you want to go and see if the pond is froze.

Richie supposed he did and the two boys kicked their heels along the stony path running along the side of the cottage and took a good long look at Ghost Hole Pond. Richie wondered whether the ghost girl was lying underneath the ice, or even frozen to the bottom of the pond, but Col said that ghosts didn't freeze and even if they did, the pond wasn't frozen all the way down because water didn't work that way or you wouldn't be able to crack the ice on the well and still draw water from it. They clambered across a field of wheat stubble and found themselves in an orchard of empty cherry trees, from where the ground sloped down to a copse. They strung twigs together with straw to make a mat, and sledged across the snow through the orchard on it, clinging to one another and bellowing. At the end of the trees, the old wagon horses watched them, blowing steam through their noses.

Over the next few days it grew colder still, and Nutty Nuttall announced there would be no more school until a thaw set in. The frost now brought a bitter crunch to the mornings and the farmers brought all their livestock in, even the sheep, but still Mr Wentworth seemed unwilling to light any fire except the one in the kitchen range, and at night ice crystals would gather on the insides of the windows and, as Richie and Col and Aunt Daisy and the Wentworths ate their tea, their breaths travelled in clouds before them. It was so cold that one night Richie woke up to find himself with his arms wrapped around old Wentworth's skinny body. Luckily, old Wentworth didn't wake and Richie kept the incident to himself. Col was his best friend, the best pal he had ever had, but there were some things you kept even from your closest confidants.

And so Christmas 1940 – the Christmas of the Blitz in London – passed uneventfully. The thaw came, school reopened, the wagon horses appeared in the fields, the air gradually warmed and it was spring. Spring in Poplar had never meant much more than a gradual elongation of the days and a frantic but ultimately fruitless house-cleaning, but here in the country, it was as though someone had laid out the fields in all their best finery, in expectation of special guests. The land around Selling filled, first with leaves and dazzling green hop shoots, then with flowers. Lambs appeared, and calves, piglets and even a few foals, and there were birds lined up on every telegraph wire. It was time to leave the Wentworths for the hop huts; Richie couldn't pretend to be sorry, though he'd grown, if not exactly fond of Mr and Mrs Wentworth, then at least tolerant of their eccentricities and grateful for the shelter of their home. But he was anxious to be outdoors again, to feel the earth beneath his feet and to be free of the stench of Mr Wentworth's elderly body beside him in the bed and of the nightly humiliation of remembering that he'd cuddled it.

The worst of the Blitz being over, the air was no longer constantly darkened by aircraft, and though Old Mr Nutty still drilled, he now encouraged his 'squad' to go out and have some fun in the country too. And so in the time between school, patriotic duties and drills, the two boys now went out egg collecting and hunting for birds and baby rabbits. Old Mr Nutty had taught them to observe, and they applied their new skills to spotting game. As the days drew out, they went farther and farther afield, as far south as the abandoned windmill in Perry Wood and as far north as Staple Street, the old road to Faversham, bringing home rabbits, ducks, bird eggs and the occasional hare, to which Aunt Daisy would add pot herbs before bubbling the lot into a fragrant stew over the fire.

During Easter 1941, Uncle Harold paid his first visit to Selling since Richie had left London, and though Richie was delighted to see his uncle, he was shocked, too, at how thin and drawn he'd become in the six months since they had last been together. Even working in the grocery business and having 'connections' in the docks, by which Harold meant access to Jack's thriving black market business, it had become almost impossible to find anything to eat in London other than potatoes, onions and a few cans of dreadful-tasting fish. When Aunt Daisy produced a bacon-and-onion pud and put her portion on to Harold's plate, cautioning Richie not to say anything, he gobbled both pieces down as though he hadn't eaten in days without noticing that his feast was at his wife's expense. Richie had once heard his mother say that the proof was in the pudding, and from Harold's uncharacteristic behaviour he deduced that things in London were really very bad indeed.

Still, food shortages and rationing aside, life was better than it had been even a month or so previously. The Luftwaffe's attacks were less frequent and Harold thought that for now, at least, the worst was probably over for the East End. There was no getting round it, Uncle Harold said, the place was wrecked, people were living in the underground shelters because there was nowhere else to go. Having barely had a decent night's sleep in six months, and lousy food, everyone was terribly, terribly tired and their nerves were stretched. It had been a bloomin' lousy time to be an East Ender, but the courage and spirit of East Enders had made Harold proud to count himself among their number.

There were times when he'd be cowering in a shelter while the ground above them thundered and rocked and sooner or later someone would strike up a song, and bit by bit others would join in and before you knew it, the shelter was so rich with the sound of human voices that you could hardly hear the horrors going on above. 'Hang Out Your Washing on the Siegfried Line' was a favourite, and there had recently been a craze for songs from the picture, *The Wizard of Oz*. Richie's mother loved those songs Uncle Harold said. When the war was over she was going to get herself a pair of red shoes just like Dorothy in the picture. He stopped and checked himself and Richie saw the smile drain out of his face. He made a consoling gesture with his hands.

Richie, son, listen, yer mum and dad's so busy. And what with travel permits so hard to come by. He bit his lip, wondering how best to continue, then, adopting a cheery voice, he said, *Tell you what, though, yer mum and dad talk about you all the time. They're always talking about you. They're missing you awfully.*

Richie looked at Aunt Daisy, who smiled, but they both knew that Uncle Harold was lying.

In the afternoon Richie took his uncle egg collecting. Back in London Uncle Harold could breed a lilac budgerigar from lime-green parents and sense when a canary was about to come down sick, but here he was hopeless. Richie would point out birds, but Uncle Harold was unable to distinguish between a dunnock and a house sparrow or between a blackbird and a starling.

Richie, son, Uncle Harold said at the end of the afternoon, shaking his head in admiration. *If you ain't turning into a proper country boy.*

The following morning, as Richie saw his uncle off at the station, he had a sudden urge to block his path and beg him not to go, but then the whistle blew and it was too late.

The summer passed and soon the hop picking season was on them once more, only more organized this year, with each farm allotted an ARP warden and, beside every hop garden and field, field-side trenches to act as shelters. Fifty thousand hoppers arrived in Kent that year, almost as many as before the war began. While the East End lay in ruins, the docks were smashed, whole neighbourhoods razed, shops, churches, pubs and clubs all burned and blasted beyond recognition, the hop was a reminder to East Enders of what small, reliable pleasures remained. Some came all the way from the West of England, or from Norfolk, to where they had been evacuated, determined not to miss out. Then the hops were done, the Londoners and the evacuees went home or back to their exiles, the nights grew dark, the days grew cold and the land fell asleep once more.

The winter of 1941 proved harsher than any in living memory. For weeks at a time the land disappeared under great snowdrifts and the trenches dug beside the fields became igloos. Birds froze in their roosts and dropped like nuts from the trees. Livestock shivered in barns. Everyone became thieves that winter. The birds stole grain from the granaries, the farm cats took milk from the doorsteps and scraps put aside for the pigs, the farm dogs pinched the cats' meat, the Land Girls stole kale and cauliflowers, the Gypsies took chickens, the hoppers dug potatoes from the fields.

But everyone rallied to the cause, too. Prisoners of war went out in teams to cut logs from the coppices, Land Girls passed their spare hours knitting hats and extra scarves for the farm workers. In Boughton, Nutty Nuttall cancelled school when one of her younger pupils got her fingers burned on the ice on a milk churn and the class spent their mornings clearing paths and spreading salt on the roads instead.

One morning, Col and Richie woke to find Old Wentworth lying stiff as a board in the bed. He wasn't dead, as it turned out, though it certainly looked that way, but he did not make a full recovery either. Having spent most of her adult life under her husband's thumb, Mrs Wentworth suddenly discovered herself. The place was cleaned, and fires were set in all the rooms, so long as Richie and Col went out to collect firewood.

Do Mr Wentworth good, she said, though whether she meant the newly warm cottage or living by his wife's rules Richie did not know.

After his attack, Wentworth was no longer able to manage the stairs, so Richie and Col fixed up a mattress for him in the front room. For the remainder of the winter the two friends had a room to themselves. Col's mother sent him copies of *The Beano*, *Champion* and *Dandy*, and for hours the two boys sat in the gloom, dazzled by the joy of sharing comics.

And then it was all over. Spring arrived and the two boys moved back to their family hop huts. On the night of 1 June, Richie went to bed beside his aunt as usual but was woken early in the morning by thudding sounds. Aunt Daisy had woken too. They threw on their coats and went out into the field. To the east, beyond Perry's Wood and the Stour, they saw a flaring of the light, like some localised sunrise making its way above the trees.

They've got Canterbury.

Richie looked on, his eyes filling with tears. Though the fires and the bombs were ten miles hence, he knew that the war had finally come to Selling. The following day, the village was full of families made homeless by the bombing and unwilling to return to the city. Sleeping in barns and old chicken coops, erecting makeshift tents in the woods or simply taking their chances out in the open fields, many were still there on 2 November, when German bombers struck the city again.

Richie's carefree days were over. He thought only about what he could do to be of use. He began by helping to fill sandbags and grow vegetables, passing his weekends collected salvageable debris and shrapnel, cleaning and supplying the local shelters. Only when his chores were done would he and Col take themselves off across the fields in search of rabbits and ducks for tea. And so the months passed and Richie Baker no longer counted them, nor thought much about the life he had left behind in London, nor much, either, of the people still living there. All his energies were focused on this place, Selling, which had become his beloved home.

In the spring of 1943, Aunt Daisy announced she intended to make a visit to London during the Easter break and hoped Richie would go with her. The thought of London worried him. He no longer felt connected to it as he once did. He had not been in London for two and half years, and had only seen his parents once in that time, when they came down for a weekend during the previous summer. He wondered whether he would still recognise his old school, the shops along the Commercial Road, the West India Dry Dock and the warehouses of the East India and the Millwall docks? Would the railway sidings, and the engine yards, the warehouses and chemical plants and factories, the pubs and breweries and seamen's missions and all the built paraphernalia of the docks, still be where he remembered them? Would he still be able to find his way to Mr Chin's puck-a-poo, to Charlie Brown's or the Wapping steps? What would Gaselee Street look like? Would the house feel like home? Would Franny and Jack still feel like his mother and father?

None of his uncle's descriptions the Easter before, nor any of his letters, had prepared Richie for what he saw all about him as the train neared London. First, in the outlying suburbs, then in the inner grids of roads and residential streets, entire rows of houses had been reduced to lines of rubble, from which dusty sprigs of buddleia sprang. Trees lay where they had been blasted from the ground, or stood in place, transformed into fragile, blackened silhouettes. Heaps of dust and debris had accumulated against the filthy walls of half-decimated factories, and there were buildings where not a single window had remained unsmashed. As they neared the terminus, he felt the scene before him retreating, as though he were looking at it the wrong way through a telescope. It was too much to take in. He thought about comics and his mother's red shoes until his mind melded the two and he saw Desperate Dan striding about in a pair of ladies' slippers and he laughed out loud, the sound unexpected and, somehow, dangerous.

At London Bridge he clambered from the train, his stomach turning and his body swaying, as though the journey had given him sea legs. He and Aunt Daisy clambered on board a bus and trundled through a wasteland of blast holes and rubble hills. The journey took hours, it seemed, before they finally arrived at a stop near Gaselee Street.

His mother must have heard them approaching, for the door opened and there she stood in her housecoat, an uncertain smile playing on her face.

Aintcha grown? she said. The war had taken its toll on the familiar terrain of Franny's face, as it had taken its toll on everything. She'd been so lovely once, but now she wore a drawn expression, her skin was sallow, there were deep hollows beneath her eyes, and her cheeks seemed quarried out. When he did not immediately reply, she turned to Aunt Daisy.

Ain't he grown?

All that country air, Daisy said.

A moment of awkwardness passed between the three of them, then Franny said:

Come in, then, yer dad's waiting.

Jack was sitting at his customary place at table. He did not get up when they walked into the room.

You may not have noticed, he said to Daisy and Richie both, *but there's been a bleedin' war on.*

He laughed, intending this to be funny. Ever obliging, Aunt Daisy broke into an uncomfortable smile.

I could murder a cup of tea, she said.

While Franny fetched the pot, Jack turned to Richie and said, *Cat got your tongue?*

There was a silence. Richie felt himself freeze. Eventually, Daisy said, *Oh, my knees and knuckles, if I ain't parched.*

Richie sat and watched his father eat. He, too, seemed much changed. The skin on his face was livid with broken capillaries and sagged at the jawline, as though someone had skinned him as you would a rabbit, then sewn the skin back on the wrong way. A smell of stale alcohol hovered around him. He looked ill, Richie thought.

Air attacks on London had recommenced that January and the RAF had attacked Berlin at the end of February. The East End had been poised for reprisal attacks, everyone was on tenter-hooks. Jack had been making one of his deliveries in Bethnal Green when he heard the siren – 8.17 p.m., he found out later. The Germans had started using lighter bombs and faster aircraft and everyone knew that the gap between the first siren sounding and the first bomb dropping was shorter now. He remembered seeing people leaping from the buses and pouring from the pubs to reach the shelter of the underground. A single 25-watt bulb illuminated the entrance and the steps were slippery from the rain and from the hundreds of wet feet that were in that instant pouring down them. It was terrible to witness such panic. Jack held back to make way for women and children and arrived at the entrance to the station just as an anti-aircraft battery set off its missiles. They were a new type, he heard later, no one was familiar with their sound and, thinking it was the start of an attack, the people queuing at the mouth of the station began to surge inwards. He heard a shout, then screaming, and from where he stood at the mouth to the entrance, he saw a sudden collapse of bodies. A woman at the bottom of the stairs had tripped. Others had tumbled into the space, crushing one another with their bodies until men, women and children were piled on top of one another like so much wet laundry. The guns continued, though, and, despite the crush, men, women and children continued to push forward in alarm. Jack stood aside, powerless to stop the human cascade. Later, he helped with the clearing of the bodies. At the end of it all, 84 women, 27 men and 62 children lay crushed to death in the stairwell.

Stories of panicking civilians being bad for morale, the official version later had it that the station had suffered a direct hit, but you couldn't keep anything from East Enders for long. The incident had left Jack profoundly shocked. For three days afterwards he did nothing but drink. He was still drinking now.

After they'd eaten, Richie drifted off along the street and began to head in the direction of the docks. At Blackwall he made his way across the river defences and managed to slip down to the Thames beach. All along the river front on either side, the quays and jetties round which his grandfather had steered his caravans of lighters were either patched up or gone. There were a couple of fireships in the channel, and some floating equipment he did not recognise, but he saw none of the busy pre-war flow of tugs and lighters. Even the water looked different. A slick of oil and debris bobbed over its surface, and what birds there had once been had disappeared. As for the air, its muddy, thick marine tang had been replaced by smells of cordite and something more disturbing still – the stench of skin, cooked flesh and burnt hair or hoofs.

He made his way back via the homes of boys he had once known. In one case, the house had been replaced by rubble, in another the whole street had gone and there were men in Home Guard uniform on practice routine in the ruins. By the time he reached Gaselee Street it was nearly teatime and there were strangers, presumably bomb-outs, sitting at the table with his parents and his Uncle Harold and Aunt Daisy, and they were all laughing at jokes Richie did not understand. Then someone struck up a tune and the adults took up the words of an unfamiliar song and began belting it out, each verse louder than the last until Richie, who neither knew the song nor most of the people singing it, wanted to run and run and not stop running until he reached hop hut number 21.

When the singing was done, his father, who smelled strongly of beer, said:

Hey, Richie, son, put a bleedin' smile on yer puss. Anyone'd think there was a war on!

Richie looked at his father. Everyone laughed.

Later that night, lying on the floor on a makeshift bed, Richie conjured his father's face, the raw web of spidery red capillaries and bulging veins, the creased and laughing eyes, and cried slow, silent tears.

In the early morning Richie and his Aunt Daisy made their way back to the station, and this time the train seemed to speed, careering through the crumbled streets of south London and out into the green spaces of Kent.

CHAPTER 12

Harold Baker missed his wife so much during their long years apart that there were times his heart could hardly bear it. The irony of their exile from one another was not lost on him. During the first summer of the war, in 1940, what with the continual raids along the Kent and Sussex coasts and the almost constant presence of enemy bombers and fighters in the skies above Kent, Daisy had suffered the worst of it. Still, if she had returned to Poplar in the summer of 1940 to escape the Battle of Britain, as he had wanted her to do, Daisy would still most likely have been in London when the Blitz began, and Harold knew she would not have left him then. He knew her well enough to be sure of that. She was loyal, was Daisy, too loyal, perhaps. If that was a fault, he hoped it was one they shared.

The first few days of the Blitz were punctuated for Harold by a strong sense of relief, not so much on account of the phoney war coming to an end, though there was part of him that was glad that the months of anticipation were at last over, as the fact that Daisy was not there to witness it. On the afternoon of Saturday, 7 September 1940, Harold had been at work in Spicer's. His ARP rota did not begin until the following day. Even before any sirens sounded, word came through that something was on its way. Women began pouring from the shops and cafés along the Commercial Road to stare at the sky. Though there was nothing to see, everyone stood on their spots, clutching their gas masks, waiting. Then the sirens began and there was instant pandemonium, men, women and children scattering like bugs in the light, making for the public shelters. Harold hurried back into the shop, locked the doors (Spicer insisted on this – he said it would give them more time to escape in the event of a German invasion, though Harold suspected it was more about preserving his valuable stock from unscrupulous passers-by) and, directing those customers who were still in the shop to follow him, he ran to the basement, where Spicer was already fiddling with a paraffin lamp and Mrs Spicer was worrying at her lip and hugging herself. For a while they sat in silence, then, when the terrible thudding and wrenching sounds began above them, someone struck up

> Up the apples an' pears, and across the Rory O'Moor,
> I'm off to see my dear old Trouble and Strife.
> On the Cain and Abel, you will always see
> A pair of Jack the Rippers and a cup of Rosie Lee.
> What could be better than this –
> A nice old cuddle and kiss –
> All beneath the pale moonlight.
> Then some Tommy Tucker and off to Uncle Ned.
> Oh what a luverly night tonight.

When the all-clear sounded two hours later, no one could think of anything to say. They tramped upstairs in single file and stood on the shop floor in a dazed state. Outside, Harold could hear people shouting for their friends and neighbours. *Ginny, you there, duck? Where's Mikey Holdsworth? Mikey, are you hurt?* Mr Spicer brought out a bottle of rum and they all had a nip. For the next hour, no one came in to buy anything, so Spicer closed up and Harold hobbled towards home. By now it was dark, and he couldn't see what damage had been done during the bombing. He picked up his ARP uniform and limped to Gaselee Street to check on his brother and sister-in-law and to beg Franny to send Richie off to the countryside. He was still at Gaselee Street when the second warning sounded. He spent the night with Franny and Richie and a handful of their neighbours in the Anderson shelter he and Jack and Richie had helped dig a few months before. No one seemed to know where Jack was. Bombs fell through the night, many landing near Gaselee Street itself. After the all-clear they came up to ground level. Looking at the scene before them, Franny began crying and clinging to Richie, repeating over and over, *God save us, God save us*. To the east, fires raged across Canning Town and Silvertown. It looked as though the entire Royal Docks was alight. Harold made tea for everyone and took Richie to one side and told him not to worry too much about his mother and that she was high strung was all and didn't know what she was saying. He left them, then, and a half-hour later, he signed on to his shift at the Poplar ARP depot.

Another 200 aircraft arrived as Harold was heading home. The moment he heard the sirens, he turned and immediately began making his way back to the depot, calling out for people to take cover. When the sound of the engines had risen to a deafening roar, he dived into a nightwatchman's hut and hoped for the best. A few hours later he emerged, shocked and covered in dust, but none the worse for wear. At the depot, he found out that South Hallsville Road School in Canning Town had suffered a direct hit, with terrible consequences. Four hundred men, women and children had been waiting at the school for buses to evacuate them out to Epping, but the buses had mistakenly gone to Camden Town, and by the time the error had been rectified, it was too late. The official death toll was seventy-three, but witnesses believed it to be in the hundreds. Between August 1940 and 10 May 1941, 5,028 children were killed in London, most of them East Enders. By the Monday, after a weekend of intense bombing, East Enders were becoming desperate. The authorities were still preventing people from sheltering in the underground. The police had forcibly removed shelterers from Blackwall Tunnel on the grounds that, if the tunnel suffered a direct hit, they'd all drown in their sleep. But the shelterers were so exhausted, so rattled and sunk by the events of the previous two days, that they lay down on the approach road to the tunnel and refused to move until the police had agreed to allow them inside again.

The lack of sleep was crucifying. Either you were tensed up, waiting for the next air-raid warning, or you were scrunched in the freezing damp of some shelter with dozens, even hundreds, of others. After the first night, Harold didn't even try. He kept himself awake with copious mugs of tea. Every so often he drifted off for a few minutes, but never for long. It was important to remain useful. Every new attack set more fires blazing, scattered more debris across the roads, left more dead or injured or homeless.

His physical capabilities limited by his leg, Harold discovered he could be most useful keeping up morale. It wasn't easy. Each night brought further bombings and everyone was terribly frightened. On Wednesday, 11 September, four days after the first attack, a high-explosive smashed the Northern Outfall Sewer at Beckton, pouring all the city's shit and waste into the river. The smell was unbearable. That was a low ebb, morale cracking as fast as ack-ack fire, with Harold limping about in his ARP uniform offering cheer.

Keep up your pluck, stay smiling, there's worse at sea. By the end of the day he could barely stand the sound of his own voice. The following morning a group of mostly women staged a protest at Stepney underground station, refusing to budge until they were given official permission to shelter there. Harold heard later that some East End communists – Daisy's old friend Sidney among them – had stormed the Savoy Hotel, which was allowing its guests to use its underground shelter. *One rule for the rich, another for the poor.* There was a great swell of anger among East Enders at that news, and Harold didn't blame them. It was all very well for the toffs, with their hotel basements and country boltholes, but East Enders were sitting targets, no one knowing what to do or where to go for the best.

In the course of his duties, Harold witnessed scenes of the most heart-wrenching horror. He saw bewildered women emerging wide-eyed and covered in dust from the rubble of buildings, screaming for their children; he saw relatives of the dead pulling the body parts of their loved ones from what had once been their homes; he saw the elderly desperately rooting in the filth for their glasses or their false teeth, the hungry scraping flour spilled from the mills and now mixed with ashes and brick dust. He heard the soft, buried cries and sobs of those trapped beneath wreckage, becoming weaker and weaker. He could never stay with any of the dead or dying for long. There was always rubble to be cleared, and walls to be pulled down and made safe, potholes to fill and the living to rescue.

Later in September, the nineteenth, he thought it was, the first parachute mines exploded across the East End. Those that actually went off had a vicious side blast that sent debris and shrapnel flying all about. Those that didn't, stuck in trees or ended up slung over telephone wires, like sinister Christmas decorations. Hearing that the parachute was made of silk, women started pulling them down to make underwear. Harold had even seen children skipping over ropes made with the things. It was typical, he thought with pride, of defiant, sometimes reckless cockney practicality.

Though he spent as much time as he could with Franny and Richie, he didn't see much of Jack in those early days. The damage to the West India was such that clear-up and fire-watching teams were needed round the clock, and Jack was usually working. When he wasn't, he could be found at Charlie Brown's or the Resolute, getting drunk and making deals. He seemed very exercised by the money that was to be made on the black market. U-boats had been out attacking merchant shipping in the Channel since war was first declared and the rumour was there was tonnage holed up in the Thames Estuary. You never really knew, Jack said, because the authorities only ever told you what they wanted you to hear, but no one had ever said what had happened to the cargo on board those wrecks. Thousands and thousands of pounds' worth of cargo. Ten to one the police had taken it, Jack reckoned, but you never knew. It might be possible to get your hands on some of it.

Harold kept himself out of his father's and brother's business now. Spicer did too. Neither had the ambition nor the stomach for black marketeering in wartime. Harold saw first hand the misery caused by rationing among the poor. Some days the queues outside Spicer's stretched beyond the parade and round the corner into the nearby street. Bacon, ham, sugar and butter had gone on the ration almost as soon as the war started, followed by meat and tea in March 1940. By July of that year, just before the Blitz, margarine, cooking fat and cheese were added to the list. Harold felt for the taut, faded faces and sleepless eyes of the women waiting. To have to trudge from queue to queue in the relentless quest for food on top of caring for their children and elderly and working long days, before retiring to the human rat nests that passed for shelters, seemed to Harold to be too much for anyone, let alone a woman, to bear. He did his best to put on a cheerful smile for them. *Never mind, duck, next week, who knows, there might be a bit of new cheese in or a batch of dried eggs.* All this time he knew where fresh eggs and cheese and even meat were to be found – in his brother's store – and he felt miserable every time he thought about his failure to speak up, but there it was, there were many kinds of loyalty and they didn't all get along with each other.

By then, he'd persuaded Franny to let Richie go and live with Daisy until the worst of it was over. Despite the continuation of air attacks on Kent, Harold did not regret seeing Richie to the train station. Nothing, he knew, could be as bad as the pounding of the East End, which carried on through the autumn and into the following year. Spring 1941 arrived and with it three huge raids on the East End, one each in March, April and May, the last leaving twelve barges blazing in the Thames beside the docks. You could see them from miles around, the thick black smoke pluming through the streets, worse than the pea-soupers and the factory waste. And there was Harold, walking home from Spicer's in the midst of all this filth and carnage, shaking his head in disbelief, thinking poor old Joe would have turned in his grave to have witnessed a dozen barges wasted so.

It wasn't until the daily bombing had subsided some time afterwards that the scale of the damage to the East End really came home to him. All along the Commercial Road, the Mile End Road, the Roman Road, the East India Dock Road and Silvertown Way, burned-out shops and broken buildings stared blankly outwards, street lamps sagged, and in the docks the crumble of bombed warehouses, sandbagged quays and drunken, half-demolished walls leaned crazily into the darkness. He noticed the destruction of entire roads of terraces with particular sadness, each one representing, as it did, the death of a little community.

After shop hours, Harold would limp back along the Commercial Road, sidestepping the sandbags, the pyramids of brick dust and spires of broken glass, the dazed, elderly and frightened men, the queues of tired, dusty women waiting at the bus stops as though none of it was really happening, and make his way back home. By now an assortment of lodgers and bomb-outs had been billeted on number 7 Bloomsbury Street. He didn't resent them, they were a good deal worse off than he was, but with strangers pacing about and his wife and nephew elsewhere, number 7 hardly felt like home any more, and it was a relief to escape to Gaselee Street, though Jack was rarely there now. If Harold wanted to see his brother, he'd usually find him in the Resolute, or at Charlie Brown's or the Prospect of Whitby. Jack seemed to be thriving on the chaos. He had removed himself almost completely from his wife and son, rarely mentioning them. Harold loved his brother, but he always felt strangely empty after these encounters. Afterwards, he'd often treat himself to a meal of rissoles and potato soup at the British Restaurant in order to feel full again, and wholesome. On the nights he wasn't on ARP duty he'd be in his bed by nine, but he was rarely able to sleep immediately. Instead, he'd pass the time writing letters to Daisy and Richie. Whenever there were night raids, he'd make sure everyone in the house got safely to the Andy, and when the all-clear rang, he'd wake those who were sleeping and fetch everyone a cup of tea. In whatever time was left before he had to start his working day at Spicer's, he would flick through his old birding books, ticking off the husbandry tips in his head and dreaming of the canaries and budgies he would one day breed and the prizes they would win.

In the middle of May 1940, the nightly bombing ceased. The East End held its breath, but May passed into June and June into July with no major incident. There was a brief revisit of the worst days of the Blitz when, during the night of 27 July, incendiaries fell across the docks, but it was also remarkable how well East Enders had adapted to this threat. The siren sound for incendiaries would have them rushing out of their houses with sand and buckets of water to put out the offending fires before they could take hold, then racing back into their shelters once more in case there were high-explosives or parachute bombs on their way.

For months during the summer and autumn of 1941 almost nothing happened, and East Enders began to pick themselves up, brush off the dust and get on with the business of living. It was only then that Harold noticed something had shifted in him. At first he thought it was the cessation of the bombs, then he began to realise that it had less to do with the bombing itself and more to do with the fact that he had survived it.

In the course of his night-time ARP duties, he had begun to notice that the streets seemed peopled with loiterers. At all times of the night, you could see men and women standing at the corners of darkened streets and in the deep shade of the alleys and turnings that ran off the main streets. At first he assumed that they were unable to sleep, but then it dawned on him that these people were waiting for someone or something. But what? He had seen prostitutes of both sexes before, and had witnessed the odd sexual coupling down some dark turning or other, but this was on a different scale. He began to linger a little, and observe. As an ARP warden he had the perfect excuse. Sometimes, after witnessing some encounter or other, he would return home in a state of such bewildering arousal that he wouldn't be quite unable to release himself from what he had seen, replaying a flash of leg, perhaps, the rippling of a skirt, a captured mouth, a sigh over and over in his mind, until he thought he might go mad from it.

The more he thought about the loiterers, the more their activities made sense to him. It was only if you'd lived through the Blitz that you could understand the surging relief of having survived it. It occurred to him that these people he saw loitering were simply expressing their joy at being alive and, if that was it, who was he to judge them? There was nothing low or dirty in *joie de vivre*; on the contrary, it was uplifting and life affirming. He thought about Daisy then. He'd gone so far as to kiss her breasts, and wedge his hand between her legs and leave it there. He knew there was more but she had never asked for it and he had not been minded to press it upon her. He didn't know why this was and didn't really question it. He knew they loved each other very deeply. The topic of intercourse had never come up. They were happy. Why rock the boat?

Now, though, he began to feel an urge to explore beyond the

confines of his marriage. He told himself that it was the madness of the war and that, once it was over, the roiling, unsettling unfolding he now felt in his groin would subside. But for now, it was impossible to ignore.

One night, when the moon was only a few degrees from full, and everything was faintly highlighted in its powdery light, Harold Baker stumbled on his opportunity. He was on one of his night-time street patrols, not ready, yet, to face the miscellany of the dispossessed awaiting him in Bloomsbury Street or to sit and listen to his hysterical sister-in-law rehearse her various grievances. He walked on south, towards the river and the dockers' pubs, until, somewhere around Tunnel Park, a wiry, weathered-looking man in a merchant seaman's uniform suddenly sprang out of the darkness and, stopping not two feet in front of him, drew a pack of Woodbines from his jacket pocket and said in a sly voice:

Got a match, friend?

It was dim and the blue light of Harold's ARP torch jarred against the pallid wash of the moon. For a moment Harold thought he was about to be robbed, but the man shot out a short, uncertain smile, displaying yellow teeth. Harold felt his weight shifting. He was nervous but something stopped him from hurrying away.

Well? Have you or ain't you? asked the man, leaning forward. *I'm dying for a smoke.*

Harold felt himself swaying backwards. He had been asked for a light before, but he sensed this was different. The Woodbine man had spoken in a particular way, as though in some kind of code. For a moment Harold could not take his eyes off the man's boots; unpolished, dust-laden boots, but newish, the soles leather, and nailed. He felt paralysed. You could never be too careful. There were fifth columnists all about. He looked up and shook his head, hoping the man could see him. The man stood there for what seemed like an age, then he lifted his hands in the air, shrugged and disappeared back into the gloom.

Back in Bloomsbury Street, Harold made himself a cup of tea and tried to settle to the papers, but he found that he couldn't. He went to bed but was plagued by the impulse to get up and return to Tunnel Park. Eventually he slept and woke to discover a cold, wet patch on the sheet. It was all very disturbing.

A few days later he was drinking at the St Leonard's Arms with Jack and one of Jack's friends, a fellow docker, who had been given a C3 permit, excusing him from the call-up on grounds of invalidity, on account of a dock hook having removed his right eye, and was working with Jack breaking cargo in the holds of merchant shipping. Forgetting Harold was there, Jack and his friend began gossiping about other gangs at the West India, and when the friend mentioned the leader of one of the Irish gangs, an old-timer, Jack threw back his head and roared with laughter.

That's the one with the bleedin' dilly bag!

The friend joined in the fun, and the two men sniggered and chewed over the words. When he'd recovered, Jack remembered his brother. He took a pull of his watery pint and said:

There's this fellow, he's got this bag, right, a ladies' bag what he brings to the docks with him.

He screwed up his face. A tear of joy trickled from his left eye.

But that ain't all. Under his cap, right, the bugger's hair is curled, with curlers, I swear, like a bleedin' tart.

The other man was shaking with mirth now, imitating the docker mincing about with his dilly bag. Harold tried to join in. It *was* funny, after all. At the same time, he felt slightly dishonourable. People had laughed at him on account of his limp and that hadn't been at all funny. Jack pushed his empty pint glass towards the barman and nodded at him to refill it.

But you can't do nothing about it, 'cause this cove is a regular fighter. He's a nancy but he ain't no sissy.

The other man thought this was hilarious and laughed heartily.

Way I see it, said the other man, *it's on account you ain't got the rorters no more. The youngsters is either evacuated or off to war and the nancies ain't fighting so they're out on the streets looking for a bit of what have you. Whereas before they might have hid a bit, you see 'em in the streets now, plain as day.*

Jack nodded wisely at this and the men turned to other topics.

Later, in the privacy of his own room, Harold returned to the subject of rorting. It was an old East End custom – boys did it to make a bit of money to take their girlfriends to the pictures. A quick fiddle in the trousers of some stranger, an outsider usually, older as a rule. A few shillings paid out. No one took it seriously. As soon as the boys started making good money at their jobs, they stopped it, got married, settled down like everyone else.

Or did they?

Harold thought about the pansies he'd seen flitting between tables at Charlie Brown's, hair pomaded and cheeks rouged, their outrageous demeanour leaving a trail of glamour behind them. He'd seen them, most often alone, stopping to chat to the tables of elderly women. They referred to themselves by women's names.

Come and sit on me knee, Betty, tell Ma Millie how you been.

He recalled the duo who busked the streets dressed as washerwomen, and sang outrageous versions of 'Mother Brown' to the accompaniment of a barrel organ and a tiny dog dressed in lace. In his early twenties, before his marriage, he'd regularly passed his evenings in one pub or another, nursing a pint of mild, while some drag act belted out old music hall numbers falsetto-style. He'd never had the money for shows like *Morning Girls, Good Evening Boys* at the Queen's Theatre in Poplar, but he'd always been amused by men dressing up as women. His birds, then his marriage, had got him out of the habit of going to the drag pubs, and for no reason that he could explain the whole scene had lost its shine.

It had never occurred to him that his taste in entertainment signalled anything in particular. In the 1920s and early 1930s nearly everyone went to drag acts. Their popularity had grown out of the music hall tradition. When the music halls began to be converted into picture houses in the early 1920s, dozens of music hall performers were forced to look for work in the pubs and working men's clubs. Among them were singers, sketch actors, burlesques, magicians and illusionists and drag acts. They were part of the East End's social fabric, as unremarkable in 1941 as they had been when Kitty Keys was powdering away her whiskers with a giant puff and belting out the music hall standards when Harold was born. If anyone associated them with homosexuality, then it was only in a barely whispered way.

For one thing, the law on homosexual acts wasn't clear. By 1941, buggery had been illegal for 150 years. The Offences Against the Person Act of 1861, along with Section 11 of the Criminal Law Amendment Act of 1885, made any act of 'gross indecency' between two men, whether private or public, consensual or forced, illegal. The Vagrancy Law Amendment Act of 1898 and the Criminal Law Amendment Act of 1912 rendered persistently importuning for an immoral purpose, cruising or soliciting, a public order offence for which homosexual men could be imprisoned for up to ten years.

It had never been illegal to be homosexual in England, only to do something about it.

Harold Baker didn't know anything about the law, but, like anyone around the East End at that time, he knew that the police almost never enforced it. To have done so, they would have had to close down half the pubs and cafés in the East End. Painted men and men in drag were commonplace, and it was the unspoken rule that so long as men were careful about who they approached, East Enders tolerated them in a way that their better-bred neighbours elsewhere in London never had. Even before the war, there were probably more opportunities to meet other homosexuals, and it was almost certainly less dangerous to conduct liaisons with them in the East End than in any other part of Britain. For hundreds of years the London docks had offered up a ready supply of merchant seamen, dockers and stevedores, creating a vast transient population. All along the river there were pubs where men could meet other men and women could meet other women, and there was no shortage of dark alleyways and cheap hourly rental rooms and public urinals where they might conduct their affairs. They were highly unlikely to be stopped by police. At the time of Harold's birth whole East End districts, among them Poplar, Whitechapel and Bethnal Green, were only very superficially patrolled, and the port police confined themselves to what went on inside the dock walls. Besides, the East End's coppers were notoriously bent. If they did catch two men having sex together, they would often be only too happy to accept payment in return for turning a blind eye.

All the same, everyone saw the papers. The scandal sheets liked nothing better than to report, usually in salacious detail, those cases of homosexual activities that did reach the courts, and everyone knew that the instant your name appeared in those reports, whatever the truth of the matter, you were ruined. In December 1935, a fifty-nine-year-old taxi driver known in police reports, and subsequently in the papers, as Edwin H was arrested with Thomas P, a forty-four-year-old bank messenger, for homosexual acts. The two were remanded on bail and released pending trial. Edwin and Thomas's case never got to trial. A few hours after he was released on bail, Edwin's body was pulled from the Thames. Thomas P was found in the water nearby, barely conscious.

During the blackout in the quiet time just after the Blitz, when almost all the friends, family and neighbours of his earlier life had gone to war or been evacuated or disappeared into their daytime work and their night-time shifts fire-watching or clearing bomb damage, ambulance driving or manning the air-raid warden stations, it seemed to Harold that the old, pre-war life was already a memory. In the deep erasure of the night, it suddenly became possible for Harold to imagine himself as someone completely different.

He was confused, and then confused by his confusion, but he could not get the Woodbine man out of his head. What was wrong with him that he had such longings? It was the war, he decided. Everything was in a state of such upheaval, it was hardly surprising that he was too. It was all so exhausting, a muddle of survival and reinvention, each day a great tangle of new and mundane experience, so much to absorb on top of the ordinary business of getting by. He told himself that his feelings were a phase brought on by the bombings and the absence of his wife, and when the war was over, and Daisy was once more with him, then he wouldn't give this time a second thought. But for now, this other life called him and he found it ever more difficult not to answer its call.

Harold's homosexual adventures began slowly. No one who knew him – not even his most intimate friends and close family – would have thought him in any way altered, and that was, perhaps, because he was not. He smiled, he went to work, he was polite to his customers with their ration cards and cheery on his ARP rounds. The only thing that had changed was that he had woken up to some part of himself that had always been there. The weathered man with his Woodbines may have been the first of his encounters, but he knew even then that it wouldn't be his last. He had no idea how to proceed, only that proceed he must.

On an early evening walk one day, he noticed a man leaving the urinal by the timber yard at the end of Lanrick Road. Nothing unusual about that, except that, shortly afterwards, another man left the same urinal and the two men walked off together. On an impulse Harold followed. The two men continued along the

East India Dock Road eastwards, and after what seemed like – and was – a long time Harold found himself in the ruins of Canning Town. A fog had come down and obscured his view of the men up ahead. His bad leg had begun to throb and he was afraid of falling into one of the many craters left by the Luftwaffe. Looking about for somewhere to rest, he spotted a pub on the corner and went in.

There, in one corner of the public bar, farthest from the door, Harold saw himself; an ordinary man, the kind of everyday man you could see in any pub across the East End, and yet somehow different. The pub, he realised, was full of ordinary different men. Out on the street, at their homes and places of work, in their service uniforms, you wouldn't know these men from any other kind, but here you could tell. Here they stood a little closer to each other, they met each other's eyes. Intrigued, Harold ordered a pint of mild, found himself a seat at a table and watched. Despite all the rubble he had stumbled through to get here, despite the fact that he was a considerable distance from home and it was dark and he was due to sign on for his ARP duties in less than an hour, he felt oddly peaceful.

He went back to the pub in Canning Town and over the course of the next few weeks, by asking the men he met there, he discovered the Liverpool Arms, the Ironbridge Tavern and the Tidal Basin Tavern, and in all these pubs there were men like him, like other men, but different.

Hello, Lola, love, how's yer father off for spots?

Maisie, dearie, give us a song.

Have you traded yet?

Oh, don't touch him, dearie, he's naff. As for that one, I never liked him, though he's got a bona ecaf. Is he to be had? I wonder.

He never told anyone where he was going, and if they asked where he'd been, he would say he'd had to go over to Canning Town to inspect a bus route or along to Orchard Place to help out a clearing team. He found the lies surprisingly easy to tell. How wonderful, how liberating, it was to be able to slip away and indulge his new and as-yet-unexplored self for a while. He hadn't felt this excited for as long as he could remember. An old, long loneliness leaked out of him and other feelings entered to fill the gap; defiance, shame but also excitement, the thrill of recognition.

Eventually, he knew, he would act on his impulses. The chance came on a Friday evening in the midwinter of 1942. A cold, puttyish mist had descended over the East End, and Harold was returning from his warden's shift when his attention was taken by some shadowy thing moving in a shop window. Stopping to get a better look, he caught the eye of a short man in his late thirties or early forties, who immediately took off before slowing down in front of a shop window two doors away. Harold peered inside his own shop window, saw a cat crouched there, then stole a glance in the direction of the short man. The man met his gaze, waited for a second then strolled back and offered a carton of cigarettes.

Out for a walk? he said. *Bleedin' foggy night for it, and all. Can't hardly see nothing.* The man had a grizzled, handsome face, which had seen a good deal of outdoor wear. He was dressed in an old but respectable blue serge jacket and trousers, and looked as though he might once have been a lighterman, before the war intervened, perhaps. He noticed Harold observing him.

Go on, have a smoke, he said.

Harold slowly reached out a hand, keeping his eyes on the man's face. He wanted to extend the moment, to keep the man there for ever, suspended in a state of permanent anticipation which would never need to be met by action.

The man took out a box of matches and struck one on his belt. Harold watched his eyes shift, noticed a mole or some kind of a wart on the left cheek, sensed experience.

I'll go on ahead, the man said finally. He turned and began pitching down the street. For a moment Harold watched him go. His mind seemed incapable of thought. In the end his legs made the decision for him. He began to limp behind, following the man a little way along the road into a small web of courts and rents. He turned right down a blind alleyway. It was so dark now that Harold knew where to stop only from the glow of the man's cigarette.

Come here. He felt a hand drawing him in close, and a rushing sensation in his belly. The man stubbed his cigarette out on the wall and put the stub in his back pocket. He pushed Harold lightly into the wall so that he could feel its green and dampening cold through the gabardine of his jacket. The man's left hand moved down to his waist, then to his groin. Harold felt the breath catching in his throat, the wild fluttering of his chest, his ears and eyes, and was suddenly aware of nothing but the man and the dark space directly around him and everything, himself included, seemed to meld together.

Afterwards, he stood in the foggy air for a while until he could no longer hear the man's footsteps. He walked home by a different route to usual, using his torch with its night cover to negotiate his way through the unfamiliar streets. At Blackwall he dropped down to the river and stood before it for a while, hoping that the air-raid siren might sound and give him something to do. For the first time in what seemed like weeks, it was quiet everywhere, except in his heart.

The following morning he dragged himself from his bed at his usual hour, put on a kettle for his tea and shave and was at Spicer's in good time for the usual eight o'clock opening. At six he returned home, made himself a sandwich, changed into his kit and headed down to the warden station. When the siren sounded he was out on the street filling sandbags. He saw the searchlights go up and block out the stars, followed by the delicate tracings of anti-aircraft fire. For a moment he stood, transfixed, following the powdery columns of light, then he made his way hurriedly down the stairs and into the basement. There he sat through the raid, listening to the men around him swapping their stories of pigeons trained and potatoes grown and football matches attended; stories of lives long since lost. For what seemed like an age Harold did his best to immerse himself in the conversation until, overcome by a sudden wave of tender feeling, he had to bite his lip to stop the tears from forming.

By the time he rose from his bed the following morning Harold knew that there would be other men. It might be months or years before he was approached in the street again, but from the snatched fragments of other men's conversations he had learned that the standing galleries of the picture houses were packed with men made reckless by their desire to escape the rigours of the war. He began to spend what little spare time he had at the Hippodrome and the Troxy. Some nights nothing happened whatsoever; on others he would feel a hand lightly brushed across his body. On a good night the hand would reach in under his coat to touch his skin.

He knew there were places in the West End, like Billie Joice's club in Little Denmark Street, where old music hall stars like Fred Barnes still performed, the Wellington and Lord Hull pubs near the Old Vic theatre and the bar of the Old World Hotel, but he was too timid to leave the comforting familiarity of the East End. Besides, he told himself, he was not a nancy boy, only curious. Around the East End, men began to recognise him. Sometimes he would exchange a few words with them, about the latest bombing or on the progress of the war, but he shied away from gossip on what he considered to be deviant topics. Most of the time he just wanted company. His sexual encounters were usually brief and superficial. Afterwards he would be content to go home alone, clamber into his bed in Bloomsbury Street or head over to Gaselee Street if Franny needed company, and drift off into whatever sleep he could get over the screech of sirens and the harsh coughing of anti-aircraft fire. He felt loved, not by anyone in particular, but in a more general way, and he liked it.

The bedroom antics, as he thought of them, though none had ever actually taken place in a bedroom, were a strange aberration brought on by the freakish conditions in which he found himself. He ignored all evidence to the contrary; the fact, for example, that, despite fumbled attempts at physical intimacy with Daisy, he had never been inside her. Instead he chose to remember their affectionate embraces, the kisses he had left on her lips, the curve of her breasts and the feeling of peace he felt lying beside her, sensing her body float into sleep. Men had *special needs*. He was like this, he told himself, because Daisy was away and he looked forward very much to her return.

The months passed and the war carried on and so did Harold. As the dust settled on the blitzed ruins of what had once been his neighbourhood, it struck Harold very forcefully that he was beginning to get used to the situation. Sights and sounds that would have chilled him to the marrow only a year before – blood splatters on the walls of bombed-out houses, say, or tattered rags of clothing, even the moans of men and women trapped beneath rubble – had now become routine. As he sat in the back room with the Spicers after the shop had closed and listened to the day's news on the wireless, he couldn't help but feel that the war was beginning to suit him.

It wasn't that he didn't miss his old life – he did, or, rather, he missed the people in it. He thought about Daisy and Richie every day and often wrote to them. In these letters he would describe in detail what he had planted in the yard – potatoes and turnips, with cabbages over the Andy. He had joined a pig club in Poplar and would send news about the progress of his pig, and keep his wife and nephew up to date on the various quirks of the lodgers at Bloomsbury Street. He made lists of the meals he had eaten. Egg and rice loaf (good), oatmeal goulash (heavy but filling at least), curried carrots (surprisingly tasty) and dock pudding (the leavings of which even the pig rejected) and he speculated on the greater variety of the country diet. He asked lots of questions – did they have eggs? Was it cold in the hop huts? Where did they bathe? – and looked forward to the replies. He was genuinely curious. He wanted to be included in their lives. He always signed off Daisy's letters *Your ever loving Harold*, and Richie's letters, *Your mum and dad send their love*, though Jack and Franny rarely asked after either Daisy or Richie.

Harold knew his letters were appreciated from the speed with which Daisy and Richie responded to them. Daisy's were full of cheerful details and reassurances. *It ain't all that warm but we are keeping fine with plenty of blankets*; the letters from Richie much shorter with many of the words misspelled in a variety of different ways – *sticulbacks, sticklebats, stiklebacks*.

Every three or four months Harold took the train to Faversham or Selling to visit. He looked forward to these visits with an intensity unmatched even by the discoveries of his new life. Daisy's endless little affirmations of affection, her jaunty, stoic smile, the spirited vitality of his nephew, brought him real pleasure. He made no mention of his other activities, but he didn't feel guilty about them either. He'd cut himself in two and each part was separately happy with itself. The two parts met rarely, and when they did, it caused him such anguish that he saw to it that they were kept apart. However much he delighted in seeing his wife and nephew, a part of him was always glad to leave Selling. He had begun to hate the dank woods with their drab little birds, the stillness and silence and the endless custardy mud, and would find himself standing on the platform straining for the first whisperings of the approaching train.

From the carriage he would watch the figure of his wife slowly diminishing and feel his throat contract with a particular kind of melancholy. And then the greens of the countryside began to be replaced by the drab greys and browns of the suburbs and the smell of cordite and ruin hit his nostrils and he would feel rooted and alive once more. The countryside, he realised, meant nothing to him, except that it currently housed the two people dearest to his heart.

After each visit, he sensed ever more strongly that his wife and nephew would not want to return to Poplar after the war. They had adjusted to their life in the country and were beginning to think of themselves as country people. Yet the thought of his leaving Poplar, of quitting his new world so soon after he had discovered it, left him with a feeling of terrible despair. He pictured himself imprisoned by trees, walled in by fields and finally buried under a wide horizon.

He was sure he couldn't go back to his old life. The war had roused a kind of passion or ambition in him which went beyond sex, and which he knew would never find expression in the countryside; there was now a part of himself that was bold and full of confidence and he was drawn to it with the desperation of a condemned man. It was ironic, but it had taken the war to make him feel alive.

For weeks he lay awake at night or sat on his bench in the Andy considering his options. The solution came to him during the latter half of 1943, when the war started to turn the Allies' way. He would set up by himself. Why not? He was confident that he knew every corner and angle of the business. Prices of bomb-outs were very low, rentals even lower. Through Daisy he had access to farmers and through Jack he knew men in the docks. He thought about all the produce he might obtain – ripe apples, succulent bacon, creamy-headed cauliflowers, treacle, bananas, raisins – and how he might distribute it fairly. Baker's General Stores, or Baker's Grocers, he would call it; or, since that sounded confusing, perhaps simply Harold's. Daisy could give up work at the laundry and do the books – she had the tidy mind for it – and Richie could assist him with stock-taking and deliveries and eventually, perhaps, take over the business altogether. He'd have a yard at the back and a shed and he could breed his canaries there. Every now and then, he might allow himself the indulgence of an evening at the Ironbridge or the Tidal Basin Tavern, but he would see to it that the real or not-so-real or real-but-temporary, nancy-boy aspect of his life, as he thought of it, would end with the war.

He began to put money aside, each week a little more, hiding the proceeds in an old cocoa tin in the Andy, safe from incendiaries and high-explosives. His night-time roamings took on a new purpose. As he wandered, he noted the bombed-out commercial properties. He looked to see where there were close-outs and shut-downs, and he took note of which stores had little remaining stock or had posted *Sorry no credit* signs in the front windows, or had failed to repair minor bomb damage, all indications that they might be doing badly. He prowled and made inventories of distress and only occasionally felt a small piercing stab of shame. One way or another the war had turned everyone in the East End into a predator.

By the middle of 1944 Harold had saved enough money to put the rent down on a modest commercial property in an area blighted by bombing. He had singled out two or three places he considered suitable and made preliminary enquiries as to the availability of leases. He spoke to friends of Jack, who reassured him that if it came through the docks, they could get it for him, and he squared that with his principles. He invested in another two club pigs. He made lists of the legitimate stock he could carry, and which items would be on the ration and which off, and other lists of behind-the-counter stock – American cigarettes, stockings, chewing gum, Jamaican rum, smuggled Canadian bacon – which he would sell for no profit to his regulars. Sitting in the Andy at night he made endless calculations of rent and stock. All he had to do now was to wait for the war to end. Everywhere the Germans were retreating. All he had to do was wait.

CHAPTER 13

While Harold was plotting and saving for the future, the boy who was at the centre of his plans was living for the hour, with no thought of what might come. Richie had changed. The lost boy who had snatched his cardboard case from his aunt, the boy who had been frightened of herons and dogged by a persistent sense of being incomplete, that boy was gone. The great adventure of the war had shaped and matured him and the demands it had made upon him had sharpened his senses and expanded his horizons. The bombing of Canterbury had galvanised him into action. The closer the war had come, or, rather, the more profoundly he awakened to the reality of it, the more he felt a strong and urgent sense of purpose and belonging. He realised that he, Richie Baker, counted, and not just in the lives of his aunt and uncle, to whom he knew that he had always mattered, but in a grander and more abstract way. Old Mr Nutty's drills and spotting rotas had given him a pride in the workings of his mind and body, but it wasn't until the arrival of the refugees from Canterbury that he fully grasped the role he had to play in this war and his portion of the responsibility for its outcome.

In January 1944, the Luftwaffe launched Operation Steinbock, a campaign of attacks and bombing across Kentish towns and villages nicknamed the 'Baby Blitz' by the locals. The RAF's response was to send out squadrons of Mosquito night fighters to engage the enemy. Richie and Col immediately volunteered for extra fire-watching and spotting duties. They knew all the aircraft now, and could distinguish one engine from another. They could sense roughly how high an attack force was flying and whether or not it was likely to be a threat to Selling or Boughton, even before the air-raid sirens sounded. All their training had been suggestive of this moment.

Filled with their new sense of purpose, they reported for duty, collected their binoculars and tin hats and set out for the hop gardens. They named themselves Unit 21 after Richie's hop hut. With air battles taking place high above them, they lay in the slit trenches and watched with mounting indignation at the enemy and a firm resolve to defeat it. Making detailed notes of the events going on above them, they entered into heated discussions with one another on strategy and tactics, everything from the angle at which aircraft must fly to maximise their manoeuvrability to the relative merits of the gun emplacements on the Spitfire Mark XIV versus the Focke-Wulf 190. When the worst of the air battles were over, they would clamber across the fields to Perry's Wood, from where they could view the blazing lights of shells falling across Hellfire Corner from Dover all the way to Maidstone, once more taking careful notes on the frequency and pattern of the attacks.

It was probably no coincidence that it was about this time that Richie discovered girls. His blood was up, his confidence high and he had Col for a co-conspirator. Being older than Richie, Col had left school more than a year ago and taken work as an agricultural labourer. Newly minted and decked out in a second-hand suit, Col had attracted the attentions of a group of local girls who welcomed his company and who would sometimes invite him to dances and other events around Faversham and Selling. At first, Col would invite his friend to come along with him, but Richie felt awkward with girls and had nothing to wear that didn't make him look like the schoolboy he still was. In the year that followed, though, Richie Baker left school, found farm work, grew three inches and developed a furze of facial hair, which he snipped into something that in a dim light might pass for a moustache. Full-time farm work had built his body and, wearing his Grandad Joe's best suit altered by Daisy better to accommodate the style of the times, the fourteen-year-old Richie discovered he could pass for someone four years older.

From time to time one of the villages around would hold a Saturday night dance. On one of these nights, in the midst of the Baby Blitz, the two boys put on their suits, oiled their hair, walked across the fields to the village hall and were admitted without a second glance. It was perfect timing. The Baby Blitz had brought in a new wave of the evacuees escaping the bombing in Kent's ports and large towns, and the new girls immediately gravitated towards the London boys, who seemed daringly raffish and sophisticated. All Richie and Col had to do was to hang around outside the Sonde Arms or the Red Lion on a Friday or Saturday night and, sooner or later, girls would appear. Having the advantage of age and superior income, Col usually got the pick of the bunch, but someone often gravitated towards Richie, who, though younger, was also less edgy and more handsome. His first sexual encounters were confined to 'the rigging', as Col put it, but Richie considered his early explorations in the as-yet-uncharted territory of sex very satisfactory. It was his intention to map out the terrain first, then come back later for the buried treasure.

From evacuees, the boys graduated to chasing Land Girls. The girls had always seemed impossibly remote and glamorous and until now neither of the boys had plucked up the courage to go after them. Some of them, Col claimed, would let you go *below deck*. In 1943, armed with their new-found confidence, they turned their sights on the Land Girls. To the Land Girls they met, Richie and Col were respectively eighteen- and nineteen-year-old railway stokers. On good evenings, they might allow Col to buy them a drink or agree to a dance, but they were still really interested only in soldiers, particularly in Americans, and would melt away the moment a group of servicemen appeared. By spring the situation had become unwinnable. Troop camps had sprung up everywhere, and the dances were so crammed with soldiers that Col and Richie didn't stand a chance. In all those spring months of 1944, only one Land Girl ever agreed to walk out with either of the boys. She was a redhead and her name was Irene. She and Col danced together on a few occasions, and he took her to the pictures in Faversham, but eventually she, too, started going with a GI and disappeared from the scene, leaving the boys to court the local girls once more.

An invasion of France seemed imminent, and those first few days of June before what became the Normandy landings were some of the most intense of Col and Richie's friendship. For a week after news of the first landings broke, they could barely sleep, there were so many facts to accumulate, so many stratagems to rehearse, so much advice to formulate. Re-enacting scenes from the invasion in their minds and chewing over tactics was something solid, almost tangible, now more than at any point in the war so far. For the first time, it seemed almost impossible that the Allies would lose the war. They would be victorious, which meant that, even if only in a small way, Col and Richie would be victors too.

As the war swung decisively in favour of the Allies, Richie began for the first time to think about his future. When the war was over, he'd apprentice to a smithy, he thought, or find work as a gamekeeper on one of the grand estates. The idea of returning to Jack and Franny, or to Poplar and to the docking life his father and his birth had both marked out for him, filled him with terror. Kent was his home now. Maybe, one day, he would settle down, get married and have children here, but the East End of London, with its bombed-out terraces, its broken docks and pinched, sallow-looking people, held no attractions for him.

One afternoon in mid-June Richie was in the hop gardens

hoeing under the bines when he heard a distant and unfamiliar buzz. For a while he ignored it. The success of the Normandy landings had given him a temporary sense of invulnerability, but four years of strafing, dumped bombs and anti-aircraft fire had also made him acutely sensitive to aircraft noise, and when after a few minutes he still couldn't quite identify this particular sound, it began to worry him. Was this some new type of aircraft, he wondered, and, if so, friend or foe? He examined the clouds, looking for clues, and saw high cirrus and, beneath them, an even layer of cumulus. The Germans preferred an overcast day. Maybe it was a German aircraft, then. Sooner or later, he imagined, the sound of anti-aircraft fire would begin. Perhaps the gunners might bring it down. In any case, Selling was unlikely to be its target. He felt himself relax a little and went back to his hoeing.

As the sound drew nearer, though, it separated. There was one familiar growl and another, newer sound, much closer and much, much lower. A Messerschmidt protecting a bomber flying at a higher altitude perhaps? But no, he knew the whine of a Messerschmidt and this was more of a throb or a pulsing buzz. He realised it had been a mistake to ignore the sound and, dropping his hoe, he hurried from the garden and, finding himself at the edge of Big Kel, scanned the sky; but he could see nothing through the cloud cover, only this thick, penetrating throb, louder and louder as if heading directly for the field. He cast his eyes about, considered making a run for one of the slit trenches, trying to recall where the nearest was, then realised there was no time. Dropping to the ground, he covered his head with his hands and awaited his fate, trying not to notice, above the sound of the machine, the thudding of his heart. In a moment, the engine throb became a screech and he felt his whole face tense and raised his hands over his head, waiting for the impact, but as he lay there, almost forgetting to breathe, the shriek transformed into a low growl and began to fade. Whatever it was had gone on its way. He looked up, smelled the air, then gingerly got to his feet, waiting for the sound to disappear; then he picked up his hoe and his training twine and began to run back along the lane towards the field where he knew his aunt was working. Just as he reached Pheasant Field he heard the tremendous and unmistakable roar of an aircraft engine in trouble. This was a very different sound from the previous throbbing, and it sounded German. It, too, seemed to be heading for the exact same spot where he stood. A ball of anxiety fixed itself like a burr to his stomach. His throat swelled. Then the sound dropped and he heard the crash some seconds later, and over the brow of the field saw a pall of cindery smoke rising. He set off for the spot where he imagined the aircraft had landed and found it, or what remained of it, about half an hour later, in a field to the north and west of Boughton. The metal corpse was blackened and there was smoke rising from the impact crater. The plane itself had only partly exploded. It was rather small, with stubby wings, a Henschel or maybe one of the new Focke-Wulfs, he thought; it was difficult to see through the blackening and choking fumes. Spotting Col among the onlookers, he made his way over. Some of the villagers were saying the pilot had been seen dragging an injured arm and running towards the railway line, Col reported; others that he had stolen a horse from Ivy Farm and was heading off on the Faversham Road. Everyone agreed that the earlier throbbing sound had been unrelated to the crash, but for now the immediate drama of the downed aircraft claimed their attention.

In the course of the next week, the rumour spread that the Germans had introduced a new and terrible weapon into the war, the Vergeltung or revenge bomb, a sort of unmanned aircraft armed with a warhead, which they were launching from sites in the Pas de Calais. Richie and Col began to speculate wildly on its features. News got round that the rocket bomb flew in a straight line until it ran out of whatever propelled it, whereupon the engine cut and the bomb plummeted to the ground and detonated where it fell. Already, the V1, or Doodlebug, as it quickly became known, had hit targets in Kent and London, and people quickly learned to dread the moments after the engines cut, for those few seconds of silence were most likely the last remaining fragments of a human life.

For now, though, the locals seemed less concerned about the Doodlebugs than about the pilot of the downed aircraft. A rumour circulated that the Gypsies had taken him in and were offering him protection, and despite the Gypsies' rigorous denials, the rumour persisted. Among those who seemed almost to take pleasure in the Gypsies' supposed treachery were the Wentworths.

Wouldn't surprise me, not in the least, those vardoes keepin' that German pilot, Mrs Wentworth said. They'd never trusted the Gypsies. The hoppers tolerated them, because they supplied rabbits and ducks and stolen chickens and offered other services, like tinkering and knife sharpening and the provision of herbal potions, but real country folk wouldn't have anything to do with anyone with Gypsy blood. They were thieves and villains, and worse than that, they meddled in the occult. Mrs Wentworth herself knew women they'd put hexes on, women who'd then become barren or given birth to dead children, or who themselves died giving birth. If she'd been Winston Churchill, Mrs Wentworth said, she'd have them all locked up along with the other foreigners and throw away the key. *Good riddance.*

The rumours and the gossip spread, and before long people began muttering about taking matters into their own hands and rooting the pilot from the Gypsy camp with guns, if necessary. Richie thought all of this something of an overreaction. He had encountered the Gypsies often over the years in the course of his farm duties; they were always friendly to him and he liked and respected them. It had been a Gypsy boy at Beckton, after all, who had first shown him how to fish and mudlark on the foreshore, and Gypsies here in Kent who had taught him how to follow stoat tracks and lay traps for rabbits. One time, when he'd cut himself badly on a scythe, two Gypsy men had staunched the blood with cobwebs until it could be properly bandaged and may well have saved his life. He knew the locals didn't like them. Whenever anything went missing, it was blamed on the Gypsies, and it was true that if you pushed things too far with Gypsies, you'd feel them closing down on you. The way Richie saw it, they had secrets and they weren't about to give them away, but that did not make them traitors.

To Richie's surprise, Col felt differently. He said he thought it was quite likely that the Gypsies were protecting the German pilot. A few days later he announced his intention to go down to the Gypsy camp and winkle him out and, after he'd winkled him, he'd pin him down and slice his bony body into tiny ribbons. If Richie didn't go with him, then Col would take all the glory himself. Imagine what the Land Girls might do for him then. He'd be going below deck every day of the week if he wanted to. At first Richie resisted. He considered the whole project absurd and pointless. Col had no hope of flushing out the pilot. On the other hand, supposing he did? The thought of Col going below deck while Richie was stuck in the rigging was too grim to contemplate so, after a seemly show of hesitation, Richie agreed to the plan and the very next afternoon the two boys made their way into Perry Wood and stopped in a clearing near the Gypsy camp to pick wild strawberries and discuss tactics. Col was all for launching an immediate attack using a pincer movement to flush the enemy.

Unit 21 will advance upon Target Vardo and engage the enemy. No retreat and no prisoners. He thought about this for a moment. *Except the stinking Jerry.*

Richie wasn't so sure. They were a crafty lot, the Gypsies, and if you wanted to catch them off guard you had to outsmart them. The two boys sat on an old log to eat the strawberries and think further. A kingfisher landed on a low branch on the opposite side of the river and for a moment Richie was reminded of the old, bird-breeding days with his uncle before the war. How much more precious this shiny gem of a bird seemed to him than those insipid little captives. It had a purity the tame birds lacked.

What if we don't find the Jerry? Being the more cautious of the two friends, Richie had thought this several times.

We'll find him all right, Col said, shovelling strawberries into his mouth.

But what if?

Col considered the possiblity.

Then we'll nick something anyway, he said. *That'll teach 'em not to mess around with Unit 21.* To Richie this seemed like an idea rooted in colossal stupidity, but he sensed that Col's evocation of their unit number was a call to unity. They were blood brothers, after all, yoked to one another by all the bonds of fantastical combat.

The boys finished their strawberries and licked the juice from their hands. The mote of sunshine speared a nearby hawthorn and illuminated another dense patch of wild strawberries.

I was thinking, Richie began, *a night raid might be better.* He stood and began to pick the strawberries. Maybe by the evening Col would forget all about the Gypsies.

They returned to their respective billets for tea, but Col came for his friend at nine that evening, ready to put Operation Vardo into action.

The friends walked slowly, cautiously, picking their way through the trees in the moonlight, and approached the Gypsy encampment downwind so as not to alert the dogs. At the edge of the stand of trees marking the outer boundary of the camp, Col motioned for them both to crouch. As the elder of the two, he'd assumed command of Unit 21 some while back and Richie usually deferred to him.

You go in to the east, I'll go west. We'll reconnoitre the exact position of the Jerry. A single whistle is a request for reinforcements. If there's no sign of the Jerry, just take what you can and get out. If caught, fire catapults at will.

Richie made his way along the path of compressed leaf mould to where the hazels and hawthorns gave out. Lamps were burning in most of the Gypsy caravans, but the exterior of the camp was lit only by the tremble of dying embers. A dirty brown dog approached, swinging its head from side to side and wagging a scrappy tail. Richie held out a hand for the animal to sniff, then he began creeping towards the caravan closest to him. A cat scattered and he thought he heard muffled conversation. He realised then that what he was doing had absolutely no purpose and, what was more, he had forgotten his catapult. He would not find the Jerry pilot and he might stir up big trouble for himself. All the same, it would be yellow to pull out now and Col would never forgive him. He moved on, inspecting the pans and knives hanging up on the hooks beside the caravan. He crouched and peered behind the caravan wheels then crept ahead, using the glint of the paintwork in the moonlight to orient himself. Somewhere around the other side of the camp, Col was busy doing the same thing. At the end of the caravan he stood upright, edged forward and raised himself so that he could see inside the window. The curtains were drawn, but through a chink he spotted a woman moving about. He slid forward and tiptoed to the next caravan, then to a third, but detected no sign of the Jerry pilot. Returning to the first caravan, he felt his way along the side where the pots and knives were hanging, reached up, felt for the largest knife, and gently began to unhook it. At least he'd come away with a good prize. His hand was now grasping the knife, but as he pulled it away, the blade clanged into something beside it, which swung and made a ringing sound then clattered to the ground. Richie froze, the large knife still in his hand. A caravan door opened and a Gypsy man appeared holding up a lantern. He tipped down the steps and saw Richie.

Jesus, Mary and Joseph.

For an instant, the Gypsy man disappeared back into the darkness. Richie heard a bell. Other faces appeared at their doors, alerted by the noise, and somewhere in the fringes of the wood a dog began to whine. Suddenly, the first man was pointing at him and shouting something in a language he couldn't understand and the other men were jumping from their caravans and closing in. Richie still held the knife in his hand. This was looking bad. He loosened his grip and held the blade out in front of him, meaning for the men to take it from him. He wanted to say, *Take it, take it*, but the words didn't come. He looked around, in the desperate hope that Col would be somewhere about to explain everything, but the men were closing in on him and he couldn't see around them. He thought about the knife and a wave of panic came over him, then a hard thump landed on his back, pushing him forward. He dropped the knife. A fist curled around his shirt and he found himself being dragged across the packed earth. A hand appeared around his face, crushing his nose. He felt a hard kick and the breath in his chest being sucked out. He stumbled forward and swung upright, swayed back a little, then forward, and all of a sudden, as if propelled by some external source of energy, he found himself lunging forward, arms flailing like a windmill in a hurricane. His right fist connected with flesh and bone then sheared away. He punched blindly with his left, missed and felt an arm reach around from behind, followed by an unbearable pressure on his neck. He was dropping at great speed and reached out his hands, but too late to prevent his face making contact with the ground. He lay there for a moment, conscious of some animal noise issuing from his mouth, then, pushing his throbbing hands into the ground, he raised himself and made to stand up. His head and neck were pounding, he felt dizzy and something on his face was leaking.

The men were standing farther back now; heavy breaths and a low chuckle came at him out of the darkness. He pulled himself fully upright, touched the damp ooze on his face and began to limp back to what he hoped was the edge of the clearing. One of the Gypsies threw something at him which hit him in the back but they did not attempt to follow. Plucking a sycamore leaf from an overhanging branch, he wiped his face so that his shirt would not get dirty. The injury to his back made him unsteady on his feet. He felt dazed and ashamed. For the first time he could remember, he wished his father were with him. Old Jack would have given the Gypsies a run for their money. He'd have shown them the size of a docker's fist.

On the outskirts of Perry Wood he spotted Col. His friend put an arm around his shoulder and helped him walk along the chalk path in the moonlight.

I ain't going back home, he said. He couldn't face Aunt Daisy fussing over him.

All right. Slowly, supporting his friend, he led them to the old barn by the Drawing Room. At the beginning of the war it had been converted into a supplies store, and was secured by a series of intimidating-looking padlocks, but Col knew a place where the clapboard was unsound, and he had soon pulled back the planks to make an entrance. Inside, it was as dark as tar. They found themselves a spot on the floor beside a straw bale and sat with their backs to it.

Christ almighty, Col said. *Them bastard vardoes, eh?*

It was so quiet in the barn that they could hear each other breathing. Col shuffled a little closer.

Ain't so warm in here, he said.

I messed that up, Richie said, *I know I did*.

Col put an arm around his shoulder.

'S'all right, he said, *I don't mind*. He was so close that Richie could feel his breath on his neck. He wanted to pull away, but Col was his friend and he was sure he didn't mean anything by breathing so close.

You hurt bad?

Nah. For some reason that had nothing to do with the pain. He felt uncomfortable, and for a moment thought he might get up and walk back to the huts, but the thought of having to explain the evening's events to his aunt prevented him. This way, she'd assume he'd gone to stay with Col, as he often did. He'd think of something to tell her in the morning.

Let's get some sleep, Col said. He pulled out some straw from the bale and began bundling it up to make a pillow. *Lie down.*

Richie settled his head on the straw bundle. He felt Col's breath on his face and turned away. The two boys lay together, feeling the silence thicken. Col pushed closer to him. Richie could feel his friend's chest and knees pressed against his back. In all the time they'd shared a bed together with Old Wentworth they had never slept this closely. Richie felt Col's breath quicken. His heart was beating very fast.

It's cold, he said. His breath was on the back of Richie's neck. Richie squirmed, trying to remove himself a little without offending his friend. Something unsettling was happening, but he didn't know quite what.

Jeez, Col, he said, *I nearly bayoneted the bastards.* He laughed unconvincingly.

Shh, said Col. Richie felt an arm across his shoulders. He tensed again.

Does it hurt? Col said. Why did he keep asking?

Nah. Richie repeated the lie. He tried to settle himself, but Col's arm was still draped around his shoulder and he didn't want to be mean and remove it. He drew his legs up to his stomach, in part to break contact between the lower part of his body and his friend.

He felt Col shift, and then something unmistakable happened. Col placed his mouth on the back of Richie's neck and kissed him. He followed this kiss with another, then another, working his way round the neck towards Richie's face. For a moment, Richie didn't know what was happening. Then he felt Col's groin, hard, pressed against his back. He bolted upright in an instant and felt his friend's body fall back.

What are you doing?

There was silence. When Col spoke he sounded angry.

Nothing. I ain't doing nothing.

But it wasn't *nothing.* Col knew it wasn't nothing and his friend was lying to him. It was something forbidden, something wrong. Richie jumped to his feet. He stood in the darkness for a moment, shaking, then he said:

I'm going back home.

Col did not answer him or try to stop him, though part of Richie wanted him to. If he could just go back and pretend that what had happened hadn't happened. He hobbled back to hut 21 along chalk roads glowing greenish white in the moonlight. Aunt Daisy was asleep and he managed to get on to his mattress without waking her. In the morning he said:

I fell out of a tree.

That so, his aunt said, giving him extra cocoa.

They did not speak about it again. Later on that day, he saw Col walking down the road beside Pheasant Field, and ducked into a turning till he'd passed. From then on, Richie went out of his way to avoid his former friend, altering his fire-watching and spotting rotas so that they did not coincide with Col's. Once, finding himself in the cookhouse with him, he turned away, and when Col said *All right, Richie?* he answered *Not bad,* and fled. Then he stopped attending Old Mr Nutty's drills altogether. He felt he no longer cared what happened in this endless war, and when Aunt Daisy asked him why Col never came around, he told the truth and said he didn't like him any more.

Doodlebugs continued to fly overhead. A few exploded near by. On 25 August the invasion of Normandy was complete. The hop season came, then fruit picking. On 8 September the first V2 rocket landed in Britain, launched from The Hague, and from then on the V2s continued to rush across the North Downs towards London. The pilot of the Henschel or the Focke-Wulf or whatever it was that had crashed in the hills by Boughton was never found and Richie did not go back to the Gypsies to look for him. At the end of October, he moved with Aunt Daisy into the Wentworths'.

He'd looked forward to this day with a mixture of trepidation and excitement, expecting Col to move in at about the same time. The best part of him was ready for a reconciliation, but the days went by and Col did not appear. In the end, it was Aunt Daisy who brought the subject up with Mrs Wentworth. The old woman looked surprised. She'd assumed they'd heard. Col had gone off to be a Bevin boy in Wales. He was down the pits digging coal. Mrs Wentworth had an address for him if the Bakers would like to write.

Aunt Daisy took down the address. All through that winter Richie wrote letters to his friend, at first accusatory, then later pained and tender, but still he could not bring himself to forgive him and he didn't ask his aunt for the address. Eventually, it was too difficult to continue to think about. His mind closed over first the wound and then the friendship, and it was followed not long after by his heart.

The winter of '44 was wickedly cold. Snow lay across the land in great drifts, obliterating its soft curves. In early January 1945, Uncle Harold arrived for his Christmas visit, delayed by a scarcity of travel permits. His appearance took his nephew by surprise. The man he'd last seen was drawn, yellow skinned and anxious. He looked like a sick canary. This new Uncle Harold was neatly and newly shaven and he'd taken care to slick down what remained of his hair with pomade. He was wearing a sweater Richie had never seen before. There was something unconvincing in his sprightliness, as though all the old clutter were still there somewhere, stuffed inside an internal cupboard, but there was no denying that he looked well and Richie was delighted to see him.

The three Bakers sat around the Wentworths' kitchen table drinking tea while Harold regaled them with stories from home. He'd said often that Poplar was exhausted, but now it was really on its knees. People were so desperate for the sights, smells and tastes of anything that reminded them of how life was before the war that they were prepared to take risks to get it. They concentrated their efforts on food. Looting was not uncommon, even though it carried a jail sentence, and the black market was burgeoning. One old woman had refused to take shelter in Spicer's basement during an air raid, saying she preferred to die with the smell of cinnamon in her nostrils than live with the taste of fear in her mouth. Spicer had had to promise her she'd get some extra cheese if she went to the shelter, and the next day she went and told all her neighbours about the cheese and the following morning the shop was swamped with women refusing to move. Spicer couldn't even call on the police to remove them since he would have opened himself up to charges of black-marketeering or profiteering or wastage, or all three. The following week, the same old woman, seemingly careless of the trouble she'd caused, called round again, but this time Mrs Spicer saw her off. They'd found out later that she'd been to every grocer's within five miles, pulling the same stunt. Every time the air-raid siren sounded, she'd dive into the nearest shop and refuse to take shelter until offered some incentive by an anxious shopkeeper to do so. She'd been dining like a queen in the basement shelters of worried grocers all over the East End for weeks.

Uncle Harold seemed particularly exercised by the D-Day landings. He wanted to know what they'd seen and whether they'd guessed at the reason for the preparations going on all around them. What did Richie think about the Doodlebugs? Had any landed nearby? Richie brushed him off with a few one-line responses and hoped his uncle would leave the subject. Already, the events of the summer seemed remote and he didn't wish to revisit them. Soon enough Harold sensed there was something wrong and began to talk about Poplar again. Of course, he said, he'd painted a bleak picture because he didn't want them to be disappointed. But on the other hand he didn't want to put them off. Everyone was so looking forward to them coming home and it wasn't that bad.

Home. The thought of it made Richie want to scream. It certainly *was* that bad, oh yes, it was.

CHAPTER 14

The Germans' six-month campaign of V2 rocket attacks in late 1944 and early 1945 left 2,754 Londoners dead, but by the end of March 1945 the Allied advance had forced the launchers beyond range. The final two V2s landed on or near their targets on 28 March 1945, one killing Mrs Ivy Millichamp in her home in Elm Grove near Orpington.

At the beginning of April, with the threat from the rockets receding, evacuees began trickling back to London. Among these was Aunt Daisy, eager to return to her Harold. Richie had decided not to go with her. He had no intention of returning to Poplar. In a month he would be fifteen, and capable, he thought, of making his own way in the world. His plan was to continue to work as an agricultural labourer for as long as the farmer would support him. After that he would find a job elsewhere in the area, or perhaps even take up an apprenticeship.

It was while he was working in the fields that he met Col's old girlfriend, Irene, again. More than a year had passed since he'd last seen her. Now she was marching down the lane by Old Ground, still dressed in her Land Girl's uniform, her flaming hair trailing after her like a comet. She looked the same, he thought, the luminous skin betrayed no sign of a year spent in the fields, and he was as forcefully struck by her as he had been when he'd first met her. She was nothing like any of the girls he knew. Sweet though they were, Irene was in a different league She was a real wow.

He called out to her and she slowed. Her hands went to her hips.

Well I never, she said.

Richie smoothed his hair. How he wished he had been wearing his suit, instead of his serge work overalls.

So you ain't in Wales with Colin, then.

No, I ain't, he said. The thought that she might still be in touch with her old beau upset him.

I don't see him no more, he said. *We ain't on speaking terms.*

Oh, she said. She didn't seem troubled by the news either way.

You look different from what I remembered, taller.

He felt warm in the glow of her attention.

I grew a moustache, he said.

She really was beautiful and there was an air of sophistication about her, which set her apart from other girls he knew, made her seem more alluring and a little out of reach.

That's it, she said. *A moustache. Makes you look older.*

He felt a sharp rush to the groin. She smiled at him, but if there was anything in the smile, he couldn't read it.

I'm going to the shop, she said. *Want to come along?*

Richie fell in with her and they walked together along the lane between thick stands of hawthorn blossom. A party of dunnocks skipped in and out of the hedges and there were honey bees massing around the blossom. She started talking but he found it hard to concentrate on what she was saying. To calm himself, he tried to focus on his footsteps on the road and immediately her voice grew sharper. She was in the middle of telling how she'd been posted elsewhere, but had returned to Selling. She had joined the Land Girl Army to avoid being sent into a munitions factory, she said. She knew girls who'd worked in munitions factories. Their skin had gone yellow and their hair had fallen out. She had lied about her age to get in.

She had hated being a Land Girl: the early rises, the roughness of the farmers, the muck and slop of farm life. She couldn't wait for the war to end and for everything to go back to normal so she could return to London.

They reached the little green and he told her he'd wait for her outside the shop. While she was gone he flitted between the hedgerows picking flowers and had a bunch ready in his hand when she emerged. She took them and kissed him once, very lightly, on the cheek, told him she was billeted with Neville and Stella Taylor at Old Oak Farm in Boughton and he should drop by next time he was passing, then she went on her way, leaving his cheek aflame.

Not wishing to seem overzealous, he left it two days before finding an excuse to visit her. He reached the gate to Old Oak, and, ignoring Taylor's old sheepdog, vaulted over the gate and went across the yard. Irene and another girl were standing behind the barn sharing a cigarette.

Having a smoke?

What's it look like? Irene looked up at him through red lashes. The girl beside her sniggered and Irene introduced her as Dolly.

Richie said it was nice to meet her and Dolly said, *Likewise, I'm sure.*

It's a wonder that anything's nice any more, ain't it? Irene said. She gave Richie a flirtatious look as she said this. He shifted uncomfortably. She had been sweeter with him when they had met in the lane. It was the presence of Dolly, he presumed, which gave her this rather alarming confidence. She flicked her cigarette to the floor and extinguished it with a twist of her foot. Richie pulled another from his pocket and held it out to her, then instantly regretted it, for she would now guess that he bought his cigarettes in singles. He checked himself, hoping that his excuse for coming would impress her. It was his trump card and now he played it.

Here, he said. *I just come this minute from the radio. They made an announcement. Hitler's gone, he's dead. They made an announcement.*

He waited for the import of this news – and of its bearer – to sink in.

Well, good riddance to him, said Irene briskly, as though it was not of enough significance to be dwelt upon. She leaned forward and took the cigarette from his hand.

Let's smoke to the death of the old bugger, she said. For a moment her fingers brushed against his. Light, long fingers with strong, even nails. She put the cigarette to her lips and waited. He realised she was waiting for him to offer her a light. He felt himself blushing and his throat tightened. He remembered then that he hadn't offered Dolly a cigarette and didn't know what to do first, light Irene's cigarette or offer Dolly his smoke and risk offending Irene. He looked at Dolly standing by, expectantly. She had a round, jolly face and the air of someone who could take a joke against herself. In that moment he realised that she understood his dilemma.

You two can smoke if you like, she said, winking at him. *I'll wait for a drink*.

That's the difference between me and Dolly, Irene said. *She'll wait but I won't*.

There was no sleep for Richie that night. His encounter with Irene had left him so helplessly aroused that he couldn't bear to contemplate wasting a moment in sleep. Everything about her moved him; the feel of her fingers against his, the shape of her mouth as she smoked, her mix of sweetness and flirtation. He feared that his groin was in danger of separating from his body and making its way to Old Oak Farm without him. The following day he was of no use to anyone, stumbling over his tasks, unable to concentrate and so distracted that he didn't even hear the bell calling him for his lunch. The moment he'd finished his chores in the afternoon he ran to Old Oak as fast as his legs would take him, only to be told that the girls had gone into Faversham to celebrate the fall of Berlin at the hands of the Russians. He hadn't heard anything about Berlin and the Russians and cursed himself for not paying attention. If there was good news going, he wanted to be the first to tell Irene.

When he went round to Old Oak Farm again the next evening, a Thursday, the girls were standing beside the barn, smoking. He listened to them talk among themselves for a while, wondering how it was that girls never ran out of things to say. Finally, he got up the courage to ask whether they liked swimming and when it turned out that they did, he asked them whether they'd like to go with him at the weekend and they said that yes, they would like that. They'd like it very much. And so it was decided.

Sunday, 6 May was bright, with high, perfect clouds sailing across the sky in a fresh breeze. Leading Irene and Dolly through a dappled tangle of wood and across a field planted with wheat to the other side, he brought them to the chalk road that led down from the great grey house and the Drawing Room to the willows beside Ghost Hole Pond. One at a time he took them by the hand and escorted them along the spongy bank to the far side, where willow branches bent down and obscured the road. Was he imagining that, as he led Irene, she squeezed his fingers? The thought made his body strain against itself, as though a creature had risen up inside him and was trying to break from its cage.

The girls sat down, removed their boots then their socks, and for a seeond or two, Richie caught a glimpse of the sweet, cool tenderness of Irene's feet before they were lost to the water. He remembered the poor drowned girl, the murdered daughter of a hopper, whose body still rested somewhere in the slime at the bottom. All through the early, bitter years of the war he and Col had kept her company. But he hadn't thought about her in months, and since he and Col had ceased to be friends he had not been to the pond. Fragments of his world had splintered off, one by one, and been lost to him. First Ghost Hole Pond, then the plum orchard where he and Col used to scrump for fruit, the fields beyond Boughton where they went rabbiting, Hogben's Hill where the aircraft crashed and the clearing in the woods where the Gypsy encampment used to be. Richie had avoided all the old haunts until this new and overwhelming need to win Irene had brought him back here.

The girls dried themselves, fussed about making a blanket of leaves and unpacked the cold mashed-potato rissoles they had brought for their picnic lunch. It was a perfect scene, a golden moment; two girls and a young man, sitting beside the water in the dappled shade of the willows, on what was to be the final day of the European war.

Suddenly, a group of Gypsy children passed them by, pointed, then ran off giggling.

Look at them Gypsies, Irene scoffed, *living in the woods like pigs*.

They carried on with their picnic but some thin thread of magic had been broken. Eventually, the girls packed up and left.

In what remained of the light, Richie took himself back to the field where the aircraft had come down the year before, and he watched the rabbits nibble at the vegetation that had grown over the impact crater, but he wasn't thinking about the aircraft or the war, or even about Col for that matter. For hours already his mind had replayed the scene by the pool, when Irene's feet disappeared under the water, and he replayed it now, over and over.

The next day, Monday, 7 May 1945, General Alfred Jodl signed Germany's unconditional surrender at Reims. The war in Europe was over.

The village of Selling celebrated VE day on the green in Selling, beside the Sonde Arms. Across the downs people were lighting fires. From Dover all the way to London fireworks and flares sparked, guns sounded. Everyone drank warm beer and they sang till the night faded into the grey dawn. All the old songs they sang and some of the new ones: 'Hang Out Your Washing', 'Keep the Home Fires Burning', 'Run Rabbit Run', 'We'll Meet

Again' and, of course, 'The White Cliffs of Dover', war songs that were once battle cries and now sounded like victory marches. And when the night was done, with Irene standing beside him, Richie took advantage of the moment, leaned in and kissed her.

The following morning at lunchtime, Richie made his way to Old Oak Farm with half a National loaf, a basket of eggs, some bacon and an old frying pan of Aunt Daisy's that had been so burned and charred over its years of service on open fires that she had given it to her nephew rather than take it back to London. He wandered with Irene along the lanes, past the first hazel blossoms, past hornbeams and hawthorns vivid with new leaves. He took her along a path running through dizzy washes of bluebells. They kissed again, then some more. She pushed him away, but in a friendly, flirtatious way, letting him know that she was playing with him rather than brushing him off. She watched contentedly while he built a little fire and began to fry the bacon and eggs for their lunch. As always at this time of year, in this part of the East Downs, the air was beginning to wear its hoppy summer pelt, but there was a breeze too, which brought with it the fresh tang of the distant sea. As the smell of bacon wafted upwards, he wanted to tell her about the loveliness of the downs, the winding lanes between sweet chestnut coppices, the beauty of the orchards in blossom, the way the cobnut trees, the fruit orchards and the hop gardens were so meticulously set in the sheltered hollows between the grassland and the scarp, but he didn't have the words.

As they ate, Irene said:

It's a wonder you ain't gone mad living here.

Perhaps I have, he said. She laughed but her voice sounded wary.

Earlier on he'd found a few early strawberries and he offered them to her now.

This dump, I can't hardly stomach it, she said, reaching over and plopping a berry in her mouth. She made a face and spat the berry out again. *Bleedin' mud and bleedin' cows. I'm sick of it.*

Richie reeled and tried to swallow back the disappointment her words had inadvertently made rise. So she hated it, then, this place that he had come to love so much. But how? He thought back to the days before the war. Nearly five years in the country had washed all traces of the city from him. He could kill a rabbit with his thumb and forefinger and barely feel his heartbeat rise, but the sight of a blue tit struggling to protect its eggs from a jay could drive him close to tears. But it hadn't always been like that. He thought back to his first months at Selling, to the grinding damp and cold, the relentless, earthy farmyard stench and the invisible air. Perhaps Irene was right and he'd been tricked by the war and its necessary compromises. Perhaps the countryside *was* terrible and he'd just become used to its terribleness. Suddenly, life in Kent seemed very small. What had he learned? How to spread muck, strangle rabbits and whittle clothes pegs. Was that all?

What about you? she said. Richie shoved his hands deep into his pockets. He thought about the places in the East End he and Irene might go; the dog track, the pictures, the music hall, the puck-a-poo cafés and the boxing. He could take her up West to a show, to the theatre even. Afterwards he'd buy her a port and lemon and a paper tray of jellied eels and they'd go back to Poplar and watch the ships coming in.

I ain't sure yet, he said. *But perhaps I'll set up in business.* The moment he said it he knew he sounded ridiculous. A country boy in business? He dared not look at Irene. If she had any sense she would be trying not to laugh. Silence fell for a while. Out of the corner of his eye he saw Irene tying her scarf tighter around her hair.

Well, good for you, she said at last.

He looked at her full in the face but saw no trace of ridicule in it, and in that moment he knew he loved her.

As the summer progressed, and the war with Japan began to edge towards its spectacular and dreadful conclusion, Richie and

Irene roamed the fields and swam in Ghost Hole Pond and lay in the straw together, with their faces to the sun, oblivious to anything but the thick pulse of their hearts. The weary, war-torn world seemed magical. When they each laughed at nothing it was always the same nothing. When something caught their attention, it captured them both. Here, now, they were completely and perfectly happy, and the heat and light of their happiness seemed to light and warm everything about them. Like all young lovers, they saw no reason to imagine a time when that might not be so. Why imagine it? Why imagine it when the sun was shining and they were young and healthy and the vicious war was grinding to an end and making victors of them. Everything that had gone before, all their past desires and disappointments, all the horror and excitement of the war, it was all obliterated. Their future lay in whatever reached out from this present moment. The world had shrunk to an infinity of two. No one and nothing mattered but Richie and Irene.

The intensity of Richie's desire came as a relief to him. He'd been frightened by the incident with Col. He thought of his friend very little, but when he did now, it was with pity rather than in anger. How could he ever have considered himself complete in their friendship? Had he been so blinded by the illusion of fulfilment he'd felt in Col's company that he really hadn't noticed that Col was in love with him? That, even as his friend had courted Irene, the object of his desire had not been Irene at all, but Richie? Col had humiliated them both. He'd done it as a cover for his own pitiful perversions. He would never, ever mention the incident in the barn to Irene, not for as long as he lived. He was sorry for Col, he really was. But he wished never to see him or his like again.

The hops ripened early that year. By mid-August hoppers were already busy whitewashing their huts and setting down rugs on the floors. Aunt Daisy arrived. Lilly followed along with Susan and Grace and a pregnant Minnie and Daisy's cousin Iris, whose son Tommy had taken Richie egg collecting before the war. Most servicemen had yet to be demobbed, so the Land Girls took on the jobs done by men before the war, as they had every year, and Irene set to the task of bine cutting. Despite working in a reserved occupation, Michael the bine cutter had signed up in 1943 and had been killed at the battle of Monte Cassino a year later, and they hadn't yet found a replacement for him.

To Richie, newly in love, the presence of the hoppers seemed an irritating irrelevance, a small subplot in the great drama that was his love for Irene.

Aunt Daisy had little to do with him this year. Though she was too discreet, too loyal, ever to say so, Richie sensed something in her manner suggesting she did not approve of Irene, and, with the self-absorption of the young lover, this made him like her less. She left before the fruit picking. There was too much to be done at home and she'd been away from Harold long enough. *Besides*, she said, *Richie's uncle had plans.* The word clattered around Richie's head. He wanted it to be made clear to Harold that he was not to be included in any plans. He had plans of his own. He could tell that his aunt was wounded by the news, but she pretended not to be. She left on a Sunday in mid-September but Richie did not go to the station to wave her off because he had already arranged to see Irene and did not want to lose a minute of his time with her.

A busy week followed. There were Bramleys and Forges to bring in, along with some of the pears. Then there were cobnuts and hazels to harvest and autumn planting to be done, cows to milk and pigs and sheep to ready for slaughter, and all the old, uncompromising routine of the land to attend to. Not once in the week did he manage to get to see Irene but he thought of little else, and the moment he was let free from his chores on Friday, he scrubbed himself down and, flinging on his suit and grabbing his torch, for it was getting dark early now, he hurried to Old Oak Farm with his wages jangling in his pocket. The old sheepdog came swinging out to meet him, thumping its tail.

Reenie! He had taken to calling her Reenie after their first proper caress. He didn't like to think of what they'd done as *going up the rigging*, in part because it seemed crude and somehow disloyal and in part because the phrase was Col's. In any case, he had not, as yet, *gone below deck*, though, of late, he had kindled hopes.

After a few moments Dolly emerged from the barn holding a lamp. She'd been squeezed out, rather, during the summer, but had never complained. Richie was grateful to her for that. She was giving by nature. One day, he thought, she'd make someone a loyal and loving wife and he hoped he'd see the day.

Where's Reenie?

She gave an amused snort, somewhere between affection and irritation.

Now you ask, I'm doing all right, she said. *Just dandy.*

He grimaced, but stood his ground.

Irene ain't here.

He felt his stomach slide. Hadn't they agreed last Sunday to meet on Friday? Had he got it wrong?

Where is she, then?

Dolly sighed.

You ain't gonna like where, she said.

Flashes of possibility burst across his mind. She'd gone back to Col? To the GI?

A letter come for her Wednesday, Dolly said. *She's gone back to London.*

Letter? Richie felt floored. She had left him for a *letter?* Was it family news? He imagined some small and temporary crisis.

Dolly registered his bewilderment and panic, and softened.

Commercial school, remember?

He let the words sink in for a moment, but no, he didn't remember.

You got a ciggy? Dolly said.

Irritated that the conversation had been stalled, Richie fumbled in his pocket, pulled out a single cigarette and thrust it at her. He waited for her to light it and take the first drag.

You know, she said, finally. *That commercial school what she was all for applying to, the letter finally come.*

Richie stepped back, away from the light of the lantern, as though the effort of trawling his memory would be assisted by a physical move in the right direction. He thought for a while but still he could not remember one time, a single moment, in all their months together, when Irene had so much as mentioned commercial school. Dolly sensed his discomfort. She took a long drag on her cigarette then stubbed it out on the gatepost and flipped the stub behind her ear.

Wait here, she said. She went back into the barn and came out a few moments later with a piece of paper on which she had written Irene's address in Stepney. Richie read it in the light of Dolly's lantern. He thought of her there, in the East End, marching down the bombed streets, her hair setting the air alight. His chest felt heavy, his throat tight. Then something struck him. He and Irene had been together for five months but she had never given him her home address.

By Saturday lunchtime he was on a train. He clambered out on to the platform at London Bridge in a daze. The bus took him through Wapping, Shadwell and Limehouse, each district more shattered than the last. In Poplar, streets that had been as familiar to him as the freckles on Irene's face had gone completely, in their place fields of rubble where buddleia and rosebay willowherb had self-seeded. Some had already been dug up and cultivated. The streets that had survived intact were ragged and filthy with dust, the pavements as rucked as hammered toffee. Parades of shops stood empty, where their owners had gone to war or simply given up and gone, leaving the flats above them boarded up. Those that remained open assumed a desolate air, and the men and women walking beside them were the shape and colour of ghosts.

He entered number 7 Bloomsbury Street in silence. After years of dust and lodgers, the place looked unkempt, the windows dust-laden, the step a mouldy grey. He was shocked by how dark and cramped the passageway seemed. There were cobwebs over the gas lamps and the linoleum had begun to crack. Uncle Harold and Aunt Daisy were very pleased to see him. Aunt Daisy put the kettle on and cut some cold slices off an onion-and-barley loaf. Harold had fetched some of his birds back from Essex and set their cages in the living room and there was a good deal of twittering. *It's That Man Again* came on the radio.

I don't mind if I do, Harold said, swiping a slice of loaf.

It's being so cheerful as keeps me going, said Daisy, pouring the tea.

They laughed at the repetition of the catchphrases and, to be obliging, Richie laughed with them.

So, sonny boy, what brings you here? Uncle Harold said. *Not that you ain't welcome, son. You're always welcome.*

Richie shrugged; he didn't want to get into any kind of conversation. He would make time for his uncle and aunt later. For now, he needed to see Irene. He intended to finish his tea and head directly out to the address Dolly had written down for him. As he drank and ate, his head spinning with excuses for leaving, Uncle Harold drew his chair closer and in a confidential tone he said:

Since you're here, your aunt and I have something we want to tell you. Harold nodded at Daisy, who nodded back. Richie felt his heart sink, but there was no way he could get out of it now. *The war had created opportunities*, Harold said, and he meant to take advantage of them. He'd done his research and discovered that commercial property situated close to bomb sites could be had at rock-bottom rents. Since the East End was one big bomb site, it meant that there were a lot of bargains waiting to be snapped up. Now the war was well and truly over, he supposed that people would be wanting two things: homes and good food. Why? Because that's what they'd been denied. If he, Harold, had had a penny for every time someone had come into Spicer's over the past few years, begging for soused herrings, potted shrimps, jellied eels or salty brawn, Eccles cakes and jam doughnuts, liquorice, cough candy, white bread and real butter, eggs and gammon ham, sugar, treacle toffee, peanut brittle, mint crèmes and Parma violets at any price, then he, Harold, would be as rich as Devon fudge. No question: the opportunities were in food and homes. Now, he didn't know anything much about homes, but he did know about food. He knew how to get it and what to charge for it. He understood inventory and storage and stock management. He was going to set up a shop. It was all very hush-hush – not even Daisy had known until very recently. He hadn't wanted to upset the Spicers because they'd been good to him. He'd been saving to be able to put down the first few months' rental and invest in some stock. Baker's General Stores, he thought, or something like it. He knew Richie was fond of the country-side, but now he'd come back to London, his future was all there for the taking. He'd have to start out small but in a few years from now, he could find himself general manager of Baker's General Stores.

Richie listened to his uncle with growing astonishment. Harold Baker, shop owner? It sounded almost as unlikely as Harold Baker, prizefighter, or Harold Baker, prime minister. The news confused him. He had come to London to persuade Irene to come back to him. Then he intended to return to Kent and take her with him. He hadn't bargained for this and he didn't know what to say. He didn't want to disappoint his uncle. For the longest time he sat speechless, idly staring at the pattern of tea leaves in his cup. Eventually his aunt said:

You won't find no answer there, duck. Tell you what, why don't yer think about it?

He nodded and stood to go.

I'm going up Gaselee Street, see me mum and dad, he said.

At the top of Bloomsbury Street he turned right and picked up the bus to Stepney. Irene's road was one in the maze of streets that spread out south from Stepney Green towards the river. Richie picked his way through the rubble. Barely a single street remained intact. His uncle had said that the housing stock had been so badly built that much of it had collapsed from the vibrations during the bombing. He found Irene's house and, trembling, rang the doorbell. After a while, an elderly woman answered the door. He asked for Irene and the woman said:

She ain't here, I don't know where she is, you'll have to fetch back later and ask her mother.

He thanked the woman and walked back east towards Mile End, then turned south, through Poplar and down Brunswick Street to Franny and Jack's house. This, too, had escaped the bombing, though the two windowpanes in the front bay had been blown in and the pieces of a dismantled tea chest which were now nailed in their place were grey with mould. The front door was open and he entered without knocking. The interior of the house gave the appearance of not having been cleaned in months, and not even the dimmed light could obscure the choking smell of rotten coal dust and the acrid tang of stale beer. Hearing the front door open, Jack suddenly appeared from the living room. Richie barely recognised him. His face was puffed and venous and a sweaty film failed to conceal the pores that had opened up on his nose and around fatty yellowed eyes. Most of his hair had gone and he scraped almost continuously at what remained. He greeted his son with a pat on the back and Richie felt his hand tremble. They went into the living room. A dank and smelly draught leaked in from the front. Franny was sitting in her chair, mending something. She had grown gaunt and drab; the last vestiges of her beauty, still startling even on Richie's visit the previous year, now clung to her face like a fragile coating of fine powder. For the first time in his life, Richie felt sorry for his parents. He sat and drank the tea Franny made and allowed such conversation as there was to wash over him, imagining himself in Irene's arms.

As soon as it was polite, he made his excuses and left. He took the bus back up to Stepney and knocked on Irene's door, but this time no one answered.

CHAPTER 15

Uncle Harold wanted to take his nephew on a tour of what he referred to as Richie's future, and Richie didn't have the heart to say no. They trudged through the tumbledown streets with their blown-out buildings, Uncle Harold cheerfully pointing out one crumbled shopfront after another, checking off his list of opportunities considered and rejected. From the neutral expression on Harold's face it was apparent to Richie that the rubble and wreckage of the bombing appeared normal to him, where all Richie saw was ruin. Eventually, they reached the shop Harold had it in mind to rent. It was set on the corner of one of the side streets leading off the East India Dock Road. The frontage itself was relatively unspoiled, though there was a long crack in some of the glass, and the paint was peeling. It had been a grocer's before the war, Harold explained, part of a larger parade including a tobacconist, a café, an ironmongery, a men's outfitters, a pie-and-mash shop and a pawnbroker's. Now it was in a row of three, the rest on either side having been blown up or burned down. It was the location which had caught Harold's attention, surrounded as it was by factories and houses and only a stone's throw from the docks. On account of the disappearance of its neighbours, the rent was cheap. He had already registered his interest with the landlord. It would take him a few months longer to save up the requisite rent, but the place had excellent prospects. Uncle Harold swept his hand over the shop sign hanging over the door.

Baker's General Store, I can see it now.

After the tour of his future, Richie left his uncle and walked along dusty, rubbled streets to Irene's house in Stepney. A stout, middle-aged woman answered the door – her mother, he supposed, from the colour of her hair – and looked at him warily, but when he introduced himself, she registered the name as though it was familiar. Irene was living in East Ham with an aunt near the commercial school, she said, but she seemed reluctant to give him an address. He asked whether he could write to Irene and requested that she pass the letters on. This she agreed to, adding that she didn't think anything would come of it because Irene had started walking out with a very nice boy from a respectable family. She whispered the word *respectable* as though it were a description of something holy and could not be mixed in with the ordinary verbal pollution of daily life.

The news hit Richie hard, but he managed to keep his feelings from his face; he wasn't going to give Irene's mother the satisfaction of seeing him crumble.

He walked round the streets for a while to give himself thinking time. Of course he was jealous of this other boy, the *respectable* one, but it wasn't as though Irene hadn't had boyfriends before he'd met her, so he knew she was the kind of girl who didn't like to be on her own. As for the boy, what boy wouldn't want to walk out with Irene? At least now he had a connection to Irene through her mother. The basic facts remained unchanged. Irene belonged to *him*, it was *him* she loved. The other boy, the respectable one, was some fancy to pass the time. He wandered on towards the East India. What a life he'd have had if the war had not interrupted it, working behind those huge crumbling walls, doing what his father did, and his father before him. He stood and watched the dockers coming and going in their shabby clothes, proud eyed and broken gaited, with immaculately laundered handkerchiefs in their top pockets. He knew the handkerchiefs signalled belonging and self-respect, but to him they suddenly looked like the flags of surrender. He thought about his Uncle Harold's proposition. It didn't seem so bad now. He turned back towards Bloomsbury Street. By the time he reached number 7 he'd decided. He told his uncle to count him in. Then he wrote to Irene saying he was pursuing a business opportunity and, once he was settled, he would come for her.

Some days later a reply arrived. It didn't say much. Irene was enjoying commercial school and had made a number of new friends. Her training was keeping her extremely busy – they gave you all sorts of work to do out of school hours – and she had very little time to herself. She made no mention of the respectable boy and Richie took this to mean that she was no longer seeing him. Feeling buoyant, he took himself down to the empty shop his uncle had shown him and looked at it with new eyes. What was the countryside to him anyway? What did it matter where he was so long as Irene was with him? With her, anything was bearable, he thought. Even this.

While they were waiting for Harold to save the last few pounds he needed, Richie went to work in Spicer's as a delivery and errand boy. He and his uncle quickly settled into a routine. Arriving at the store, his uncle would open up, while Richie checked the mousetraps and laid new bait. Then he'd sweep and polish the parquet flooring, wash the pavement outside the shop and, in fine weather, put out the display bench and stack it with items from stock. In the afternoons, he went delivering. At six thirty he would help Harold fold the flour, rice and sugar sacks, return the butter and cheese to the cold room and lock up the store, then uncle and nephew would join the flow of thin, sallow-faced men and women making their way along the Commercial Road back home. Aunt Daisy would greet them with a hot meal of bacon pud or a rissole made from the dense, liverish fish that everybody knew, but never said, was whale, and while she was doing the washing up and Harold was sorting his accounts, Richie would feed and water the birds and clean out their cages. Afterwards, he and his uncle might go down to look at the shop, stopping off in the Resolute for drink. Sometimes, they'd go on from there to the Crown in Sclater Street and discuss the husbanding of canaries, budgerigars and finches. His uncle didn't seem to notice that Richie was no longer interested in these conversations, nor much in the birds themselves, which, when compared to the wild birds of east Kent, seem artificial and pointless.

They kept their plans a secret from Spicer.

Another few months, just you wait, Uncle Harold would say. He'd lean in and pinch his nephew on the cheek.

And so month after dreary month passed, the seasons slipped by unnoticed, the streets remained the same grey tumble of smuts and rubble, the men and women the same half-starved bunch it seemed by now that they had always been. Nothing much of interest happened, but Uncle Harold held fast to his dream. One particular evening, as he and Richie reached the top of Bloomsbury Street, Harold turned and said:

How's about calling the place Baker and Son?

To keep himself sane, Richie daydreamed about Irene. He continued to write to her regularly, though the replies came less often now. Several times, Richie begged her to allow him to visit, but each time the stiffness of the reply was its own clear message. He figured that she was terribly busy at commercial school and wanted to finish there and to establish herself in a job before she turned her thoughts to settling down. He didn't blame her. Wasn't he doing the same, after all?

Only one incident stuck firmly in Richie's mind from that period. It happened one afternoon in the summer of 1946. Richie was sweeping the parquet floor at Spicer's and Uncle Harold was behind the counter counting bars of laundry soap when the bell above the door clanged and a tall man with a soft smile walked in. There was something about this man, in the way he walked, loose hipped and with a swinging motion, which made him stand out from the usual run of customers. And it wasn't only Richie who noticed. From the opposite corner of the room where he was slicing cheese into neat and exact two-ounce ration-ready slices, Spicer looked up and stared momentarily. The man sauntered up to where Uncle Harold was stacking soap and said:

Hello, dearie.

That was it, that was all he said, but it was the velvety, almost flirtatious voice in which he said it which struck Richie.

Putting down his soap, Harold went around to the front of the counter.

Can I help you, sir? Nothing out of the ordinary in that, except that while he was speaking, it seemed to Richie that Harold was trying, as subtly and discreetly as he could, to herd the man towards the door, but, instead of being driven back, the tall man moved closer and, leaning forward, whispered something in Harold's ear. Richie saw his uncle turn, flustered, and quickly limp back behind the counter, as though trying to protect himself, but the man followed him, still talking. His voice had taken a hostile tone, and he was speaking in a foreign language now. Richie saw his uncle cringe then blush. Reaching for his pocket, Harold took out a wad of money and handed it over to him. The man inspected the wad, nodded, smiled, then turned and sauntered slowly out of the door, leaving Harold standing stiff and poised, as if waiting for something that had already happened. For a few minutes he just stood there, then he returned to his soap, but as he did so, Richie noticed he was shaking.

No reference was made to the event that evening, or afterwards, and Richie put it to the back of his mind. He got on with his work and tried to pretend he was happy in the city, though the smallest thing could still bring back Kent so vividly and forcefully to mind that it winded him. Walking past Charrington's, say, the smell of hops would hit him and suddenly he was in the gardens pinching cones. Sweeping manure from the road to take to the allotment his uncle had taken on, his mind would wander to the broad, hawthorn-hedged fields, churned and mulched, awaiting the slow, steady thud of a pair of Suffolk Punches. So taken was he with the scene before him that he would forget where he was and once narrowly missed an oncoming bus.

The winter progressed; 1946 became 1947. On a freezing morning in the middle of January, Richie and Harold arrived at the shop to find two policemen waiting. They asked to see Richie and Uncle Harold in private and as they all made their way into the back room, Richie felt his pulse quicken. He hadn't been mudlarking in years and he'd stopped pilfering, so what could the police possibly want with him? The thought crossed his mind that Col had reported him and that the police were about to arrest him for being a nancy and a great swell of fear rose up and he felt like a tug caught in the wake of a vast and sinister ship.

In the back room, the policemen broke the news. The body of Jack Baker had been found early that morning by a passing baker's apprentice in a small turning in Limehouse, partially buried in a pile of bomb-damaged bricks. The police said it looked as though Jack had stumbled into the turning drunk and had managed to dislodge a pile of rubble. He'd lain there for a while, unconscious most likely, then had been sick. It appeared that he had choked on his vomit.

Richie heard his uncle thanking the policemen and watched them leave the room. He felt oddly unmoved by the news. It seemed abstract, as though it wasn't about him. If he felt anything, it was relief. Uncle Harold, on the other hand, seemed floored. He sat down on Mrs Spicer's chair, head in hands, sobbing, and when Richie went to pat him on the back, he grabbed his nephew's hand and held it to his face.

The funeral was held at East London Cemetery. More than

a dozen of Jack's drinking friends turned up, ate all the Spam-and-mustard sandwiches and drank so much beer that they forgot they were at a wake and started a brawl. Asking around the West India in the week after the death, Richie and Harold discovered that at the time of his death Jack Baker had been hocked to the hairs on his head. He'd had something of a gambling habit, which he'd always kept secret from the family. He'd borrowed from a number of unsavoury sources and now they all wanted paying back.

Franny was hysterical about the news. It wasn't a woman's job to understand money, she said, it wasn't fair, the situation Jack had left her in.

In order to keep Jack's creditors at bay, she sold her furniture and the trousseau she had taken from Elsie's drawer all those years before, along with her little mink and the dog brooch Ruben had given her, and moved into number 7 Bloomsbury Street to save the rent. Harold paid off the remainder of Jack's considerable debt from his savings for the shop and, when that proved inadequate, he took out a loan from Mr Spicer to cover the remainder.

Not long afterwards, the little shop on the corner of the East India was rented out to an outsider from Hackney, who turned it into a cobbler's and engraving business.

After Jack's funeral, Richie wrote to Irene with the news. He needed to know she loved him and that, once she'd finished commercial school and he'd found work, they would be together. The collapse of his uncle's plans was a blow, but not one Richie would allow to soften his resolve. He wanted Irene to know that he was prepared to do whatever it might take to make her happy, even if that meant following his father into the docks for a while. At Jack's funeral, his father's old gang had promised to take him on if that was what he wanted. In less than a year, when he was eighteen, he would be called up for his National Service, and who knew what opportunities might present themselves then to a young, healthy man like himself. He might end up running a farm in the colonies. He could see himself swanning around India, with tea and servants on tap. He would write to Irene on embossed notepaper sprinkled with exotic perfume, sending money for her to join him.

He waited two weeks after posting the letter and, when he got no reply, he went round to Irene's mother's address in Stepney, but Irene's mother said it had been a while since she'd heard from her daughter and that Irene had always been *the sort to go her own way.* He took a bus to East Ham and found the commercial school but the secretary said that Irene had already left and the only forwarding address they had for her was her mother's. They kept a list of employers who often recruited to their typing pools from the school's graduates, but they didn't know whether she'd got a job with any of them. He took the list all the same. It was mostly big firms – Shell, Keiler's, Venasta's, British Petroleum – based in the East End and in the City, and over the next week or two Richie worked his way down it in his lunch breaks or during his deliveries, asking for Irene by name; but no one had ever heard of her. He wondered, with a sinking heart, whether it was something he had said or done.

The months that followed were desperate ones for Richie. Irene was seldom out of his mind and he determined to put all his spare money and energy into finding her. Back and forth he went to the firms on the list, then to the school itself. Once he took a train back to Selling and knocked at the door of Old Oak Farm, but no one there knew the whereabouts of Irene or Dolly. He tried to find the Land Girl Army office, but it had been disbanded and its archives dispersed. He kicked himself for never having asked for Dolly's address. Several times, he went back to Irene's house, but each time her mother's response was the same. She hadn't heard from her daughter and had no idea where Dolly lived. Eventually, she asked him not to come round again.

Look, sonny boy, she said, *some things jess ain't meant to be.*

Still, Richie remained convinced that Irene loved him and wanted him. He began to think something terrible had happened to her. He went to the London Hospital, then to the parish records, but there was nothing to suggest she had ever checked in or been treated, or that she had married, had a child or died. And in any case, her mother would have told him. The summer passed into autumn and still he could not forget her.

One early evening in the autumn of 1947 Richie had just sold a hatch of linnets and he was standing in Whitechapel High Street waiting for the bus home, when, out of the corner of his eye, he thought he caught a flash of red hair. He felt his heart shudder. The street was full of people heading home from work. It was dark, the remains of a pea-souper hung in the air and the gas lamps cast a pallid light across the murk. To look again for confirmation that the hair he'd seen belonged to Irene was almost more than he could bear. Yet, if he did not, he would never be able to forgive himself. Everything in him, the whole of his body and his mind, felt it was she. It was almost as if she were a magnet and he a nail. In a moment of decision he turned, and there she was, hurrying along the pavement past him. In the months since he'd last seen her, she'd filled out. She was wearing a suit, and looked, he thought, spectacular, like someone in the pictures. He called out. In an instant she slowed and turned her head. She stood on the pavement looking at him, blinking off the rain that was just beginning to fall. She leaned one hand on her hip and smiled. She looked so beautiful, so extraordinary, that he stood fixed on the spot, fearful that if he moved, he might miss something of her. His head throbbed with thoughts he couldn't catch. He slid through the crowd towards her.

Reenie, Reenie!

She met his gaze. Her eyes were the colour of summer wheat on the turn.

You look the same, she said.

Do I? he said, and regretted it instantly. It was a vain thing to say, a soft, weak, vain thing, he thought. She responded to it with a shrug.

Are you . . . are you . . . He had no idea how to finish the sentence, but he couldn't leave it without sounding an idiot, so he went ahead. *Are you all right?*

She nodded. He thought she looked bored suddenly, and awkward.

Come for tea, he said, conscious of wanting to keep her near him. *A cup of tea, a piece of something nice.*

She shook her head. He felt his belly lurch.

I've got to get me bus. She stared into the middle distance, refusing his gaze. *Look,* she said, fumbling over the words, *I'm getting married.*

He blinked and started looking up and down the road. The world was strangely disconnected. A woman walked by pushing a pram. Someone bumped him then moved on. A bus for Canning Town pulled in to the stop.

Her eyes moved away again and he could see that she was going to get on the bus, that she wanted to get away from the situation, to get away from him.

He felt his eyes filling. She saw it and took pity on him. Reaching out, she touched his elbow.

I couldn't never have married you, Richie. Sooner or later, me dad would have put a stop to it, between you and me. Yer old man was an awful boozer and he couldn't keep off the horses. Then there's yer uncle Harry, or whatever he is . . . well, there ain't no decent word for Harry, is there? Me dad wouldn't have stood for the likes of Harry in the family.

She dropped a dry little kiss on his cheek, stepped on to the bus and was gone.

He stood at the bus stop for a minute, or perhaps it was longer. Several buses went past but he didn't get on any of them. Then he began to walk. All his expectations, had been turned on their head. His legs began to rush him eastwards, towards Poplar, and as he went, he turned Irene's words over and over in his mind. He put his hand in his pocket and worked the money he'd been given for his canaries between his fingers. By the time he reached Bloomsbury Street and opened the front door, he was fighting back his tears. He went straight to his room. When Aunt Daisy called out later, asking whether he wanted any tea, he said he wasn't feeling well. He wasn't. He was sick and rucked up, like a ball of used paper. Sitting on his bed, he went over and over Irene's words. Over the next day or two, he thought of nothing else. Finally, he decided to go back to Irene's mother's house.

I don't know no more than you do, Irene's mother said. *He's some gent from the office. She ain't told me nothing about him. Some executive gent. No good asking me, I don't know nothing about it.* Richie let the tears come then. He no longer cared who saw him. Shocked by his response, Irene's mother looked about to make sure none of the neighbours was listening, then waved him into the passageway of the house. As he entered she put her finger to her mouth and, pointing to the living-room door, she whispered:

'Er dad's awful fussy, you see. When he come back from the war, he was terrible picky. He wouldn't have let Irene go with no one . . . She cleared her throat and looked directly at Richie *. . . certainly no no one with a you-know in the family.*

Richie looked uncomprehending and Irene's mother's voice took on an impatient tone.

You know, a wassname, she said. *One of them whadyercallems.* She lowered her voice to an almost inaudible whisper. *Nancies.* She looked put out at having to say the word.

For a moment Richie had no idea what she was talking about, but then it came to him. Colin had betrayed him. He'd revealed what had happened between them, the disgusting, unforgivable thing that *he*, Colin, had done to Richie. The injustice of it winded him. He was back on the doorstep now. He turned to Irene's mother, but she was already closing the door.

Aunt Daisy was standing in the passageway when he got in. He must have been looking pretty bad because she put her hand on his arm and asked him what was wrong. He said it was nothing but he saw his aunt didn't believe him. He felt ashamed of his feelings and of lying to her.

It's Irene, he said finally. *She's getting married.*

And before his aunt could respond, he had pushed past her and was heading up the stairs to his room. He sat himself up on the bed, and began a letter to Irene, but after several starts, he still could not find what he wanted to say. As he began his fourth or fifth draft, something came back to him: a sudden image of the tall man in the shop, the man to whom Harold had given money, so sharp, so complete in all its details that it was as though the event was happening again in the room. He thought about the way the man moved, the slight tone of threat in his voice. *Hello, dearie.* He saw his uncle fumbling in his pocket for money, then he remembered what Irene had said to him at the bus stop. And the mother. All three events seemed connected. But how? He leaned back into his pillow, thinking. The sudden surfacing of the truth brought a lurch to his stomach. It was as though he'd been in a submarine in the deepest part of the ocean all these months and now he was finally rising. Of course!

It was Uncle Harold.

Richie rose from his bed. He couldn't stay in his uncle's house a moment longer. He would have to leave completely and decisively. Taking his cardboard suitcase from under the bed, he slung a few clothes in it, along with some savings, then he went downstairs and in the passageway he called out to Aunt Daisy that he was going to the pub. He picked his cap up and opened the door, then he threw it as hard as he could down Bloomsbury Street.

He found himself in the Commercial Road and hopped on

to a bus heading east. Aunt Daisy must never know what her husband was. He would have to put himself out of her reach, go somewhere where there would never be any danger of his blurting it out. At London Bridge, he bought a single ticket to Faversham with the money he'd made from the canaries and boarded the next available train. It was cold and late when he arrived, so he went to the nearest pub and ordered a pint of beer and an egg and made both of them last. At closing time, he went down to Shepherd Neame's and found a warm spot next to the mashing tuns. There he waited out the night and, first thing in the morning, having washed his face and hands in the creek, he knocked at the office manager's door and offered himself for work. He found lodgings with a family in a house not far from Oare Creek. From there it was a walk past the gunpowder mill and the gravel works to the brewery. All the winter he worked in the brewery yard, rolling barrels, loading and unloading. He was neutral about the work. He enjoyed the camaraderie of the workers but he didn't try to make any close friends. On his eighteenth birthday he would be called to do his National Service and he was in no mood to make casual or temporary friendships. He passed his spare time alone, wandering Ham marshes as far as Nagden marshes, as far east as Cleve Marshes and the Seasalter levels where they bordered the mud and sands of the Oaze and gave out to Whitstable Bay.

Once he felt settled, he wrote a letter to his aunt apologising for the manner of his leaving. Something had happened, he said, and he'd needed to get away. She wrote back, sounding older and sadder, and he felt bad, for her, for his mother and his grandad. He cursed the Baker brothers, his father, Jack, and Uncle Harold. He'd loved both of them, but what had they ever done but wreck his life? First his father's debts and now his uncle's perversity, his filthiness. It was a disease, a sickness, he felt himself tainted by it. Together, these two men had lost him the love of his life and he hated them both, hated them so completely that he could not ever imagine a situation when his heart would not boil with it.

In the late spring of 1948, his call-up papers arrived. He packed up his lodgings and left what few belongings he couldn't take with his landlord. Before he left Faversham, he went to one of the shabbier pubs and got himself a tattoo, reading, simply, *Irene*.

CHAPTER 16

Daisy put her nephew's disappearance down to Irene's engagement. She had witnessed the intensity and the depth of his feeling for the girl and knew that, beneath the self-contained, sometimes bluff air, there lurked a delicate heart. She did not, or not then at least, imagine that it had anything to do with Harold. Eventually he would return, or at least write and let them know where he was. She remembered her own mood when Sidney had left and felt confident that Richie would get over his current crisis. People did get over things, other people. So long as they put their mind to it a human being could get over almost anything.

Predictably, Franny went into a tailspin about Richie's leaving. Knowing nothing about the existence of Irene, for Richie's sake, Daisy and Harold had thought it best to keep quiet on the matter, Franny tortured herself with the likelihood that her son had committed some crime or racked up gambling debts. Having ignored Richie for most of the past eighteen years, Franny had discovered a need for her son, or, rather, a need for his money, around the same time as she'd been widowed. She had sacrificed to bring Richie into the world. After all, if it hadn't been for his existence, she would not have suffered the shame of debt and the loneliness of early widowhood. Had she not become pregnant with him, she might have gone on to marry anyone – God knew, she hadn't been short of offers – and she expected payment on the debt. If Richie had got himself into trouble, he would be no good to her. The thought of having to go out and work full-time filled her with terror. She was too sensitive for mangling or making up brushes or for any of the other hard, joyless labours that were available to women of her station.

The family waited a week, and when Richie still did not return – this was before Daisy had received a letter – Daisy decided that it was only fair to pass on to Franny the one fact in the situation that she knew; that Richie had suffered a disappointment in love. She felt bad saying even this much. Richie was a private person and she did not want to give away his secrets. After all, she and Harold had secrets too, and would have hated them divulged.

He'll have gone back to the country for a bit until things have settled down, Daisy told Franny, as she brushed her sister's hair.

Franny waited for Daisy to divide the hair and begin clipping in her curlers.

He wants to remember what's important in life, like his family. Daisy flustered with her sister's hairnet and tied a scarf over the curlers.

He wants to remember his old mum, Franny said. She looked in the mirror and, content with what she saw, patted her scarf. Not so old. She brushed away a dry tear. *Mind you, I always said that boy never come to nothing. Like his father that way. Me a widow too. Shame on him.*

Daisy took a breath. Her sister was certainly making the most of her newly widowed position. For the first few months she'd insisted on dressing in widow's weeds, though hardly anyone of their generation did this any more, relishing the attention the outfit brought her on the street and, most particularly, among Poplar's male shopkeepers.

There you go, Mrs B, a bit extra for you today. Build you up after your loss. A cheeky wink, a surreptitious little smile. *Next time, perhaps you'd like a home delivery? I could come round meself.*

Sometimes, Daisy suspected, her sister liked being a widow more than she'd enjoyed being a wife, but there were so many widows about with husbands whose deaths had been rather more honourable than Jack's. There was only so much sympathy the widow of a man who'd drunk himself to death could expect to get. Franny's currency as a widow was losing value rapidly and Daisy sensed that her sister would find a way to play Richie's disappearance to her advantage.

I don't suppose we'll ever really know what really happened, Franny wailed, dabbing a dry eye with her handkerchief. It sounded like a line from one of her beloved pictures. Perhaps it was, Daisy thought.

He's bound to get in touch sooner or later, Daisy said, in an effort to sound comforting. *He's a good boy really*.

Then the letter addressed to Daisy arrived, while she was at work in the laundry. Recognising her son's handwriting, Franny opened it.

Richie wrote me, she announced that evening, when Harold and Daisy had both returned from work. *Something come up, apparently, but he'll write again soon. He's got a job in, um . . .* She tried to summon the details but quickly gave up. *Anyway, he put a five-pound note in the envelope for his old mum. He always was a thoughtful boy.*

Daisy found the letter the following evening when she was clearing up a pile of Franny's *People's Friend* magazines. Surprised to discover that the addressee was herself and not her sister, she pulled the letter out and read it. The moment she'd finished she sat down at the table and wrote a response and, since Richie did not give an address, she addressed the envelope care of Shepherd Neame's in Faversham. On her way to the Apex Laundry, she posted it. The following week, as she was dusting, she came across the pile of *People's Friend* magazines again. Franny had turned them over looking for a knitting pattern but the letter lay where Daisy had left it. Franny had not reread it, nor, Daisy assumed, had she chosen to answer it.

No reply came.

Just before Richie's eighteenth birthday Daisy sent a card signed by herself, Harold and Franny. Harold inserted a five-pound note into the card with a short covering note encouraging Richie to spend the money on *some nice togs*. Franny said she wouldn't send anything this time. She'd never been much of a writer.

A response arrived soon afterwards addressed to Daisy and, this time, Daisy was the first to open it. In a short half-page Richie thanked his aunt for her card. He said he had been called up and was due to report for training the following week. He did not give an address, or say where the training centre was. The letter ended with a promise to write, and a request that his uncle not write to him again, nor attempt in any way to contact him. He asked his aunt not to mention her husband to him in any subsequent letters she might write. He realised his request was unusual but he and Harold had had a *falling out* and Richie didn't want to hear from him. He was sending Harold's five-pound note back and enclosing two of his own which Daisy was to give to his mother. Once he'd began receiving his National Service wages, he'd try to send a few pounds regularly for her. He hoped Daisy would understand.

She read the letter to Harold and Franny, keeping back the hurtful parts, and adding thanks for Harold's gift. Then she burned the letter. She realised that she'd been wrong to ascribe Richie's disappearance to Irene alone. But why had Richie taken against his uncle? Harold wasn't someone people fell out with. Gradually, it dawned on her that Richie might actually have stumbled across the truth. Oh, and she knew how much pain lay in *that*. But how? Who would have told him? Only she and Harold and a few, mostly anonymous, men knew who Harold really was – *what* he was.

A while ago, not long before Richie disappeared, a tall man had followed her along the road from the Apex Laundry. There were people in the street so she knew that it wasn't his intention to rob her and, besides, she had nothing worth taking. All the same, he continued to hover behind. Eventually, at the corner of the East India Dock Road, she decided to turn and confront him. She already knew what he wanted. Months before, in a fearful and shamed state, Harold had finally confided in her. He hardly knew the man, he said. He was a docker and he'd first met him through Jack's business. He'd encountered him again during the war. The man had been exempted from the call-up on grounds . . . well, Daisy could guess what grounds from what followed. It was the middle of the Blitz and there were bombs dropping night after night. It had been a kind of madness, he said, brought on by the war. He had been lonely and in constant fear of his life. He couldn't understand it himself. The man had got himself into some kind of financial trouble and he'd come to Harold threatening to reveal their liaison. Arranging to meet the man in a quiet spot down by the ruins of the docks before the bomp-on, Harold had taken £50 from his savings jar, almost all the money he and Daisy had managed to save since they'd paid off Jack's debt, and waited for him, but the man hadn't shown up and Harold had had to leave to get to work on time. He still had the fifty pounds in his pocket when the man found him at Spicer's later. So as not to arouse the suspicions of Richie and Mr Spicer, Harold had very quietly asked him to rearrange their meeting for the evening, but the man became aggressive and accused Harold of trying to stall for time.

She forgave him, absolutely and completely. It took her by surprise how easily and instantly she forgave him.

Looking back, the news had come as a shock rather than a surprise. Daisy had always known that their marriage lacked certain elements, but she had never missed those elements and had never considered them necessary. Perhaps this in itself made her as peculiar as Harold. She supposed she had assumed they were each as innocent in bedroom matters as the other. In this respect, she saw she had been naive. All the same, she had never had anything to reproach him with. On that point, she was absolutely clear. The only lack in her marriage that she had ever felt had been their failure to produce children, and Richie had made up for that. The years of friendship and love between them had more than compensated for the absence of sex. She hadn't ever considered leaving him. He was what he was: a loyal and loving husband and a good man. She believed him when he said that his night-time antics were a temporary aberration brought on by circumstance. Hadn't the war made them all a little crazy? While it was true that she might have wished Harold's *particularity* to be otherwise, he probably felt the same about her. Who was she to set herself apart?

She told the tall man that he could spread whatever dirty stories he wanted to whomsoever he liked, but he would not continue to rob her and her husband of their cash or their happiness. The tall man looked taken aback, and opened his mouth as if to say something, then thought better of it, shrugged and walked away. As she knew now, he'd done what she'd given him permission to do. He'd spread his dirty, nasty little stories and she supposed Richie had somehow got wind of them. But then, how did that explain Irene's behaviour? Coincidence? Somehow, Daisy didn't think so. She remembered Harold saying he had met the tall man through Jack's business. Was it possible that the tall man had told Jack what he knew about Harold? Could Jack have passed the news on to Richie? The thought was sickening. For all his faults, she didn't think Jack Baker capable of such disloyalty. If she knew Jack as well as she thought she did, he would have boxed the tall man all the way to West London if he'd so much as tried to gossip about Harold. Still, she began to feel that Irene must have found out somehow. She recalled Richie saying that Irene's father was a docker and that he was very protective of her. Was it possible that he and the tall man had got talking one night in one of the many dockers' clubs and pubs down by the West India and the tall man had fired one of his disgusting, rotten little arrows then? Though she had never met Irene's father, Daisy thought she knew the type. Bluff, bristling, as hot and angry as a range stoked for a washing copper. That must be it, or as near to it as made no difference. Irene's father had come to hear about Harold's little secret and, as a result, he'd banned his daughter from seeing Harold's nephew. At last, she thought she understood at least something of what Richie might be feeling. She had never liked Irene, didn't consider her good or kind enough for her nephew, but she could see that, in Richie's eyes, he'd lost the great love of his life because of the stain on the family reputation that had resulted from Harold's 'condition' being exposed. In trying to exact revenge on Harold, the tall man had actually wreaked it on Harold's nephew. Why had she stuck so stubbornly to her principles – principles that seemed laughable now – when she could have given the tall man what he wanted and sent him on his way. Daisy felt weak with the knowledge that it could all have so easily been prevented. What would it have cost her? Her vain, ridiculous attachment to abstract principles and a few pounds?

Well, there was nothing to be done now, but to protect those she loved from knowing the whole. Harold must never know that Richie had discovered his secret and Franny must never find out that Harold had been the cause of Richie's disappearance. For the foreseeable future, there must only be partial truths with white lies set about to guard them. Later, when Richie was older and wiser, when another woman had replaced Irene in his affections, she would put all the pieces together for him and ask him to forgive Harold, Franny and herself – who had each, in his or her own particular way, let Richie Baker down.

At the end of the summer of 1948, Daisy took herself hopping. Here, at least, it was almost possible to believe that the war and the sad events that followed it had never happened. The fields had been cleared of much of the detritus that had been left on them to prevent aeroplanes landing, the sheds and barns had been restored to their pre-war uses and the hop huts had been painted their pre-war white. There were Fuggles, Goldings and

Challengers in the gardens, Bramleys, Grenadiers, Coxes, Laxtons, Worcesters, Fortunes and King Harrys in the apple orchards, Williams and Conference pears, Newtons, Victorias and greengages in the plum orchards. There were cherries growing in Gushmere Court and the farm had returned to cultivating strawberries and blackcurrants. The number of pickers was only slightly down from the late thirties. Nonetheless, all was not quite well in east Kent. Another battle had begun in the hop gardens, only this time the enemy was a hop disease. At the end of the thirties, verticillium wilt had spread from the Continent and it was gradually advancing westwards. The first sign of it in a hop garden meant that every bine in that garden and many in the gardens either side had immediately to be grubbed up and burned. Some east Kent farms had lost their entire hop crop the previous year on account of the disease, and if the wilt continued to spread as it had, the whole of the Kentish hop crop, which made up the vast majority of the hop output of Britain, would soon be under threat. Many Kentish hop growers were already considering quitting. Unless the price rose substantially, it was hardly worth the risk of growing hops any more. British brewers were already beginning to import their hops from the United States, which was, as yet, untouched by the wilt. Everyone was saying that the Americans would eventually take over the world hop market just as they were taking over everything else.

Another American import arrived in Britain about the same time. The first US-built hop-picking machine was trialled at Smugley Farm in Goudhurst, not far from Selling, in 1937. To the delight of the hoppers, it hadn't worked well in damp conditions and was soon sent back, but everyone in the hop business sensed that it would only be a matter of time before someone came up with another machine more suited to the conditions in Kent and, when that happened, the era of hand picking would be over. You could never stop the tide, Joe Crommelin used to say. The tide came in and out regardless.

When the hop came to an end, Daisy returned to the ragged remains of the East End and her family. She continued to receive occasional letters from her nephew, the addresses always typed now, or written in an unfamiliar hand, so that neither his mother nor his uncle would guess the sender. Whenever Harold asked where the letters came from, Daisy would say they were from hopping friends, which was sort of true. Franny never asked. Her interest in Richie seemed to begin and end in the envelopes of cash he sent her.

He's a good boy, remembering his old mum, Franny would say, patting the money. Daisy got the feeling that Franny didn't miss her son.

After his initial training, Richie had been sent to Frankfurt and was garrisoned there for the foreseeable future. He had learned to drive a lorry and got himself a reputation as a quick learner. His NCO was talking about promoting him to lance corporal. In her replies, Daisy kept the promise he had extracted from her never to mention Harold, though it felt like an act of great treachery. Instead, she told him he was loved and missed and would always be welcomed home.

The East End continued to change, if anything more rapidly during the late forties and early fifties than during the Blitz. It looked so different now that Daisy wasn't sure her nephew would recognise it. Certain streets had been 'slum-cleared', razed, awaiting redevelopment. Others, already ruined by the Luftwaffe, became proposed sites for vast new council estates. For now, though, the ground was either vacant, temporarily converted into allotments or filled with prefabricated homes. Despite all this activity, though, the East End still seemed empty. The population of West Ham had fallen from around 35,000 before the war to about 12,000, statistics repeated in each of the East End's many districts. Many of those who had left to live with relatives or friends or been evacuated to the country during the war decided not to return. Poplar had lost a good deal of its neighbourliness, Daisy thought. You could no longer walk up the East India Dock Road and expect to pass a sea of familiar faces. So much change. Sometimes Daisy wondered where it would end.

Among the leavers were Lilly and her family, who moved to a council house on the Becontree Estate in Dagenham and were now working at the Ford plant nearby. When Daisy went to visit her there, she found her old friend changed, more concerned to show off her new bathroom than to catch up. Eventually, Lilly moved farther out to Basildon new town. After that, the friends hardly saw one another.

I swear I don't know why you stop in that place, Lilly said, referring to Poplar.

Had the remark been framed as a question, Daisy could have answered her old friend with a single word: Harold. Poplar hadn't felt like home to Daisy for many years, but the horrors of the war had seemed only to increase Harold's attachment to the place. The ongoing replacement of whole neighbourhoods of streets and terraces with faceless council blocks, the removal of families from houses to flats, the construction of roads cutting through the heart of old communities, and all the other changes seemed to fire an intense loyalty to the place in him.

You can't stop progress, he'd say.

But was it progress? Or was it the excitable and egocentric opportunism of a group of urban planners who had been handed the gift of a vast building site by the Luftwaffe on which to test out their newest theories about city life? Had any of these people actually lived in the old East End? Daisy wondered. Did any of them understand the steady heart that beat beneath the seeming chaos, the soul that was embedded in the streets along with the smuts and factory stink? In Daisy's mind, Harold was a dutiful captain standing fast on the deck of a slowly sinking ship. His loyalty was admirable but it would kill him all the same.

She longed to get out, and by out she meant really out, not out to some dead zone whose residents had been placated by internal bathrooms and back gardens, but out to the real countryside, to the hills and wooded valleys, where the air smelled of sea and hops and where things changed slowly and with no fuss and you could almost hear the trees breathing, to a place where she could forget everything that had happened in the East End and start afresh.

But Harold would not move. Mr Spicer was an old man now, and there were certain things – such as climbing the stepladder or heaving coal sacks – that he and Mrs Spicer could no longer do. Since the death of Henry and May – of pneumonia, within six weeks of one another, during the hard winter of 1947, the same winter during which the government finally recognised the inhumanity of the casual labour practice of bomping-on in the docks and introduced the National Dock Labour Scheme to regulate dockers' pay – the Spicers were the nearest Harold had to parents. They'd been good to him over the years and he felt a duty of obligation towards them.

If this was all true – and it was – then why did it feel to Daisy like an excuse? Was he hoping to take over the shop when Spicer retired? If he was, he had never said so. The real reason for refusal to move eluded Daisy. It wasn't as though he wasn't interested in nature. On the contrary, he'd become rather obsessed with his allotment and had taken to growing giant vegetables of the sort suited only for entering into vegetable competitions: vast parsnips, football-sized swedes, and cabbages you could barely lift. They were quite inedible, useless really, but he didn't even bother to enter them into the competitions. It was during this time, too, that he began to expand his canary collection. By the early fifties, he'd taken to breeding strange and ugly birds, like the hunchbacked Scotch Fancy canary and the bizarre, swirly Parisian Frill. The aviary now filled most of the backyard and he kept the birds in cages stacked up against the walls in the scullery and the passageway. How many were there? A hundred? Two hundred? Not even Harold seemed to know. They made a racket and they were smelly too, but he wouldn't divest himself of any of them. Franny, who was still living at Bloomsbury Street, was always complaining about them.

He's gone barmy for them bleedin' birds. Ain't you gonna do nothing about it?

If that woman don't like it she knows what she can do. Harold had taken to calling Franny 'that woman'.

Don't let him talk to me like that. I was living in this house before we'd even heard of Jack and Harold Baker, and better for it.

In 1952 Mr and Mrs Spicer announced their retirement and, if Daisy very much hoped this would spur Harold into action, she was to be disappointed. The news seemed to send him into a carnival of dithering about whether to take up Spicer's lease on the shop and, after many months, Spicer eventually let the lease go to a fellow with an Indian name, a Lascar Daisy would have called him once, though she knew that term was no longer popular or, perhaps, even acceptable. The Indian man installed his family in the shop and didn't need any more staff. Harold found a job at a dry goods store on the East India Dock Road, but after so many years at Spicer's he found it hard to settle. Yet even this did not seem to galvanise him into moving elsewhere, and it wasn't long before he grew irritable with Daisy if she so much as mentioned the idea. He began to spend more time in the pub but he wouldn't talk about his drinking. He wouldn't talk about anything.

He's away with the bleedin' fairies, that one, Franny said. *Typical bleedin' Baker boy. Ain't no good to nobody in the finish.*

This was also the year in which a letter arrived for Daisy from Canada. It was from Richie. He was sorry he hadn't written for so long, he said, but the two years after National Service had been hectic and he was only just drawing breath. He wanted his aunt to know that he was getting married, to Julie, in Toronto. He had met her in Germany and it had taken a while to get his

Canadian immigration papers sorted out but now they were. Canada suited him, all that space. He couldn't believe how lucky he was, really, landing such a lovely fiancée in such a lovely country. He signed off *Your loving nephew Richie* and noted in a postscript his intention to write separately to his mother with the news, but only after the wedding. He didn't want Franny to start demanding passage to Canada. He didn't have the money and wasn't sure he'd want her at his wedding anyway. It was better this way.

The letter arrived a few days before Daisy was due to go hopping and it made her doubly glad to get away. It was a burden on her, keeping a secret like Richie's wedding. There seemed to be so many secrets now, so much unsaid and not talked about. Elsie's illness, Franny's pregnancy, Lilly's affair and *her* pregnancy, Harold's wartime quirk, and now there was Richie's wedding to add to them. She wondered what purpose all these secrets served. Reputation? Respectability? It seemed absurd, really, that a generation who had lived through two wars, who had witnessed what they had witnessed, suffered all they had suffered, should concern themselves with respectability. But then again, she thought, perhaps having seen what they had seen and suffered what they had suffered, respectability was the only sure and certain thing left them.

It didn't seem so long ago that East Enders could rely on the hop as the highlight of the East End year, but that, too, had changed. So many East Enders had moved away, the old neighbourhoods had broken up and people didn't need the money as they did before the war. Gone, then, were the days when whole streets had made the journey together and London neighbours had lived side by side in the huts, cooking, singing and picking all together, minding each other's children.

Sooner or later, machines would come in and replace human pickers. After the disastrous experiment at Goudhurst, Kentish farmers had given up on the idea of importing American machines. Conditions were too different. In 1954 only 7 per cent of hops grown in south-east England were machine picked. But it wouldn't stay that way. A single hop-picking machine staffed by two men, six to ten women and four to six cutters could strip and sort as many hops as 160 to 200 hand-pickers. Before long, someone would devise a reasonably priced, efficient picking machine designed specifically for the conditions in Kent.

For now, the only major technical change to the harvest was that the hops ceased to be transported to the hop exchange in Borough on special trains and began instead to be moved by lorries. During late August and early September you could see them trundling along the old Roman Road from Dover to London in convoys, the identifying labels on the hop pockets turned inwards to discourage rival farmers from sabotaging each other's crops.

Lying under her eiderdown in hut 21, listening to the owls and the scratchy squeal of bats, Daisy thought about Joe and how he had been right to say that no one could stop the tide. But at least, Daisy thought, by going hopping she could stem it for a while.

Back in London, more change was on its way. The Apex Laundry announced its intention to remove to West London to be nearer the West End hotels that made up much of its clientele, so Daisy found work in one of the new launderettes opening up across the East End. Physically, the work was so much easier than in the old days of poshers, mangles and dolly tubs. She simply filled machines with dirty clothing, poured in laundry soap, emptied the wet clothes out after the cycle, bunged them in the dryers and supervised the customers. All the same, Daisy found the adjustment harder than she had anticipated.

In the long, slack spaces at the launderette she made cups of tea and thought about how everything was going to the dogs. Machines had made people sloppy. Stains were left in, laundry was delivered with the buttons and pins still attached and people didn't even bother to turn out their pockets or pull skirts and trousers inside out to protect their nap. Service washes came in covered in untreated grease stains, with paper still in the pockets and pieces of chewing gum stuck to the sleeves. People handed over bags of smalls covered in what she could only describe as 'filth' – soiled nappies and worse. Nobody seemed to care any more. No pride. The shamelessness and want of respect were baffling. Day after day perfectly good clothes were being ruined by people dazzled by new technology. Poplin, silk and fine embroidery all went into the machines. Such laziness. Did no one have working hands any more? No spin dryer was a patch on a mangle, say what you liked. And as for the new so-called iron-free fabrics – lustre, then the rayons, nylon, crimplene and polyester – well, they were just pandering to people's carelessness. But people these days wouldn't get their hands dirty, they wouldn't work at it, they gave up far too easily. There weren't many things on which Daisy felt fit to pass judgement, but this was most certainly one of them. It was all very sad.

That was another problem with machines. They left you with too much thinking time.

It must have been around the same time – the older Daisy got, the more inexact she became about the present and the more precise about the past – that she took the Cambell bus to see Lilly, who was now living out in Basildon. Arriving, it seemed to Daisy as if a fragment of a city had broken off, drifted into the countryside and got stuck there. Lilly seemed to like her new surroundings, though. She had a fancy house, with a bathroom suite, a refrigerator, a fitted kitchen and a back yard that she referred to as *the garden*. There were wall-to-wall carpets in most of the rooms and everything was much easier to keep clean than it had been in the old days. A quick dust, a run round with the sweeper, a little elbow grease to shine the taps. No blacking of the range and the fireplace, no whitening of the step, no boiling laundry in a copper, no film of dirt on everything, no encroaching bugs or accretions of mould. Everything about Basildon was clean. Over lunch – Lilly called it lunch now, not dinner – Lilly announced that she didn't intend to go hopping any more. It was too far to travel, she said, and now that she and Jimmy were both working and young Grace was off their hands, they didn't need the money. Lilly wondered whether Daisy would do her the favour of visiting the spot where they'd buried what they had buried, lay some flowers, say a prayer, or sing a verse or two of whatever came to hand.

Walking to the bus stop to catch the bus back to Poplar, Daisy could see that Lilly was right. Basildon was admirably clean. Still, the visit left her feeling empty and vaguely soiled and she thought it unlikely that she'd go again, or that Lilly would invite her.

Nevertheless, when she returned to Selling that summer, she saw to it that she kept her promise. The hop garden had been grubbed up, the dividing hedge taken down and the burial spot was now covered by the stubble of newly harvested wheat, awaiting burning. Daisy left a bunch of campions, ragwort and summer vetch and sang a verse or two of 'All Creatures Great and Small'. She left out the prayer because she didn't in all honesty think that anyone was listening.

Like many Kentish farms, Gushmere Court had reduced its hop output, but the Berrys had not yet invested in the new picking machines and they still welcomed those pickers who wanted to come down from London and pick. Most of the farms around had made the change. By 1960, nearly half of all Kentish hops were being machine picked. The machines stripped the bines clean of hops and leaves, then separated out the hop cones. The way it worked was that two men travelling on the back of a tractor would cut the bines from their wires and another couple would load the bines into a trailer. When that was full, they'd drive it round to the farm shed where the machine was kept. Four or five women would then feed the bines into the machine, which would strip them of their cones and, using blowers, separate the lighter cones from heavier leaves, twigs and other unwanted detritus. A couple of women would some-times stand by to ensure the process ran smoothly and to pick out the odd bit of twig or leaf or, occasionally, a body part of some unfortunate rodent. The hops would then go out to the drying rooms of the oasts. Some farms had dispensed with their oasts too, investing instead in a Morden drying machine, a modi-fied herb dryer. The machine required none of the skill and judgement nor any of the dedication of the kiln men – men like Old Wentworth – who used to move into the kilns during the drying season so they could keep a close eye on progress. The drying machine could not tell by eye when the hops were dry, but would be set to cut off the moment the cones reached their optimum 4 per cent water. In that sense they were more accurate than the kiln men. All over Kent, oasts were steadily abandoned, or converted into storage sheds.

You can't hold back the tide.

Imported American hops were arriving almost daily in the London docks now, from where they would have to be moved by lorry the three or four miles to the Hop Exchange in Borough. Despite the depredations of the Luftwaffe and an ageing infra-structure, the Port of London continued to be the largest and one of the busiest in the world, the lush, thumping heart of empire, sucking in raw materials from every part of the rapidly shrinking dominions and pumping Britian's economic lifeblood, its manufactured goods, across Europe, to America and beyond.

At number 7 Bloomsbury Street, not all hearts were beating with quite such vitality. At the end of 1959, Harold's birds began to die. At first, when he found one or two of his older canaries stiff at the bottom of their cages, he put it down to them catching a chill, but then the dying stepped up pace until barely a day went by without another three or four bright little corpses. Harold consulted his handbooks. He sealed the windows in the house and laid bolsters along the doors to keep out the draughts. When that did not help, he took each bird from its cage, washed its little spindle legs in a mustard bath and poured drops of olive oil into its beak, then he cleaned out and disinfected all the cages, but the birds continued to die.

Harold was bewildered. He brought in a few of his bird-breeder friends, but they, too, could not account for the devastation. Among them all, only Franny seemed unmoved.

Such nervy little things, them birds, she said. *Can't hardly say boo to a goose without one of 'em snuffs it.*

By Christmas time, all but three of Harold's collection of 120 canaries had died. Harold measured their deaths in drinking binges.

It was probably no coincidence that, not long afterwards, Franny found herself a fancy man and left Bloomsbury Street and London altogether. The man's name was Michael. He was a widower and, as Franny became very fond of reminding everyone, he was at the end of a posh career as a middle manager in an insurance office and was about to retire. Michael was one of those old-fashioned men who like to fuss over women as though they are children or beloved pets. He nicknamed Franny his little pearl. Within a few months they had married and moved to a house in Nottingham. They didn't visit much and didn't invite Harold or Daisy up to stay. What with their regular holidays in Clacton-on-Sea (and once to the Costa Brava, which Franny found far too hot), they were kept about as busy as any two people could be, Franny said. No time for anything. Eventually Michael bought a caravan and they began to spend more time in Clacton than in Nottingham. In both locations they played a great deal of bingo.

CHAPTER 17

Daisy used Franny's departure as an excuse to try to heal the now long-standing rift between her nephew and her husband. In 1965 she wrote to him in Toronto, suggesting that, now Franny wasn't around and there was space in the house, Richie might consider visiting them. Daisy was keen to meet her grand-niece and nephew, Sam and Patsy, and, of course, Julie. In a brave and deliberate move, she added a PS reading: *Harold would be so pleased to get to know them too*. It was the first time she had broken her promise to Richie in nearly fifteen years, but enough was enough. It was time for family feuds to end.

By now Harold's health was poor. He was drinking a great deal, his leg was twingeing, the knee was playing up and he seemed at a low ebb generally. He hadn't replaced the canaries he'd lost and he'd failed to cultivate his allotment two years in a row so the council had taken it back. He spent most of his nights in the pub now or hunched over the racing form, though he didn't seem interested in the horses or dogs. It was almost as though he'd given up. As to the cause of his decline, Daisy could only guess. The loss of his birds didn't explain all of it. Perhaps he was still haunted by what had gone on in the war and its aftermath, his estrangement from Richie? It had even occurred to her that she herself was the cause of his miserable state. It was because he loved *her* that he'd stopped seeing men. She sometimes thought that the seeds of Harold's decline had been sown much, much earlier, though, on that night so long ago when, running for a bag of toffee, he had fallen through the banisters and landed on his little brother. For over a half a century he had carried that burden, but now he was old and the burden was too heavy.

A reply to her letter arrived not long after. In it Richie enclosed a photograph of Julie, Sam and Patsy, sitting on a rock surrounded by trees. Sam looked like Joe, she thought, though Patsy was quite unlike either Franny or Elsie. It was odd to think that her grand-niece and grand-nephew would speak with Canadian accents. Perhaps she would have trouble understanding them? She remembered from the war that Canadians were always very touchy about being mistaken for Americans. It was the same, now, with the Indians and Pakistanis or with Jamaicans and Ghanaians. There always seemed to be some new division or other. Secrets, divisions. Time would make a nonsense of them all, Daisy thought, but then she was just a laundress and all she really knew was how to remove stains from dirty laundry.

In his letter, Richie went on to say it was too expensive to visit, which was a blow, though not an unexpected one. Well, then, the photograph was better than nothing, though Daisy wished he had sent one of himself and wondered why he hadn't. But he'd always been funny like that. A bit self-contained. Most likely he didn't even realise that Daisy would have liked to know how he looked at – she thought about it; Gordon Bennett – thirty-five. She thought of her own face, still with its spindly neck and it oafish ears, only now folded and corrugated too. Time and tide!

She would write again, she thought, and this time she would include something about Harold in the main body of the letter. Not much, just a line or two. Then she would wait to see how Richie responded. She had a telephone now so that she could keep in touch with Franny, even though they only really ever wrote, and then not often. But it was one of those things. Having the telephone made her feel that one day she and Franny might be better friends. Most likely Richie had a telephone too. They had all sorts of things in Canada. Perhaps he might even call one day, though it would probably be terribly expensive, and she remembered there was a time difference between the two countries.

How much Daisy wished her father were still alive. Joe had always known how to steer a safe path through rough waters. It was in his blood. He'd been gifted that way. Daisy would have to move more slowly with Richie than Joe would have done. All the same, she was determined to see Richie and Harold reconciled. They were a long way from that, she realised, but the letter was a start, and for the first time in years she felt light, her mind spacious and sweet, like a hayfield newly mown.

That year, 1965, was a landmark one in other ways. In the spring, Harold retired, and in the summer rumours began that the London docks were in trouble. It was hard to understand. The Port of London remained the largest in the world, handling more and more cargo. Only a year or two before the Port of London Authority had invested £2 million in the vast new refrigerated warehouse at the Royal Albert Dock in Silvertown, and both the PLA and the unions had seemed buoyant about its future. People said it was all about 'containerisation'. The first containers had begun to be unloaded from American ships in the late 1950s. They were easier to handle and track than traditional cargo, harder to steal from, didn't shift during shipping and didn't require warehousing at either the outgoing or the incoming end. More importantly, the new containers didn't need manhandling. They could be loaded and unloaded directly from trains or lorries on giant cranes, then transferred direct from quay to ship and vice versa. In a single stroke containers rendered stevedores, breaker gangs, hatchmen, manhandlers, winch operators, porters, warehousemen, bondsmen, tallymen and lightermen redundant. All you needed now were container ships – and since it was much easier to stabilise containers than loose cargo the only limit to the size of the ships was the size of the docks at which they loaded and discharged their cargo – the containers themselves, cranes and some form of land transport at either end to bring the goods from manufacture to market, plus a few people to operate the cranes and to oversee and administer the whole process.

The PLA, the shipowners, the dockers' unions and the dockers themselves hadn't seen what was coming, maybe because it was too frightening to contemplate. By 1965, the situation was becoming impossible to ignore, though still no one anticipated, even then, the speed at which the new technology would take over and the devastation it would leave in its wake. In response, the PLA invested millions in a new container port at Tilbury, thirteen miles downriver from the West India, and for a while the deep-water port at Tilbury grew at the expense of upriver docks like the West India. The National Dock Labour Board moved some dockers to Tilbury, a four-hour round-trip commute for some, and offered others voluntary severence, and this, coupled with the general air of anxiety, stirred up by activists in the dockers' unions, led to a series of stoppages and minor strikes that continued throughout the sixties. Having success-fully resisted the Luftwaffe only twenty years before, the East End became a battleground once more, with communists and fascists taking turns to capitalise on the anxiety and discontent of generations of East Enders who had fought a world war to protect a way of life that was about to be taken away from them by their own government. One week it was Jack Dash, the next Enoch Powell. Whichever, the outcome was the same. Shipowners began diverting their cargoes to rival ports, at Rotterdam, Hamburg and elsewhere. The strikes escalated, but by now they were a death rattle. The end was rushing towards them, gathering speed.

With Franny gone, space opened up in Daisy's life for new

friends, and Harold's drinking, which brought with it dark chasms of depression, created a need for them. On Tuesdays and Fridays Daisy would go out to the bingo with women from the launderette. Harold, meanwhile, continued to slide softly into alcoholism as though he were on a muddy slope in heavy rain. A couple of pints in the evening became five or six, then one or two at lunchtime, plus a nightcap after his return from the pub. Unlike his father, he was not an aggressive drunk. The drink seemed to send him farther into himself and he became superficially cheerful but locked away; the deeper parts of his personality played out remotely, perhaps even to himself.

Daisy tried to focus on the things she most looked forward to – her nights out with the girls or one of Richie's infrequent letters. The highlight of her year continued to be the annual hop, though it was no longer about stripping bines, there being fewer and fewer bines to strip and more and more machines with which to do it, but about catching up with old friends and, most of all, about being in the soft, calm beauty of the North Downs. If Harold had been willing to move, she would have gone, then, escaped London for ever and never once regretted it. For so many years, it was what she had longed to do, but her life was with her dear Harold. While he lived, she would stay in London.

No one expected Harold to make old bones. In the early 1960s, his bad leg became arthritic and began troubling him, and he was in almost constant pain, too, from a crumbling vertebra set off, the doctor thought, by the impact of his childhood fall, which had gone unnoticed at the time. To quell the pain, Harold began to drink more. In the mid-1960s, he began to suffer bouts of the kind of minor illnesses that plague drinkers before the major ones set in – gout, circulatory problems, memory loss – but it was during this time that Daisy drew closer to him.

It's being so cheerful as keeps us going, he'd say, sadly, squeezing her cheek as he had many years before when Joe had died. She bought him a new breeding pair of canaries, and when he became too ill to look after them properly, she boned up on breeding techniques herself, so that she could present him with a nest of hatchlings, which gave him tremendous pleasure. She wrote to Richie, explaining that Harold was really very ill. She knew Richie couldn't come over, but she hoped that he might call or write to his uncle, who loved him dearly and still talked about him a great deal.

A letter came back a couple of weeks later. Though for years now Richie had typed her address on the envelopes or got someone else – Julie, she supposed – to write it by hand, this time Daisy recognised his handwriting instantly and knew what it meant. He had stopped hiding from his uncle. She opened the envelope with trembling hands. Inside there was a letter for her and folded between the pages an envelope containing a card, addressed to Harold. A wave of relief came over her. For years now she had colluded in the deception that had kept Harold from his nephew; hiding letters, keeping secrets. It had been that or lose touch with him altogether. Now, all that was over. Her nephew had finally come round. She picked up the card and brought it to Harold, who was sitting in his chair talking to his canaries. Harold opened the envelope and stared at the picture of a maple leaf superimposed on a street scene.

It's from Richie, Daisy said.

Harold nodded, slowly opening the card and tipping it upwards, as though trying to avoid spilling any of its precious contents. He reached for his glasses and his magnifier and, while he was reading, Daisy went to fetch a pot of tea. When she returned, the card was on his lap. He held it out to her.

So that explains all them letters with Canadian stamps, he said.

I'm sorry, duck, she said. All these years she'd lied, telling him the letters were from a hopping friend of hers, her loyalties hopelessly conflicted, but Harold shook his head reassuringly and, taking her hand, patted it.

I brought it on meself, he said, but with no self-pity. *Family curse, the drinking. And all that other stuff, that wartime craziness.*

Daisy felt the old love for him bubbling up. It all seemed so distant now, the cause of the rift lost in the mists, like the call of an extinct bird.

Not long after this, Harold Baker was cut down very suddenly by a stroke which paralysed his left side. For a while he lingered on, just as his brother Archie had done decades before. His world seemed split down the middle, his one good hand, the right, roaming up and down the blacked-out side, seeking confirmation of the whole.

Oh well, he slurred, speech eroded by the trauma to his brain, *left leg was none too clever in any case.*

He had always been a cautious man, slow to tread unfamiliar paths, and in the business of dying Harold Baker was no different. Daisy struggled to look after him, plumping his pillows, massaging his legs, both good and bad, and, towards the end, feeding him pulped food on teaspoons. She wrote to Canada and, not having a telephone number for Richie, begged him to call, which he did, though by this time his uncle was in hospital and couldn't speak to him directly. Daisy brought news of the phone call, though, and he seemed to take it in. She thought it no coincidence that he took his last breath two days later, on 22 May 1967. There was nothing to wait for any more.

Daisy Baker telephoned first Richie then Franny to tell them the news and a week later Harold Baker was cremated with his favourite manual on canary husbandry. Franny and Michael came down from Clacton, where they were now living permanently. Lilly and Jimmy arrived with Millie and Grace (Susan had moved to Scotland and couldn't get away). Iris's boy, Tommy, middle-aged and balding, came with them, then there were a few of Harold's birding friends, some old men from the allotments and Billy Shaunessy's son and daughter, Phil and Dotty. Daisy had worried someone unexpected might turn up and was relieved when no one did. Richie Baker sent flowers through Interflora, directing that the card be signed *from Richie, Julie, Sam and Patsy with love.*

Afterwards, neighbours and friends from the old days gathered in Bloomsbury Street and in true East End style they made a song and dance of their grief. There was a great deal of drink but, out of respect for the deceased, only a few very minor brawls. The guests all said the event had done Harold proud and what a good send-off it had been, as though Harold were a ship they were waving from the docks. Then they went back to their lives and Daisy was left alone, shipwrecked by grief.

While Harold had been struggling with the thankless business of dying, a committee had been meeting in central London to discuss the recommendations of the 1957 Wolfenden Report on homosexuality and prostitution, or Huntley and Palmers, as they were known, so as not to offend the ladies on the committee. At 5.50 a.m. on 5 July 1967, only six weeks after Harold died, the result of their deliberations, presented as a bill to parliament by Leo Abse and Lord Arran, finally limped through its final stages in the House of Commons. The Sexual Offences Act legalised consensual homosexual acts between men aged twenty-one or over. It was now a matter of law. Society had finally accepted that which Harold Baker had been unable to accept in himself.

After the funeral, and for want of any other direction, Daisy headed out to the hop gardens. The downs were looking particularly beautiful that year. Rain had kept everything fresh and caterpillar green. The tiny blue butterflies that were, for her, so redolent of this part of Kent scribbled across lacy hedgerows and hayfields brindled with seed heads. When the picking was done, she sat beside hop hut number 21 and thought back across the landscape of her marriage; from Harold standing at the door in his best suit, holding a canary, at its most distant horizon, to the sunny, forgiving arrival of Richie's card. There had been rocky interludes, steep cliffs up whose slopes they had both struggled, but all that seemed trivial now. Whenever she thought about Harold, her chest swelled with gratitude. Diligent shopkeeper that he was, he'd taken her off the shelf just at the moment she supposed she'd been completely forgotten. He'd dusted her down and, not minding her physical imperfections, found her to be just the thing. Plain women couldn't take love for granted the way that beautiful women like Franny could, but Harold never seemed to mind that he had married the ugly sister. She marvelled that he had been able to love someone as blankly ordinary as herself. In those early days, his careful, considerate love had rescued her from the feeling that her life belonged to her mother, her sister, her father, but never to herself. There had never been a moment across the years when she hadn't loved him.

As for sex, well, they always said you didn't miss what you'd never had. In any case, none of the women Daisy knew had given sex a particularly good write-up. They took pleasure in kisses and cuddles but could do just as well without the rest. Harold had always been affectionate but he'd spared her the fuss and mess of the rest of it. And while she didn't doubt that she'd missed out in not becoming a mother, her childlessness aroused in Daisy only a gentle sense of fading, like watching the first leaves of autumn fall. Being childless saved you a great deal of pain, of which the birth itself was only the first and most fleeting.

She and Harold had lost sight of one other, but his death had separated them only physically. In her mind, he was as continually and vividly present as he had always been. He was speaking to her now, telling her what she already knew, that his death had presented her with an opportunity and that she'd be a fool not to take it. Harold would have found it impossible to have left Poplar, even though the Poplar he knew had abandoned him long ago. But now he'd given her the chance to get out before she became too old or frail to be able to manage the move.

At the end of the hop she returned to Poplar excited by her prospects. She'd have to save and make arrangements, but just the thought of moving to the countryside gave her days a new energy. She continued at the launderette, pouring soap powder, scrubbing stains, folding and unfolding as the old Poplar she knew continued to crumble. In 1967, the same year as Harold's death, the East India Dock was filled in and replaced by a new power station. The following year, the innermost dock of the Upper Pool, St Katharine's, was closed, and in July 1970, Prime Minister Edward Heath declared a state of emergency and put troops on stand-by after 50,000 dockers around the country walked out for two weeks over pay and conditions. In 1971, five union men were arrested for blacking vehicles bypassing the docks and 170,000 dockers went out on strike in support of them.

As late as 1968, London remained the largest port in the world, and both the Port of London Authority and the unions seemed confident that by managing the monumental change required to convert the port from a series of upstream docks developed piecemeal over hundreds of years by private enterprise to a modern, high-tech, downstream deep-water port capable of handling vast new container ships, the London docks could be saved. Fifteen years before, 250,000 men had made their living inside the docks, and double that number in the ancillary businesses: driving lorries, railway work, ships' supplies and ship repair. By the early seventies there were only 16,500 registered dockers working in the London docks. Thousands had taken up the voluntary severance scheme and retired early, set up new businesses, got themselves employment elsewhere or headed out for sunnier lives on the Costas, but in east London 10,000 ex-dockers remained on the dole.

You couldn't stop the tide. For a while the unions and the

PLA imagined that as long as you ran fast enough, you could keep up. But they were wrong. After 400 years during which the Port of London had been one of the world's great trading hubs, it was all over. They were rearranging deckchairs.

In 1974, it was announced that the two remaining Poplar docks, the West India, where Henry and Jack had spent so much of their lives, and the Millwall, were scheduled for closure, and that was when Daisy Crommelin finally decided to retire from the launderette, gather up her savings and get out. By working well beyond the usual retirement age, she had accumulated enough money to buy a small house somewhere outside London, and she had no trouble deciding where she was going to go. She left the house in Bloomsbury Street where she had been born and lived all the years of her life without a trace of regret, and moved to a tiny cottage on the outskirts of Faversham in east Kent, only a few miles from Selling. The cottage had a view of a cemetery on one side and a stretch of fields and orchards on the other. Still vaguely bruised by Harold's forays into giant vegetables, Daisy grew flowers in her garden and watched the seasons turn. All year round, chirpy brown dunnocks and house sparrows bounced and fussed about on the crazy paving outside her living room, picking up the seed she left for them. Unassuming little birds, they were, and so drab that most people barely noticed them, but Daisy looked out for them and looked forward to their company. They were nothing much to look at, it was true, but their cheerful, resolute little spirits moved her in ways that flashier birds never could.

When she wasn't doing her laundry, keeping the cottage clean, watching the birds and making cups of tea, all of which took up a great deal of time, Daisy would take herself off on country walks. Her favourite route led past Lady Dane Farm along the footpath to Goodnestone, where there was a little stream. Sometimes the stream dried up a bit, other times it ran almost flush to its muddy banks, but it was always there. It was a bit like mangling, she thought. The water moved and turned and moved, but it always wound up in the same place.

Every once in a while, a letter would arrive from Richie. Daisy liked to think he was all right but it was difficult to tell from his writing, which consisted mostly of pithy little descriptions of Sam's ice hockey team outings and Patsy's swimming triumphs. She did notice that he rarely mentioned Julie any more and gave almost nothing away about himself. This last didn't surprise her – even as a little boy, he'd been opaque – but the disappearance of Julie seemed ominous.

She supposed that, if his marriage went wrong, Richie would stay in Canada to be near his children, but whatever happened, she was sure he would never return to Poplar. The news from there was mostly bleak. In 1978, in order to try to limit its financial losses from the upstream docks, which were running at £9 million a year, the PLA announced its 'Radical Approach' plan for the docks, changing working practices, reducing manpower and transferring all its cargo handling to Tilbury. But losses on the upstream docks, the Royal Albert and King George V in North Woolwich and the Royal Victoria in Silvertown, continued to increase. In 1980 the government announced a rescue package on the understanding that PLA operations be self-supporting by 1983. It meant closing the last of the upstream docks. The Royals closed for general cargo handling at the end of 1981. The last vessel to be loaded left the King George V dock on 7 October 1981, and the last vessel discharged its cargo on the dockside three weeks later. A few more dockers transferred to Tilbury, but most were given redundancy payments and sent on their way. By the early 1980s, 80,000 East End dockers were still on the dole. The London docks, which together had made up what George Lansbury, first socialist MP for Poplar, had once grandly termed 'The Road to Empire', swiftly became roads to nowhere: bleak, fenced-off, bricked-up dead ends fringed about with the disgruntled remnants of former communities and patrolled by skinheads, who were often themselves the sons of redundant dockers.

Finally, in April 1989, a century after the Great Dock Strike won the dockers a sixpenny hour, the 'Dockers' Tanner', and the right to at least a half-day's labour if they were called up, the National Dock Labour Scheme, introduced during the Second World War to provide dockers with guaranteed employment, was abolished under the Thatcher government and cheap, casual labour once again flooded into the ports. But by then it was too late for London. The docks had been taken over by the London Docklands Development Corporation, and were being targeted for 'redevelopment'.

Despite all this, or perhaps because of it, the annual hop persisted here and there. Farms like Gushmere Court reduced their hop production and began to take on students to strip the bines. The students were cheaper and more pliant, they had no proprietorial feeling for the hop gardens as the Londoners did, and they were willing to stay on for fruit picking. East Enders still came to those farms willing to accommodate them, sometimes travelling hundreds of miles with no promise of work, just so that they might soak up the atmosphere and exchange gossip with friends and former neighbours they rarely saw, sing fireside songs, eat potatoes and windfall apples straight from the ashes and remember the good old days together.

Daisy would go down herself for a few days, stay in the hop huts, and feel the old connectedness. Each time she kept her promise to Lilly, visiting the spot where her baby was buried and laying a bunch of wild flowers. She was by no means alone. Bouquets were left for departed friends, ashes were scattered. One old-timer celebrated her centenary in the huts and had the Queen's telegram to prove it. Children grew up and had children of their own and regaled their youngsters with stories of the old days, and the children would shake their heads in disbelief and say, *What, no hot water, no toilets, no TV?*

Once or twice Lilly came down to visit. After her retirement, she'd taken on part-time work as a dinner lady in a local school and in her spare time she told fortunes. There was always a great demand for clairvoyance in Basildon. Lilly was convinced of her powers of mediumship, and swore she had heard from Mrs Shaunessy and even from old Nell. In spite of this, though, she'd never been contacted either by Michael the bine cutter or the spirit of the baby she had never had, and in her dark moments she sometimes wondered whether they hated her. She said it would be unlucky to revisit Michael's old cottage so neither of them ever ventured up the path that led to it. Daisy wondered whether they would even be able to manage it now. Lilly had a hip replacement and Daisy's knees played up. From time to time Lilly wrote and moaned about the hip, but both she and Daisy realised how lucky they were. Aside from the usual run of aches and pains brought on by the gradual depredations of age, they were both remarkably healthy.

For this reason it came as a great surprise to Daisy when she began to develop pains in what she called her private parts. Eventually, and for the first time in decades, she took herself to the doctor. The doctor was an Indian gentleman; a Lascar, Joe would have called him, though Daisy knew you couldn't say that any more. A lot of them were doctors these days, the Lascars. When Daisy had been a little girl they'd been sailors; now they were doctors. Daisy couldn't see anything wrong with that. Good on 'em.

Do you have relations? the Indian doctor asked.

Daisy was taken aback by the question. Of course, she said, she had a sister and a nephew, but she didn't see them often.

The doctor coughed.

I meant sexual relations.

Oh, she said. The penny dropped. Silly her. Well, not really, she said, she'd been perfectly happy without, thank you very much.

The doctor looked at his notes for a moment as though trying to locate written evidence. Daisy just let him get on with it. The only thing that mattered to her wasn't written down in any notes, and that was that Harold had loved her and she had loved him in return.

The doctor coughed once more, smiled politely and referred her to a specialist.

It was one of the ironies of Daisy's life that the parts of her body she had not used were the ones harbouring the cancer. It was in her ovaries. The silent killer, they called it. No real symptoms until it was too late.

She wrote to Richie and ten days later received a phone call. He would be on a plane by the end of the week, he said.

After thirty-seven years − *thirty-seven years* − he was coming to visit her.

By then, she was in hospital and hooked up to machines. They'd given her drugs that made her feel by turns light-headed and sick, but on the agreed morning she paid for the hospital hairdresser to give her a shampoo and set and she put on her best matinee jacket in recognition of the occasion. The nurse had pulled her curtain around to give her some privacy, so she had no warning of his arrival until a face appeared through the gap and a voice she would know in an ocean of voices said:

Auntie Daisy!

And when he held out the bunch of flowers he had brought it was as much as she could do to keep reminding herself that she was here in hospital and he was a grown man and the days of Pheasant Field and Franny and Jack and Harold were all long, long behind them. She smiled and blinked a greeting.

Got any of your rock buns for me, Auntie Daisy? he said.

She scoffed at him, delighted. Tipping her head towards one of the machines that appeared to be attached to her by tubes, she said:

Do that look like an oven? She shook her head and tutted playfully. *He buggers off for nearly forty years, and now he wants rock buns.*

As for him, he seemed the same, she thought, though that might have been the drugs they'd given her. A bit heavier, maybe, not so much hair, but her Richie.

You been to see your mum, yet? she said.

He shook his head. He'd driven directly from the airport to Faversham. She noticed, then, that his voice twanged somewhere between cockney and what she took to be a Canadian accent.

He didn't stay long that first time. He was tired from the journey, and she was always better in the mornings herself, but he came again the following day, and the next, and gradually, one by one, they caught up on the years. After National Service he'd had any number of jobs, but nothing you could call a career. Still, he didn't mind, because he'd got to work outdoors, which is what he loved. He'd loved his wife Julie too, but things between them had deteriorated and they were about to split. He adored Sam and Patsy, his kids, but they weren't kids any more. Sam had got a job in computers and gone to live in California and Patsy was thinking of moving to the UK. They'd both had children. He showed Daisy the pictures. It was a shame about Julie; it was a long marriage but during the last two decades they had only really been together out of habit. The fact was that he'd never quite got over Irene. Daisy had never liked her, he knew, but it was as though a splinter of her had been left inside him, and over the years it had only worked its way deeper. He had loved Julie insofar as he was able. He had been faithful to her, they had both been good parents and, for a while, they had made each other happy, but, as much as he hated to admit it, he had never managed to love his wife as he had loved Irene.

For the first two weeks they made no mention of Harold, each wary of upsetting the other. At the end of the first week, Franny arrived from Clacton with a Victoria sponge, and talked mostly about Michael, but the following day she told Richie that Daisy's condition jangled her nerves, which was bad for anyone of her age, and said that the least Richie could do, after what he'd done to her, was to drive her back home. By the time he returned, Daisy had taken a turn for the worse and the doctor had increased her morphine dosage and said that he didn't think it would be long now before she began to lose consciousness.

It was then that Richie decided to bring up Harold. He knew it was too late for Harold's forgiveness, he said, but he wanted to explain. He told his aunt about the incident with Col in the barn, about his terrible shame and the rage he'd carried with him as a result. He said he realised now that Daisy had been happy with Harold, but back then he was young and judgemental and all he'd seen was a man who had first betrayed first his wife and then deprived his nephew of the woman he had loved, a woman for whom he had never found a satisfactory substitute. Once he'd moved to Canada, his life in London and Kent had frozen in his mind and he hadn't seen, through his correspondence with Daisy, that the memory of his presence had taken on a life of its own, separate from himself. He bitterly regretted that now. He said he wished he could have stopped the tide, but dazzled as she was with drugs, Daisy knew that this was the one thing he could never do, that no one could do, that she could not do herself, even as the tide washed in all around and took her away from him.

CHAPTER 18

After Daisy died, Richie spent a while in her house, sorting his aunt's belongings. Every so often his mother would call, remembering some old trinket of his aunt's that she now wanted for her own. He boxed them up and, when he was done sorting, he sent them to her. He said he would visit when he had made up his mind about what he was going to do. He already knew then that he couldn't simply settle back to his old life in Canada. His time with his aunt had stirred up too much of the past and fragments had now lodged themselves at the front of his mind.

In his spare time he revisited all his old Faversham haunts – the creek side, the marshes, the pubs beside the brewery. It was odd how little the place had changed. The shops were different – the chains had moved into Faversham as everywhere – and the town had spilled out, but the centre was still dominated by the giant barrel sheds, the chimneys and mashers and the hoppy, yeasty aroma of Shepherd Neame's.

After a few days, he plucked up his courage and took himself for a drive around Selling. As he drove up to the old station building, the years peeled away and he was a boy once more, alighting from the train with his cardboard suitcase, his aunt coming towards him along the platform. One of the pubs – the Old Century – had been converted into cottages, but the Sonde Arms was still there, and the soft path that had led down to the chalk lane. He left his car and walked west towards Pheasant Field. The road itself was wider than he remembered it, and it

had been asphalted over, but these were the only changes. He
passed Ghost Hole Pond and the Drawing Room and made his
way by the big grey house to the gates of Gushmere Court Farm.
It was a bright, sunny day and he could see beyond a series of
newish-looking farm buildings to a strip of sea in the distance.
A man was bent over a Land Rover in the courtyard, and for a
moment he thought about calling out to him, but the overwhelming rawness of his feelings stopped him and he decided,
anyway, that it was best to keep this image only in his mind,
with no distracting accompaniments. What if the man said the
place was no longer a working farm, or that they no longer
grew hops there? What if he knew nothing, if the history of the
place was of no importance or relevance to him? Richie thought
about whether to carry on to Pheasant Field, but the possibility
that the past had been erased there too prevented him from
walking on. He turned back, found his car again and drove past
the Tudor manor of Rhode Court, which had always formed the
eastern boundary of the territory he'd roamed with Col. The car
put a comforting distance between him and the scene before
him. He tuned the radio to a local music station, then turned
south and drove down to Stone Stile Farm, following New Forest
Lane to Shottenden. How short the journey seemed. He was
surprised, too, by how well he still knew the lie of the land;
even though in all the years he'd lived in Selling, he had only
ever taken a route to Shottenden that passed through the fields,
he was able to direct himself there via the roads and had not
once had to stop and look for a sign or consult his map. He
stopped at Shottenden for a while, before heading north again
up Goldups Lane to Perry Wood. The music and the drive had
together made him feel both more confident and vulnerable.
He parked his car in a shallow layby and walked up the hill
through the sweet chestnuts to the Mount, from where he and
Col used to look out for the glow of artillery fire and plan how
they would use their superior knowledge of the land to wage

war on the Jerries in the event of an invasion. He saw now, of course, that Col's advance on him had almost certainly been experimental and that Col had probably gone on to get married and have children, but even if he hadn't, what difference would it have made? They could have remained friends, best friends even. The thought of it made his throat swell and started his eyes itching. Afraid of his emotions, he turned back down the hill, got back in his car and drove along Vicarage Lane past Poppington Bungalow to Danecourt Bridge, from where he watched the trains passing. There were Gypsies living nearby, in Meadow Wood. He saw their caravans, but did not stop to talk to them. His heart was so full his ribs ached.

After paying a visit – final, as it turned out – to his mother to drop off those of his aunt's effects to which she had laid a claim, Richie Baker returned to Canada. A few weeks later his aunt's solicitor contacted him. Under the provisions of her will, Daisy's little house in Faversham was to be sold and the proceeds divided equally between her sister and her nephew. He telephoned Franny, who was clearly irritated by what she saw as the inequity of her sister's will, but agreed to leave the arrangements for the sale to Richie and the solicitor. It was while he was waiting for the money that Julie finally filed for divorce. Under the terms of their separation, he offered her half of the money he'd been left by Daisy, but she would not take it. She'd been a good wife to him and he was grateful for this, her last generous gesture towards him. She seemed to harbour no sour feelings for him, as though she knew how hard he had tried to make her the love of his life. He was relieved when, a few months later, she met an old friend at a school reunion and started dating him.

While his divorce was going through, Richie returned to England. For a while he rented a flat in Bexleyheath, found work as a gardener for the council and spent his time mowing park lawns and planting snapdragons and busy Lizzies. One day, about six months after his return, he took it upon himself to get on a train and visit Poplar. He picked up the Docklands Light Railway at Tower Gateway and headed east. The fact that the train was driverless unsettled him, as did the train's Toytown look and the elevated position of the rails, and he was glad when it slowed into Poplar station. He'd been concentrating so hard on staying calm that he hadn't noticed the scene around him, and when he alighted from the train and stood on the station platform he had to reread the sign several times to reassure himself that he was, indeed, in Poplar, as the announcement on the train had said.

He was aware that the area immediately to the south was no longer officially referred to as the London Docks, nor as the Isle of Dogs, but as 'Docklands', a newly desirable place in which to work and live. He'd seen a few of the newspaper reports on the regeneration, not least because it was two Canadian brothers, the Reichmanns, who were leading it. He thought of himself as a child, setting out for the alley beside the West India with Bird picking over the stones on the foreshore beach, and laughed. The Reichmanns hadn't known the place then, as he had, and he didn't suppose they would appreciate being told that it had a fast-beating heart and that the rich blood of belonging pumped through its arteries.

Richie had already witnessed the transformation wrought by the Luftwaffe, but what the Reichmanns and others had done in the last few short years was astounding. Before him stood a great huddle of glass and steel so tall it pierced the clouds. So many skyscrapers competed for the eye that he was dizzied by the endless tiny grids of windows that seemed to be glass ladders inviting an infinite climb. Had this been Toronto he would have believed it, but here in East London, the towers seemed so incongruous that it was difficult to look at them and not suspect that this was some kind of optical illusion, one of those new-fangled holograms that everyone was talking about. The sheer scale of the development seemed to make no concessions at all to what had been there before. Worse, it had simply wiped the old Poplar away. All that remained, the bascules and swing bridges of the old dock locks and the odd stretch of water, had become mere adornment, a nostalgic little theme. Canary Wharf, from where oranges and tomatoes and, Richie guessed, his uncle's birds had first arrived in the capital, was now an immense skyscraper topped with a flashing light to warn off planes. The West India itself had been filled in and studded with towers, a section of the old dock wall and a small area of the dock itself retained as a water feature, complete with newly minted fountain. The towers thrust from this piffling substrate as though reminding the world of its irrelevance and their own generosity for conceding the continued existence even of this much remnant.

Richie descended the stairs to ground level. The concrete pillars were daubed with racist graffiti and advertisements for the BNP, and the prevailing smell was of urine. Following a chain-link fence, he made his way past the brown struts of the new Billingsgate market towards the towers. The sun appeared from behind a cloud and cast the great forest of glass and steel before him in spangles which sent out illuminated traces that reminded him of the anti-aircraft fire over the Kent sky during the war, and he felt himself torn between disgust and wonder. Inside, Canary Wharf was a city in miniature, with shops and offices and connected to the railway and to the towers around it by a series of marbled walkways and shining escalators. Inside, people in suits moved about hurriedly, neither talking to one another nor making eye contact, looking not so much like real people, Richie thought, as actors in a TV drama. He walked on and out the other side of the complex to a series of building lots studded with giant cranes. Beyond them were scenes of desolation: potholed roads lined with graffitied walls and half-terraces of houses beached on squalid tracts of wasteland.

The dockers' pubs where men had once collected and spent their wages were all boarded up and many had been vandalised, but the strip of land beside the river had been lined with new developments of apartments. White *For Sale* signs stared blankly out, as though surrendering to the river water.

Slowly, Richie made his way back to the DLR and took the next train east across the oxbow in the River Lea, past the Pura Foods factory at Orchard Creek. He got off at Royal Victoria, on the edge of the now deserted dock, beyond the reach of the development 'miracle' on the other side. The platform was bounded by link fencing through which brambles struggled to maintain a foothold. On the north side of the dock the rows of shops were mostly boarded up, and those that remained sold either fried chicken or kebabs. The Connaught Inn was still standing there on the dockside, but of all the warehousing and administration buildings, only the Millennium Mills and Silo D remained, and the whole area was fenced off with chain-link topped with barbed wire. Farther off, Richie was amazed to see that what had once been the quayside dividing the Royal Albert from the King George V had been converted into an airport runway. A few small planes busied about beside a boxy blue-and-silver terminal building which now directly overlooked the huddle of old terraces in Silvertown and, beyond them, the tremendous, stinking mess of the Tate & Lyle sugar refinery. The remainder of the dock had all but gone back to nature.

Richie returned to Bexleyheath and his job in the municipal gardens, but his trip to London had flushed too many memories from their habitual hiding places for him to be able to settle, and he returned to London a month or two later. The degree and speed with which history was being erased from Poplar had given him a new sense of urgency. From the moment of his divorce, he had begun to fantasise about rekindling his relation-ship with Irene, and now it felt as though all trace of her old haunts might at any moment vanish, leaving no trail. He took a week off work and went up to the Family Records Office in Islington, then to the Public Records Office in Kew and to the Metropolitan Archives. He spent an afternoon in the local history section of Tower Hamlets Library and a morning sifting through parish records of weddings and funerals. He tramped old and now unfamiliar streets, looking for Irene's old house, but the place where it had once been had gone, replaced by a sixties housing estate predominantly inhabited by Asian families. He tried to recall the bus stop where he'd last seen her, but could no longer quite work out where it must have been. He took the District Line to East Ham, went into the library looking for the old commercial college where Irene had studied, and was directed to the Newham Borough local history library, where he found a list and realised that he never knew the college's name.

When the week was up, he sat down in his kitchen and tried to bring to mind everything he could remember about Irene. The exercise shocked him. It was much less than he'd realised. He'd never thought about her as a collection of known facts, only in the context of his feelings for her, but now that he did, he realised he couldn't remember the colour of her eyes or how tall she was or in which month she'd been born. He didn't even know her middle name.

He wondered what he was doing in Bexleyheath and realised that he didn't really know. He had only ever felt truly happy in east Kent. When his second week of holiday entitlement fell due he got into his car and drove east down the M2, stopping off at various places and staying at cheap bed-and-breakfasts. He drove himself along the Roman Road in the direction of Canterbury, then north again to Horse Sands and the mud flats at South Oaze and as far as the North Sea. He stayed in Faversham for a night, then headed south to Selling, where he spent some time driving along the still-familiar lanes. Parking beside Selling station, he walked along the old chalk road, now asphalted over, past Ghost Hole Pond and the Drawing Room and along to Gushmere Court. This time he did not turn back but carried on along the lane until he came to the old, familiar mossy gate which stood at the bottom of Pheasant Field. He hardly dared look up the slope for fear that the flood of memories would overwhelm him. He mustered his courage and raised his eyes and there it was, the gentle curve, filled with dandelion clocks as it had been back before the start of the war, and to his amazement, at the top of the field, he saw a single line of hop huts, remains of the double line that once ran along the fence beside the wood. He did not go up then, but carried on along the road, past familiar orchards, towards the farm where Irene had been billeted. As he stood at the farm gate he could almost see the old sheepdog, whose name he had long since forgotten, come swinging its way towards him. He turned his back to the farm, giving himself a moment to collect his thoughts, then he set off once more up the lane in the direction of the field where the V1 had landed. All day he walked, retracing the old routes he'd walked with Irene. He didn't know what he was looking for; his legs seemed driven by some old impulse.

That evening, exhausted, he checked into a nearby bed-and-breakfast. For the first time in almost as long as he could remember, he felt perfectly happy. He made himself a cup of tea and sat watching the tiny TV for a while. A thought entered his mind. At first he tried to ignore it, but it worried at him for so long that he could no longer concentrate on the TV. He switched it off. While he'd been watching it had grown dark but he wasn't minded to turn on the light so he sat in the dark for a while with the thought bouncing around in his mind. He tried to set his mind to bed, but the thought wouldn't let him; it was so subversive, so counter to everything he had told himself over the years, that he felt as though someone had peeled off his skin and scattered the parts, and he had no idea how he was going to gather them all back up again. And yet the knowledge contained in the idea wasn't anything new, it was something he had known all his adult life, but it had been so buried that he hadn't been able to recognise it. He realised now how completely mistaken he had been and how far he had allowed that mistake to proliferate until it had taken on the character of truth. He thought back to his earliest memories, of women leaning over him, asking where his brother and sister were. His life so far had been a search for missing people, as though they and only they held the key to his happiness. One after the other he'd clung to friends and lovers – even to his dog – hoping they would be his route to happiness when all he had ever needed to feel complete was here, in the soft hills and gentle orchards. All these years, it hadn't been Irene he'd yearned for, it had been this countryside in Kent. Everything he wanted and needed was right here.

He slept long and fast that night, undisturbed by the screeching of owls and the squeaks of foxes. In the morning, he got up, washed his face, shaved and went down to breakfast. The land-lady appeared and said, *Good morning, Mr Baker, will you be having tea or coffee?*

He asked for tea and she disappeared into the kitchen, returning with a jug of milk and some toast, and asked him, very politely, whether he knew the area. He explained that he'd been billeted there as a child during the war and she said:

I expect it's changed a good bit.

The kettle began to whistle and she went back into the kitchen, returning with a mug of tea.

Still, she said, brightly, *you can't hold back the tide, can you?* She put Richie's tea down on the table. *Now, what can I get you for breakfast?*

Eggs, he said. *I'll have eggs, if you don't mind.*

EPILOGUE

Richie Baker returned to east Kent and lived there until his death not long after I began writing this book. At Gushmere Court Farm in Selling, Julian Berry continues to grow hops, apples and pears and other fruit crops, carrying on a Berry family tradition stretching back in the records to 1720 and most likely much earlier still. Julian's brother farms in nearby Boughton. Despite the fact that British hops have almost disappeared among the major brewers, there are a sufficient number of microbreweries preferring the flavour of unseeded Kentish hops like Goldings and Fuggles, to the German or American seeded varieties, to make it worth the Berry family's while – just – to continue to plant and grow them. Like all farmers, the Berrys have had to move with the times, and this has meant hiving off those parts of the farm which do not contribute to the profitability of the business. One of the first things to go in recent times was the grand house that was once attached to the farm. It is now occupied by a dentist with a clinic in nearby Faversham. Other things have changed too. You can still see the distant smear of the sea through the farm buildings, but the horizon is now interrupted by wind turbines. The high-speed Eurostar railway line passes not far from Selling, but any passenger who happens to look out of their carriage window as they whoosh by will see a landscape remarkable not only for its beauty but also for its persistence. From a train travelling at speed the countryside around Selling looks pretty much the same as it did a hundred years ago.

What has changed most is not the land itself but the way the land is used. Most of the old hop farms have now moved out of hops altogether. One of the largest and most famous, at Beltring, until recently owned by Whitbread, now operates as a museum and country park and runs an annual nostalgia-laden 'war and peace show'. Beltring also claims to house the world's largest collection of oast houses, though none now operates as a commercial hop dryer. Most of the remaining Kentish oasts have long been converted into rather swanky homes. Their characteristic circular footprint – which was once thought, erroneously as it turned out, to dry hops more efficiently than a rectangular kiln – meant that they were unsuitable for conversion into working farm buildings. As a result most were saved from being knocked through, added on to, reroofed in corrugated iron or otherwise altered. Their white cowls remain the most recognisable symbols of the Kent countryside, as redolent of the garden of England's history as old tin mine workings are of Cornwall.

Gushmere Court Farm still runs four working kilns, each built in 1903, the same year Harold and Daisy were born. The kilns dry the product of 18 acres of hop gardens. Julian Berry uses a 1958 Worcester-made Rotobank hop picker with a Brough cleaner and chopper to process his hop crop. Though he has got rid of most of the old hop huts, he retains a few post-war examples, which he refers to as 'The White Huts'. Every summer, ex-hoppers continue to arrive from the East End of London and from parts of the cockney diaspora – Essex mostly – to spend their holidays in the huts. They don't pick hops any more, but they feel a great affinity to the land and are almost proprietorial about the farm. Quite recently, one ex-hopper held her hundredth birthday party in the huts, and Julian Berry says he still comes across bunches of flowers by the side of the hop fields left, often, at the spot where a hopping family scattered the ashes of a loved one. Julian Berry keeps in touch with those hopping families who wish to keep in touch with him, but some have found it hard to forgive the Berry family for moving with the times. When Julian put on a barbeque for ex-hoppers in 2004, only two people turned up.

The Berry family continued to employ hoppers during the picking season, as they have done for at least the last three hundred years, though their numbers are reduced from several hundred in the interwar period to not more than a dozen, and their job is not to pick cones manually but to cut the bines, stack them on to trailers, take them to the hop shed and feed them into a picking machine. The pickers are no longer East Enders but, for the most part, East Europeans.

Fittingly, perhaps, the most recent immigrants to arrive in the East End of London are also East European. Over the past few years tens of thousands of Poles and smaller numbers of Hungarians, Romanians, Czechs and people from the republics of the former Yugoslavia have made east London their home. These new arrivals don't remember the 'old' East End of alleys and turnings, and understandably assume that the current arrangement of streets, office buildings and apartment blocks represents the definitive version. Just as the passengers on the Eurostar rush on, through a countryside that remains in large part unchanged, so these new East Enders settling in the new developments springing up everywhere in east London in the shadow of the Olympic site remain oblivious to the persistence of the old East End, whose physical remains have long since been torn down or redeveloped, but whose soul lives on in many respects unchanged. The East End of London has always been a roiling, fluxing sort of place, a district constantly shaped and renewed by the energies of incomers: the valve through which new people, languages and cultures continue to flow into the capital. The only difference now is that, with the demise of the docks, the products of British industry and innovation no longer flow out from the East End. It has become a place cut off from its anchor in the sea trade.

Like many 'old' East Enders, I mourn the loss to the area of the docks and of all that the docks represented, not just in economic terms, but in cultural ones too. London is a colder, more abstract city for the loss of its port. To my mind, no amount of stocks or futures or derivatives or shorts traded in the new skyscrapers of Canary Wharf can make up for the filthy, wondrous bustle of physical trade and manufacture that used to characterise the eastern reaches of the capital. But it does not do to wallow in nostalgia, not least because the East End has always fundamentally been about East Enders, that resilient, energetic, resourceful, multifarious bunch of people who make the district of London between the Tower and the Essex estuary home. And in that most profound sense – the sense most worth celebrating – nothing much at all has changed in the East End of London.

ACKNOWLEDGEMENTS

I should like to express my intense gratitude to those people –
too many to name individually – who shared their memories of
hopping with me. They came to me through friends, notices put
out in print and on the Internet, by word of mouth and in very
many other ways. Without them this book would be a thin affair
indeed.

Thanks are due to the friends and family who took an interest
in the project over its long gestation and continued to provide
encouragement and support. Dr Teresa Bridgeman has been my
first and best reader as well as my great friend over many years
and many books. *Hopping* is dedicated to her.

The staff of Tower Hamlets Local History Library, the Museum of Kent Life, the British Library, the London Metropolitan
Archives, the East of London Family History Society and The
Faversham Society helped ease my research. Vivienne Archer
and John Newman have together made the Newham Bookshop
a one-stop shop for everything East End. I have relied on their
judgement and knowledge on many an occasion. Thank you also
to Hop Farm Country Park at Beltring, to Shepherd Neame
Brewery and, most especially, to Julian Berry of Gushmere
Court Farm. My great gratitude to Professor Bill Fishman, who
helped me begin my East End journey many years ago and
continues to be a source of great inspiration to me, as to countless others.

At Fourth Estate, my thanks to Nicholas Pearson for believing in the book and to Louise Haines, Liz Woabank, Jessica Axe and Julian Humphries for seeing it through its various stages. I am grateful to literary agents David Godwin and Peter Robinson for their friendship, support and good advice.

Finally my love, thanks and admiration go to Simon Booker, who put up with me throughout the writing of this book. Though I'll never know quite how he did it, I am boundlessly grateful to him that he did.

Though this book is a team effort, any errors are my own.